THE ELECTION OF THE CENTURY

THE ELECTION OF THE CENTURY

THE ELECTION OF THE CENTURY

and what it tells us about the future of American politics

★ ★ ★ ★

Stephen J. Wayne and Clyde Wilcox
Editors

M.E.Sharpe
Armonk, New York
London, England

Library of Congress Cataloging-in-Publication Data

The election of the century and what it tells us about the future of American politics /
edited by Stephen J. Wayne and Clyde Wilcox.
    p. cm.
Includes bibliographical references and index.
ISBN 0-7656-0742-5 (alk. paper) — ISBN 0-7656-0743-3 (pbk. : alk. paper)
    1. Presidents—United States—Election—2000. 2. United States. Congress—Elections,
2000. 3. United States—Politics and government—2001– I. Wayne, Stephen J.
II. Wilcox, Clyde, 1953–

JK526 2000m
324.973′0929   2001042660

Table of Contents

Introduction

Stephen J. Wayne and Clyde Wilcox

In a government "of, by, and for" the people, popular sentiment, electoral choice, and public policy are extricably linked to one another. Campaigns and elections provide this linkage. They provide information that helps the electorate evaluate candidates and make voting decisions. These decisions, in turn, help determine the personnel and shape the policy agenda of the new administration. They also provide the foundation that enables elected officials to build a governing coalition and gain support for the public policy decisions they make.

Although the electorate–government–public policy linkages are ongoing, the political environment is constantly changing. Policy decisions and their impact are one source of these changes. External events and the reaction to these events by the government and governed also affect the environment in which subsequent elections occur and policy decisions are made and justified. In short, political climate cannot help but affect porous electoral and governing processes in a democracy such as the United States.

Although the campaign-governing cycle is continuous, there are moments when it is possible to take a snapshot of them. The election provides one such moment. At this brief point in time, the views and judgments of the electorate can be assessed within the context of the campaign that precedes the election and the policy and personnel consequences that follow from it.

This book provides such a snapshot. Its objective is to examine the American polity at its first point of decision in the twenty-first century. What does the 2000 election tell us about the composition, disposition, and

aspirations of the American people, about their perceptions and evaluations? What does it reveal about the attitudes, beliefs, and opinions of the
electorate, their level of political knowledge and understanding, their activity or apathy? And on the basis of this information, what can we say
about the vitality of the American polity, the representative character of
the government, and the operation of a political system that purports to be
democratic?

Campaigns and elections matter. They generate interest; they encourage
group activity, funneling that activity into a decision-making, public arena.
They connect positions and promises to candidates and their parties,
thereby providing an issue debate that often results in a governing agenda.
They jog memories of past actions, thereby enhancing the accountability
of those in government. They emphasize personal qualities. By exagger-
ating the candidates' strengths and weaknesses, they bring these personal
attributes and potential liabilities into sharper focus. The media and candidates also bring out the policy inconsistencies and contradictions of those
running for office, thereby influencing the judgment people make when
voting.

Whereas campaigns provide a forum for debate, elections provide the
mechanism for choice. Not only are officials selected, but the campaign
has a lot to do with their selection of staff, both those they will bring to
help them in government and those they may nominate for political and
judicial positions. Elections can provide direction for the new government,
political support for that government, and, in general, legitimacy for its
decisions and actions. In short, despite the blurring of campaigning and
governing, of voting and polling, and of promising and performing, campaigns and elections do matter. They affect who governs, what policies
those in government pursue, and when, and whether there is sufficient
support within the institutions of government to convert these proposals
into public policy and among the populous to obey them as the law of the
land.

As the United States moved into the twenty-first century, its public mood
was ebullient; optimism abounded. Public satisfaction with the economic
condition of the country was at an all-time high. Three out of four Americans believed that their country was headed in the right direction. Most
saw the nation's economic condition as good or excellent. Additionally,
they saw their own personal finances improved over the last four to eight
years.

No single issue was cited as of pressing concern by more than a small
percentage of the people. Only when asked about the moral climate did a
majority say that the country's condition had deteriorated. Other social

issues such as drugs and crime did not generate as much concern as they had in previous elections. The strong economy muted these issues as well. Finally, with the end of the Cold War, the public did not perceive a direct threat to the security of the United States. Interest in foreign policy issues had diminished. There was less foreign news on the major broadcast networks.[1]

Public perceptions coincided with economic data. High growth rates, low unemployment, a bullish stock market, expanding exports, and low inflation all reflected the prosperity that the nation was enjoying as the 2000 election cycle got under way. Historically, these data, along with the popularity of the president, have been used to predict election outcomes at the presidential level.

President Bill Clinton's job approval ratings remained high throughout his second term, despite the political and personal scandals that plagued him and his administration. In fact, as the political rhetoric heated, as Clinton himself became the object of more strident partisan criticism, and as doubts about his character increased, his job approval ratings actually rose, reaching a high of 70 percent in the first national poll after the Senate voted to acquit him of the impeachment charges which the House of Representatives had initiated.

The economic and social conditions clearly favored incumbents. The political climate was mixed. Washington was deeply divided along partisan and ideological lines while the country was evenly but not as deeply divided. The major parties were at parity with one another. This environment set the stage for the 2000 election.

All the political scientists who constructed and applied their models which were based on past elections predicted a victory for Vice President Al Gore with a winning margin between 3 to 5.5 percent of the vote.[2] They made this prediction despite the fact that Texas governor George W. Bush led Gore throughout 1999 and into the fall of 2000 in the public opinion polls. But the predictions were wrong. Anne Marie Cammisa examines several explanations of why the models failed to predict the vote accurately. Did they make improper assumptions, errors in analysis, or was the 2000 election simply unique and therefore unpredictable? In answering these questions, Cammisa describes the role the economy has played in the retrospective judgment of voters in past elections, explains why the 2000 vote did not generate such a judgment, and then goes on to discuss what role economic conditions played in the election outcome.

If it's not "the economy, stupid," then what was it? Did foreign policy matters play an unexpected role in the 2000 presidential election? Andrew Bennett and Troy White suggest that the answer may be yes. They begin their discussion by explaining why the candidates, who monitored public opinion so closely, devoted so much time and energy to debating foreign policy issues when those issues have become less salient for most voters. After documenting the foreign policy debate, the authors argue that this dialogue was important because it helped the electorate to assess the competence of the candidates on truly presidential matters. In 2000, it also helped the electorate get a handle on the "character" issue. Thus, even when foreign policy issues themselves may not capture attention, energize the electorate, or divide it along partisan lines nearly as much as domestic issues do, they still constitute a criterion for judging presidential potential.

Unlike foreign policy issues, social problems have captured more public interest and concern during recent presidential campaigns. Of these problems, none have been more explosive and emotive than civil rights. Since 1948, when Strom Thurmond led a splinter movement of white southerners, protesting the Democratic Party's stand on civil rights in its platform, out of its national nominating convention, the issue of civil rights has divided Democrats, leading to a partisan realignment in the South and a weakening of white, middle-class support in the North. Conversely, it has helped the Democrats increase their support from white liberals, African Americans, and Latino voters. What role did race relations play in 2000? Did the candidates take traditional positions to maintain their bases of support or did they try to reduce the partisan wedge that this issue has produced for so long? Jeremy D. Mayer addresses these questions in chapter 3. He provides a brief history of the race factor in presidential elections and notes the impact of civil rights issues such as affirmative action, legislative redistricting, and equalized educational opportunities on the 2000 campaign. Mayer also analyzes the racial composition of the vote, concluding that the divide among the races is as great as ever.

From race, we turn to gender issues and the so-called gender gap in voting behavior. Political scientists began to notice differences between the voting patterns of men and women in the 1980s, differences that got larger in the 1990s. Attitudinal distinctions between men and women on a range of policy issues, from the role of government in the domestic arena to the use of force in international affairs, were also evident. Melissa Levitt and Katherine C. Naff examine the gender-based literature on vote choice, partisanship, and policy preferences in chapter 4. They then apply the conclusions of this literature to the 2000 presidential election, assessing the candidates' gender strategies and tactics, their issues positions and policy emphases, and the impact of gender on voting. Levitt and Naff's title suggests their conclusion, "Gender As a Political Constant." The authors see gender, like race, as an independent variable that affects the perceptions people have of the parties, the candidates, and the issues, ultimately influencing their choice of candidates.

Another electoral trend evident in recent years has been the inattention and general apathy of Generation X, the youngest age cohort in the voting population. Molly W. Andolina reviews the political behavior of this group and why so many in the younger generation seem to be "turned off" to national electoral politics. Is it because candidates do not address their issues, take positions with which they can identify, or seem so uninspiring, insincere, or just plain irrelevant? Andolina examines candidate and party appeals to younger voters in the 2000 campaign, the receptivity of these voters to those appeals, and the turnout and voting behavior of these young Americans. In her conclusion, she looks to the future impact of this age cohort on American politics and government.

Religious preference is also related to voting behavior. One group that has grown in size and influence during the 1980s and 1990s has been the Christian Right. A quarter of the electorate, the Christian Right has become a core component within the Republican party's electoral coalition. Clyde Wilcox explores the evolving impact of this group on internal Republican Party politics. He examines the disagreement between the purists and the pragmatists within the Christian Coalition, the role Christian fundamentalists played in the 2000 Republican primaries, and the activities and voting behavior of the Christian Right in the general election.

From the behavior of groups within the electorate, we turn to the influence of partisanship on the electorate. For years, the allegiances people have toward parties have been viewed as the most important long-term, stabilizing factor in American electoral politics. Seen as a motivation for voting, a catalyst for vote choice, and a rationale for the voting decision, partisan attitudes have been the basic building block upon which the electorate decides and by which analysts have explained those decisions. Since the end of the 1960s, political scientists have observed a weakening of partisan bonds in both loyalty to the parties and the strength of that loyalty, more split ticket voting, and more personality-based factors that influence why people vote as they do. But beginning in the 1980s, political analysts have also noted sharper ideological distinctions between the major parties, more partisan unity in Congress, and much more strident partisan rhetoric in national politics. Are these trends in partisanship consistent with one another? Do they augur a new era of partisan realignment or one of continuing dealignment?

The next three chapters explore the partisan dimension of the 2000 elections. Stephen J. Wayne examines partisan perceptions, attitudes, and voting behavior over the course of the election cycle. He notes the stability of partisan beliefs and voting behavior in the American electorate from the onset of the 2000 primaries through the general election, the Florida vote controversy, and the beginning of the Bush administration, explaining this stability in terms of the compelling nature of the partisanship prism as the basic story line of politics and government.

Separate chapters then deal with the organized attempts by congressional Democrats and Republicans to control Congress. Michael A. Bailey and Keiko Ono focus on the Democratic congressional campaign: its high hopes but disappointing results, at least for the House of Representatives. They look at the resources that the Democrats employed, their strategy and tactics, issues and personalities, and explain why that party did not achieve its goal of winning back the House. G. Patrick Lynch and Hayden Milberg do the same but from the Republican perspective. They too assess the congressional party's strategy and tactics, indicating how the Republicans learned from their 1998 disappointments to run a stronger and less presidentially-oriented campaign in 2000. Both chapters indicate the re-surgence of the congressional parties in terms of recruitment, resource development, and strategic focus. But the chapters also indicate the powerful forces of incumbency and constituency, both of which act to inhibit change.

Incumbency is one reason that women still trail men in election to office. Although more women were elected in 2000 than in previous elections, women are still underrepresented in Congress and in state legislatures and elective executive positions. The gap between the proportion of women in the electorate and in government continues to be sizable. The next chapter explains why this is the case. The authors, Sue Thomas, Courtenay Daum, and Beth Stark, describe the magnitude of the gender gap in elective government, the reasons the gap exists, and why it makes a difference in public policy. Their chapter also looks to the future with more optimism than a statistical analysis of the past would suggest.

Although incumbency is usually an advantage, especially with a strong economy, peaceful international climate, and a president with high approval ratings, it did not win the presidency for Vice President Gore. Why? Did he sever his ties with Clinton too completely or did the remnants of the Clinton scandals dog Gore's efforts and undermine his credibility and electability? Margaret Tseng explores the Clinton factor in the 2000 election. She examines the competing claims of Clinton fatigue and nostalgia that pundits used to explain the absence or presence of Clinton's shadow. She also discusses Clinton's actions during the election and uses the Voter News Service exit poll to assess the president's impact on the party and its presidential candidate.

In addition to incumbency, technology also has a major impact on electoral politics. The age of radio and, later, television greatly changed the way in which campaigns were conducted and voters informed, the techniques that candidates employed and the attributes they needed to demonstrate, and the attention that the electorate displayed, the knowledge they possessed, and the evaluations they made. The candidates who effectively utilized these electronic media were benefited. Franklin Roosevelt, John Kennedy, and Ronald Reagan enhanced their campaigns by being effective communicators in the age of the electronic mass media and instant information and messages.

The next chapter turns to the latest communications revolution, the Internet. Although some candidates for the 1996 nominations and election had Web sites, all of the presidential candidates and more than half the candidates for the House and Senate[3] had them and used them in 2000, as did the political parties, which trumpeted their new interactive sites for their national nominating conventions. News networks and major print media also got onto the Internet by providing up-to-the-minute campaign information and commentary on their Web sites. There were even academic studies to measure the impact of Internet usage on the electorate. Jeffrey A. Wertkin examines the role of the Internet in the 2000 election. With access to a comprehensive Internet survey, Wertkin analyzes how the Net was used, by whom, and to what effect. He postulates the potential of this communications technology for future elections.

In addition to determining who is elected to office, how else does an election campaign affect governance? Lynn C. Ross addresses this question in her chapter on party platforms, campaign promises, and governing agendas. She explores the literature on platforms, promises, and performance as well as the linkage between issues, promises, and voting behavior. Concluding that elections have meaning and do matter for governance, she provides alternate interpretations of the 2000 election and explains how the Bush administration used that election as its mandate for governing and its agenda for the beginning of the 107th Congress.

Our concluding section summarizes the lessons of Campaign 2000: what it tells us about the American polity, about electioneering in the new millennium, and about how issues and candidates connect to agendas and administrations and, ultimately, public policy decisions. We highlight the trends within the electoral environment, the continuities and changes that are apparent as American democracy moves into the twenty-first century. In this way, we provide a snapshot of the predilections, preferences, and political judgments that were revealed in this, the election of the century, and are likely to influence the future of American politics.

Notes

1. "The Media at the Millennium," *Media Monitor* (July/August 2000): 4.

2. Robert G. Kaiser, "Is This Any Way to Pick a Winner? To Researchers, Election Is All Over But the Voting," *Washington Post*, May 26, 2000, A1, A4.

3. "Congressional Candidate Web Sites in Campaign 2000: What Web Enthusiasts Wanted, What Candidates Provided." *The Annenberg Public Policy Center of the University of Pennsylvanaia,*" January 2001.

THE ELECTION OF THE CENTURY

THE ELECTION OF THE SENTRY

I

Traditional Wedge Issues and Their Impact

1

Is It the Economy, Stupid?

The Role of the Economy in the Election

Anne Marie Cammisa

The economy is strong, the president ends his second term with high public approval ratings, and his vice president, an experienced and seasoned politician, runs for the White House. Under ordinary circumstances, the vice president would be expected to win. Indeed, the *Washington Post* reported in August 2000 that "for one group of political scientists who study U.S. elections, Campaign 2000 is effectively over. And the winner is . . . Vice President Gore, narrowly but clearly."[1] In the 2000 election, however, the circumstances were far from ordinary, and Vice President Al Gore failed in his attempt to gain the presidency. On the one hand, the vice president did win, at least in the number of actual votes cast. On the other hand, such numbers provide scant comfort to a politician whose opponent is the one taking the oath of office and settling into the White House. For years to come, scholars will attempt to explain what exactly happened in 2000 and what it means to American democracy. One particular question to be addressed is what role the economy plays in an election and whether election 2000 defied the conventional wisdom that presidential elections during times of peace are won or lost on the state of the economy.

At issue is the theory of economic retrospective voting. According to this theory, voters make their decisions on today's election based on what happened in the last administration, or last few administrations. Voters use party as a cue in making their decisions, evaluating the merits of a party's candidate based on the state of the economy and on who currently holds the White House. If the economy is strong, voters tend to vote for the party that holds the White House. If there is a recession, voters tend to vote for the candidate whose party has been out of office. In other words, credit or blame for the economy goes to the party in office. And voters have memories, so while the current state of the economy is of primary importance, so too is the state of the economy under previous administrations. Based on retrospective voting theory, which has been relatively accurate throughout the modern presidency, Vice President Gore would have been expected to win the presidency with a strong lead over Republican George W. Bush. Under eight years of Democratic leadership in the White House, the economy had continued in almost unabated growth, with high employment and overall consumer satisfaction. In fact, some say that Bush's father lost the 1992 election when he was blamed for the economic downturn of the early nineties.[2]

The economy plays another role in the election. While voters make independent evaluations of the state of the economy and the party in office, candidates take policy stands on ways to continue or spur economic growth, and those positions add to voter knowledge about a particular candidate. Whether or not this knowledge plays a crucial role in voter decisions is another question. Nonetheless, it is important to examine the differences between candidates Gore and Bush to evaluate the role of the economy in the election. Voter decisions are affected by issues as well as by the economy (although the retrospective voting model posits that issues are far less important in voter decision making), and economic issues were among the defining factors of the Bush and Gore campaigns.

This chapter examines the role of the economy in the 2000 election, providing at least a preliminary answer why voter forecasting models, which rely on economic retrospective voting theories and have been accurate in the past, proved insufficient to predict the results in November 2000. First, the chapter discusses the role of economic issues in the 2000 election. Then, it explains economic retrospective voting and what voter forecasting models predicted for 2000. Third, the chapter examines the 2000 election in light of the models, addressing the factors that made 2000 unique and that may account for the failure of the forecasts. The chapter concludes with an assessment of the role of the economy in the 2000 election.

Economic Issues in 2000

A strong economy and a budget surplus provided both challenges and opportunities for the two candidates in 2000. Beyond taking credit for the strong economy, the incumbent party's candidate, Gore, needed to outline what he might do with the surplus. Bush obviously had the problem of making the case for change in a time of prosperity, and he also had to explain what he might do with the surplus. Both candidates proposed cuts in taxes as a way of spending the surplus, although Bush's proposed cuts were deeper. Bush's plan included cutting tax rates at all tax brackets with the end result a reduction of $1.7 trillion over ten years. He also suggested tax breaks for education, child care, health care, married couples, and the "inheritance tax." Gore's tax cuts added up to about $500 billion over the same time period, using tax credits (for low-income workers, education, child care, and after-school expenses, among others) rather than tax rate reductions.[3]

Gore planned to use more of the surplus money for increased spending than for tax cuts. Gore planned to spend $115 billion on public schools, on school construction, teachers, computers, and reductions in class size. Not surprisingly, Bush's education plan included tax cuts, as well as a program to give parents of students in failing schools money toward sending their children to private or religious schools. His plan included both increased flexibility for local school systems and new federal standards. Gore proposed expansions of Medicare to address the rising cost of prescription drugs, while Bush planned to address those costs through privatization. Finally, Gore called for an expansion of the Earned Income Tax Credit and Social Security.[4] Bush, on the other hand, favored at least a partial privatization of the social security program.[5]

Clearly, the two candidates differed in their approaches to spending the budget surplus, with Gore favoring increased spending and Bush preferring decreases in taxes. In terms of the economy more generally as an issue, voters seemed, first, not to place too much importance on it, and second, not to give Al Gore much credit for it. (Whether or not Gore sufficiently attempted to claim credit for the economy is discussed below.) When asked what the most important issues were in the 2000 election, voters were divided between education and the economy: 21 percent and 20 percent of voters selected education as the most important issue in Roper public opinion polls conducted in August and October 2000. Just 15 or 16 percent of voters rated the economy as the most important issue in those same polls. And in a November 3 Roper poll, 45 percent of voters said that it made no difference to the economy whether Bush or Gore was elected, although 34 percent of voters said that Gore would more likely keep economic prosperity going (only 16 percent said the same about Bush). However, opinion appeared to have changed somewhat at the time of the election. In the Voter News Service (VNS) exit poll, 18 percent of voters listed the economy/jobs as the issue that mattered most, compared to 15 percent who listed education. Of the 18 percent who believed that the economy and jobs were the most important issues, 59 percent voted for Gore.

Economic issues in the 2000 election proved difficult to pin down. There were differences between the two candidates on how best to deal with economic issues, and it appears that voters understood those differences and had at least some tendency to believe that Gore would be better at handling the economy. On the other hand, it seems clear that Gore did not get as much credit for the economy as would be expected for an incumbent vice president. In addition, the general aura of economic prosperity meant that the economy was not an issue of overarching importance in the 2000 election. That said, how did voter forecasting models based on economic variables fare in this election? Not very well, as the next section demonstrates.

Using the Economy to Forecast Votes in the 2000 Election

Voters make their decisions about presidential candidates based on a variety of factors, including party affiliation, issue positions, and personality. Such factors impact both an individual's voting decision and the aggregate outcome of an election. Clearly, no one issue will affect each voter in the same way. In the aggregate, however, scholars have demonstrated that the state of the economy has affected the outcome of most elections. In the last twelve elections, the state of the economy has been an accurate predictor eight times.[6] Morris Fiorina in 1978 noted the relationship between the economy and the vote, calling it "economic retrospective voting."[7] Retrospective voting in general refers to the tendency of voters to make their decisions based on their knowledge and interpretation of each party's past successes; economic retrospective voting posits that the economy is the most important factor in such retrospective voting patterns. Research throughout the 1980s solidified the belief among scholars that perceptions of the economy have an impact on the success or failure of presidential candidates.[8] Analyses of the 1992 and 1996 presidential elections also indicated that economic retrospective voting models were appropriate: The economic downturn of 1990–1991 apparently cost the senior George Bush votes in the election, while the sustained economic growth of the mid-1990s helped propel Clinton to his second term.[9]

By the time the 2000 election rolled around, the smart money was betting that Al Gore would win. "Common sense says that a growing economy during a presidential election year ought to favor the party in power."[10] Indeed, not just common sense, but also sophisticated political models predicted that Al Gore would win handily—with anywhere from 52.8 percent to 60.3 percent of the two-party vote[11] (see Table 1.1) The reasoning behind the predictions was that the economy was in a period of unprecedented economic growth, the incumbent president had high public approval ratings (albeit combined with low personal approval ratings), and the country was at peace. The voting models all included statistics that measured both economic growth and approval ratings of the current president. All of the models also assumed that both major party candidates would run solid campaigns. Based on statistical techniques, political scientists were confident in their predictions of a Gore win. What happened in November 2000 was obviously contrary to these expectations. In effect, the election was a virtual tie. Each of the major party candidates received about 48 percent of the vote. Technically, Al Gore won the popular vote, albeit by a very slim margin. Not only were media pundits left floundering to explain how they could have called the election for Bush, only to change their minds twice more, political scientists were left grasping for explanations as to why their sophisticated and highly developed statistical models were so far off the mark. Given the relative accuracy of their models in previous elections, why weren't the models closer to reality in 2000? Were the models actually wrong? Was there something particular about the 2000 election that limited the accuracy of the models? Or was 2000 just an outlier election in an overall pattern of relative accuracy of economic prediction?

Explanations for the Failure of the Model in 2000

The remainder of this chapter evaluates a variety of explanations as to why the 2000 election did not fit economic retrospective voting theory generally and the models specifically. Six explanations are examined: (1) Since Gore technically won the popular vote, the models worked after all, (2) the presence of a third-party candidate on the left damaged Gore's chances for reelection, (3) the economy is no longer an important issue to voters, thus invalidating the models, (4) Gore ran a bad campaign, contrary to an assumption of the models, (5) the models would have worked with a different mixture of variables, and (6) there was something different about the 2000 election and the models just could not work.

1. Gore actually won the election, so the models did work.

Technically, this is true. Gore did win a slightly higher percentage of the total national vote than did Bush (Gore won just over 48 percent of the total vote, while Bush won just under 48 percent), but this does not let the

Table 1.1

Vote Predictions (in percent)

Author	August forecast of Gore vote
Campbell	52.8
Abramowitz	53.2
Norpoth	55.0
Wlezien and Erikson	55.2
Lewis-Beck and Tien	55.4
Holbrook	60.3
Lockerbie	60.3

Source: Christopher Wlezien, "On Forecasting the Presidential Vote," *PS* (March 2001).

models off the hook. The models cannot account for oddities of our political system, such as the electoral college, and did not attempt to predict the margin of votes there, but rather stuck to predictions about the national popular vote. However, the models predicted that Gore would get anywhere from 2 to 10 percentage points more of the two-party vote than would Bush (see Table 1.1 above), so they failed to predict the closeness of the election. (In fact, Gore received only 50.2 percent of the two-party vote, compared to 49.8 percent for Bush.) Some might argue that voting irregularities in Florida and other states gave Bush an inflated number of votes, but even conceding that such irregularities were in Bush's favor, the marginal votes Gore could have obtained in their absence would still have left a much slimmer margin of victory than these political scientists would have predicted.

2. The presence of a third-party candidate on the left did irreparable damage to Gore.

Admittedly, Ralph Nader, the Green party candidate, did take more votes from Gore than from Bush, and further, the models did not even attempt to make predictions about three-way races. Each model only suggested the percentage of the two-party vote that each candidate would receive. (In other words, the models ignored the votes for Nader and simply added up all the votes for Gore and Bush, determining what percentage each had of those voters who voted for a major party candidate.) Even so, the race was close. Each candidate had only about 50 percent of the two-way vote, and assuming all Nader votes actually would have gone to Gore, the final result would have been below the models' predictions. "If Nader's votes are added to Gore's (and Buchanan's to Bush's) the result is a combined Gore-Nader vote of 51.4%, 1.1% closer to the forecasts."[12] In fact, a survey of Nader voters indicates that a percentage would have voted for Bush had Nader not been in the race. Thirty percent of Nader voters surveyed claimed they would not have voted at all without Nader in the race, 47 percent claimed they would have voted for Gore, and (perhaps surprisingly) 21 percent said they would have voted for Bush.[13] Yes, without Nader present, Gore would likely have won the election, but again, this is not enough to prove the models correct. The fact that the models do not allow for a third-party candidate is a flaw in the models, but the presence of a third-party candidate cannot be used to explain why the models did not work in this case.

3. Credit for a good economy no longer goes to the government.

This argument is twofold. In the first place, the economic boom at the turn of the millennium had been going on for so long (almost ten years) that many young voters could barely have a memory of an economic recession, especially given that the most recent one (1990–1991) was of record short duration. In this scenario, voters have gotten so used to economic growth that it becomes an expectation, rather than a luxury. Therefore, voters are less likely to make their decisions based on economic considerations, since they would expect both parties to fare the same. The November 3 Roper poll quoted above lends some credence to this notion, given that almost half of voters surveyed (45 percent) said it would make no difference to the economy who was president. A second reason may be that voters now are more likely to give the credit for economic growth to the "new economy" based on high-tech industries and stock market investments, and less credit to the government. And voters who see economic prosperity as more a credit to business than to government would be more favorably disposed to a Republican candidate. A *Wall Street Journal*/NBC News poll in June of 2000 found that 27 percent of voters had confidence that the economy would remain strong under Gore, while 30 percent said they lacked such confidence. On the other hand, 31 percent of voters said they had such confidence in Bush, and 28 percent said they were "not at all confident."

What voters thought of each candidate's ability to handle the economy did not seem to be the overriding factor in making voting decisions. This would seem to indicate that an economic retrospective voting model is not valid in a period of economic growth that lasts a long time. The model is based on the assumption that the economy is of primary importance in voters' decisions. If the economy is relatively unimportant, then the model cannot be used. It is not that voters were unaware of the economic boom in 2000, but rather that they did not think that either candidate would have much effect on it. But there is another explanation for the lack of importance of the economy in the 2000 election. Perhaps it was Al Gore's fault. Perhaps he should have made the economy more important in voters' minds. That leads us to the next explanation.

4. Gore ran a bad campaign.

This argument is related to the one posited above. In both cases, Gore didn't get credit for the economy, either because he didn't claim it or because voters no longer link the economy to the government, regardless of what the candidate claims. Each of the vote models operates under the assumption that the candidates run reasonably good campaigns. If the candidate who is expected to win runs a poor campaign, the models cannot be faulted for the candidate's own failure. The question is, did Gore run a bad enough campaign that he effectively lost the election he rightfully should have won? Interestingly, political commentators who say that he did tend to be members of the Democratic Party. (Presumably, it hurts less to lay the blame on an individual candidate rather than on the party, or rather than giving credit to the opposition candidate.) The evidence that Gore ran a bad campaign revolves principally on the question of whether or not he sufficiently emphasized the administration's economic achievements. The theory goes something like this: The economic models are predicated on the belief that the candidate runs a good campaign, which means taking credit for a good economy when your party is in power. Gore, however, attempted to distance himself from Clinton and shied away from touting the Clinton record, thus losing the opportunity to credit the administration for the strong economy. "The Gore campaign short circuited the models this year. All of the models (excepting Norpoth's [which predicted 55 percent of the two-party vote for Gore]) are premised on the idea that one of the candidates will find it in his interest to emphasize the economic record."[14]

The first question to be asked is whether, in fact, Gore avoided taking credit for the economy that had boomed under Clinton. It is true that Gore did much to distance himself from Clinton: barely mentioning Clinton's name, asking Clinton not to campaign on his behalf, stressing his own moral rectitude and thirty-year marriage. His stump speech, however, did include boasting about economic growth, the booming stock market, and jobs creation, although he also emphasized that "this election isn't about the past, it's about the future."[15] Focusing on the future meant, at least in part, avoiding discussions of the past, and Gore was criticized for avoiding the economic good times as an issue in the election.[16]

Even if the Gore campaign did ignore the economy, it seems that voters should be capable of giving credit for a good economy to the administration, without having to be told to do so. The retrospective voting model in general posits that voters make their decisions on the state of the economy itself, not on whether or not candidates take credit for it. Could voters figure out that the economy was good? It seems that they should have been able to do so. Public opinion polls throughout the year 2000 gave evidence that voters consistently ranked the economy as strong.[17] Interestingly, however, 57 percent of voters in the VNS exit poll thought the national economy was not good. Not surprisingly, the majority of those voters voted for Bush. Worse, 66 percent of voters in the same poll though the economy would be worse a year from now, and they too had voted for Bush. At least in the VNS exit poll (though not in earlier polling data), voters did not think that the economy was good and that it would get worse. If the retrospective voting model assumes that the economy is good, and yet the voters do not believe that it is, is that a problem with the model or with the voters? On the one hand, perhaps the voters by election day were seeing some evidence of an economic downturn (although 54 percent of voters in the same VNS exit poll were not too worried or not at all worried about the future of the stock market). On the other hand, 68 percent of voters in the VNS exit poll said that Clinton was somewhat to very responsible for the economy, and 52 to 79 percent of those said they voted for Gore.

Another question is whether voters had faith in either candidate's ability to maintain a strong economy. Asked which of the two candidates would do the best job of keeping the economy strong, 46 percent of voters said Gore, compared to 38 percent for Bush in a Roper poll in September 2000. A similar question on November 3 elicited similar numbers: 44 percent for Gore and 37 percent for Bush. Of course, other polls indicated a lack of trust in Gore. The June *Newsweek* poll quoted above found a slightly smaller percentage of voters having faith in Gore's ability to handle the economy than those who had confidence in Bush. Another poll question in the November 3 poll has an interesting response. When asked whether economic prosperity would be more likely to continue under Gore or Bush, 34 percent said Gore, 16 percent said Bush, and 45 percent said it makes no difference.

The data are confusing. One interpretation of those numbers could be that the bad Gore campaign hypothesis is correct. If only Gore had been out there telling people the economy was good and then claiming credit for it, he could have convinced some of the 45 percent who thought it made no difference who was president that indeed it did make a difference and they should vote for the Democrat. Of course, another interpretation is that the voters truly did not think it made a difference to the economy who was president and that campaigning was not going to change their opinions.

The main difficulty with the argument that Gore ran a bad campaign is that it fails to acknowledge the untenable position in which Gore was placed as Clinton's vice president. While Clinton did have consistently high public approval ratings, he also had consistently low personal approval ratings. Perhaps Gore could have associated himself more closely with Clinton, gaining more credit for the booming economy in the process. There was a cost associated with that strategy, however. Associating closely with Clinton meant associating with his personal problems as well as his political strengths. Clinton's personal approval ratings were less than 35 percent, and Gore's support among those who believed the country was "headed in the right direction" was 50 percent, compared to the usual 66 percent vice presidents receive in similar circumstances.[18] In addition, after the election 44 percent of voters rated the Clinton scandals as important.[19] Gore had to decide whether to risk associating himself with Clinton's negatives or risk not getting enough credit for the economy. It was a difficult decision. To say he made the wrong choice is not to say he ran a bad campaign. And it is not at all clear that Gore would have won handily had he associated himself more closely with the president. Whether or not Gore should be faulted for not running on economic prosperity, it is clear his campaign decisions were handicapped by association with an impeached president.

The evidence is mixed, even as to whether voters realized the economy was good. Gore initially attempted to take credit for the economy while distancing himself from Clinton, a strategy that might have hindered his claims on the economic boom. He also attempted a prospective campaign, focusing on the future rather than past accomplishments. Polling data in some instances showed Gore to be favored as the candidate who could best help the economy, while in other instances Bush came out ahead. And some data showed that a large number of voters thought it made no difference to the economy who became president. What is evident is that Gore did not get sufficient credit for the economy to win the election on that factor. It is unclear whether he or his campaign could have done anything differently to lay claim to the good economy, particularly if voters did not see it as such.

5. The models would have worked, if we had only had the right mix of variables.

Perhaps this is true. Although the models did not predict the percentage of the two-party vote that Gore received, at issue is whether or not there was something else they could have taken into account to more accurately predict the outcome. Various other variables include Gore's campaign strategy (discussed above), the fact that Gore was not actually the incumbent president, whether or not the economy was as good as the indicators led scholars to believe, whether income growth rather than gross domestic product growth is the more appropriate economic indicator, and the tone of the news coverage.[20] Could other variables be added to the mix to come up with a better forecast? Possibly, although none of the forecasters has yet come up with a model that is accurate in describing the 2000 election.

This points out a flaw in the models: Once we find a model that seems an accurate way to predict an election, another election comes along that flummoxes political scientists and commentators, causing a return to the drawing board and a search for new and better variables. The models seem based on the assumption that there is some absolute "formula" that can tell us who will be president, if only we could find it. And although the vote forecasters are loath to admit it, it seems obvious that each election has its own unique set of circumstances that sets it apart from others.

Does this mean that the models are never accurate? Not at all. To judge vote forecasting models based on one election is to not see the forest for the trees. Still, political science will never have a perfect prospective model. The best we can hope for is to come up with ways to predict past elections. Or, as one of the forecasters put it, "what this analysis really tells us is that forecasting models 'work' as long as voters and candidates behave as they have in previous elections. When that assumption is violated, then all bets are off."[21] No matter how close the models get to reality, reality always gets in the way.

6. The models just plain did not work this time.

Perhaps this election was such a different set of circumstances that it cannot fit into a more general model. The sitting president, albeit with high public approval ratings, had been plagued by financial and sex scandals, dogged by investigations, and ultimately impeached in the House of Representatives. The vice president had had his own fund-raising scandal. Moreover, he was widely known as being "wooden" and lacking in "likability." Gore's performance in the debates, which should have showed him off to advantage, instead played up his negatives: a general aura of smugness and a tendency toward exaggeration. His opponent should have been a relatively weak candidate. Although he had high name recognition as the son of a former president, Bush was prone to malapropisms and mispronunciations, and had relatively little political experience beyond the Texas governorship. He was more easygoing and likable than Gore, however. In addition, there was no overarching issue that united (or divided) the country in one direction or the other. It may simply be that "Clinton fatigue" set in with some number of voters and neither Gore's positives nor Bush's negatives were sufficient to overcome it. The voter forecasting models cannot take into account various personality factors. And perhaps economic retrospective voting just was not going to take place in the 2000 election.

It is obvious that there are no easy explanations of the outcome of the 2000 election. And in the long run, it is difficult to determine how individual voters make their decisions and what impact various issues ultimately have on voters. If any election is going to defy all predictions, surely the 2000 election is the one.

Conclusion

Economic issues did not work at all in the way one would expect in 2000. The economy was excellent, the nation was at peace, and yet the sitting vice president barely won the popular vote. It stands to reason that something other than the economy decided the election this year. Was it that rather than being wrapped in the success of the economy under Clinton, Gore was wrapped in the failure of Clinton's personal life and his impeachment in the House? This situation was so unusual that one might well imagine that Clinton's personal problems played some role in voters' evaluations of his administration and, by extension, their evaluations of Gore. Was it that Gore did not play up the economy as much as he should have? Perhaps, but this still leads us back to Clinton's problematic presidency. Could it be that Gore's personality was just so unappealing that voters were disinclined toward him regardless of the economy? It seems unusual that voters would make their decisions solely based on personality, and while Bush's personality was more appealing than Gore's, this advantage would seem to be balanced by voters' perceptions that Gore was more experienced and ready for office than Bush. Or was it simply that the economy was not an important issue this time?

It will probably be generations before historians tease out the reasons for Gore's failure to take the White House. It probably is a combination of all of the factors mentioned above. One thing is clear: It's not *just* the economy, stupid.

Notes

1. Robert G. Kaiser, "Academics Say It's Elementary: Gore Wins," *Washington Post*, August 31, 2000, A12.
2. See, for example, Alan Grant, "The 1992 U.S. Presidential Election," *Parliamentary Affairs* 46 (April 1993): 239–255.
3. Lee Walczak, Richard S. Dunham, and Howard Gleckman, "The Politics of Prosperity," *Business Week*, August 7, 2000, 96–100.
4. Ibid.
5. See Edward Walsh, "Bush Pushes Social Security Plan," *Washington Post*, October 20, 2000, A10.
6. See Jeffrey H. Birnbaum, "Is the Economy Destiny for Gore?" *Fortune* 142 (August 14, 2000): 57.
7. Morris Fiorina, "Economic Retrospective Voting in American Elections," *American Journal of Political Science* 22 (1978): 426–443.
8. See, for example, Edward R. Tufte, *Political Control of the Economy* (Princeton: Princeton University Press, 1978); Morris Fiorina, *Retrospective Voting in American National Elections* (New Haven: Yale University Press, 1981); D. Roderick Kiewiet, *Macroeconomics and Micropolitics: The Electoral Effects of Economic Issues* (Chicago: University of Chicago Press, 1983); Gregory B. Markus, "The Impact of Personal and National Economic Conditions on the Presidential Vote: A Pooled Cross-Sectional Analysis," *American Journal of Political Science* 32 (1988): 137–54; Steven Rosenstone, *Third Parties in America: Citizen Response to Major Party Failure* (Princeton: Princeton University Press, 1984); and Ray Fair, "The Effect of Economic Events on Votes for President," *Review of Economics and Statistics* 60 (1978): 159–173, and "The Effect of Economic Events on Votes for President: A 1984 Update," *Political Behavior* 10 (1988): 168–179.
9. R. Michael Alvarez and Jonathan Nagler, "Economics, Issues and the Perot Candidacy: Voter Choice in the 1992 Election," *American Journal of Political Science* 39 (August 1995): 714–744; R. Michael Alvarez and Jonathan Nagler, "Economics, Entitlements and Social Issues: Voter Choice in the 1996 Presidential Election," *American Journal of Political Science* 42 (October 1998): 1349–1363.
10. Birnbaum, "Is the Economy Destiny for Gore?"
11. See Christopher Wlezien, "On Forecasting the Presidential Vote" *PS* (March 2001). Wlezian reports predictions based on economic forecasting made by James Campbell; Alan Abramowitz; Helmut Norpoth; Christopher Wlezien and Robert Erikson; Michael Lewis-Teck and Charles Tien; Thomas Holbrook; and Brad Lockerbie. The predictions were presented at a panel at the Annual Meeting of the American Political Science Association in August 2000.
12. James E. Campbell, "The Referendum That Didn't Happen: The Forecasts of the 2000 Presidential Election," *PS* (March 2001).
13. Wlezien, "On Forecasting the Presidential Vote."
14. James E. Campbell, "The Referendum That Didn't Happen."
15. Ceci Connolly, "Short on Time, Nominees Boil It Down: In Sum, Gore Vows to Fight for Middle-Class Prosperity," *Washington Post*, November 3, 2000, A20.
16. Dan Balz and Mike Allen, "Gore Pins Hopes on Economy," *Washington Post*,

October 19, 2000, A1; Bob Herbert, "In America: Why So Close," *New York Times,* November 6, 2000, A39.

17. Campbell, "Referendum That Didn't Happen."
18. Birnbaum, "Is the Economy Destiny for Gore?"
19. "And Still No Winner," *Economist* 357 (November 11, 2000): 35–37.
20. Campbell, Wlezien, Bartels, and Zale, "Presidential Vote Models: A Recount," *PS* (March 2001); Holbrook, "Forecasting with Mixed Economic Signals: A Cautionary Tale," *PS* (March 2001).
21. Holbrook, "Forecasting with Mixed Economic Signals."

2

Foreign Policy in the Presidential Campaign

The Attentive and "Apathetic Internationalist" Publics

Andrew Bennett and Troy White

Did Foreign Policy Matter in the 2000 Presidential Election?

The conventional wisdom maintains that in the absence of wars or international economic crises, foreign policy has played little role in American presidential elections. This view has become particularly pronounced since the end of the Cold War. In this interpretation, the complexity of post–Cold War policy dilemmas and the absence of a powerful foreign adversary have caused an inattentive and uninformed American public to return to its history of isolationism and unilateralism on foreign policy. This view became especially prominent after the 1992 elections, when Democratic candidate William Clinton, with little foreign policy experience, focused his campaign on the domestic economy. The incumbent president, George Bush, had wide foreign policy experience and enjoyed extraordinarily high approval ratings after the victorious Gulf War in early 1991, but voters perceived him as out of touch with the domestic economy. Clinton's victory therefore created the impression that domestic affairs would far outweigh foreign policy in post–Cold War presidential elections.

This conventional wisdom was reinforced in 1996, when foreign policy received little attention from the public and the media, the substantive foreign policy differences between the presidential candidates were limited, and Clinton easily won reelection in the midst of a strong economy. By the late 1990s, the majority of policy-makers polled in one study viewed the public as unwilling to support an internationalist foreign policy, critical of the United Nations, skeptical of peacekeeping, and extremely averse to casualties.[1]

As is often the case, this conventional view contains grains of truth and a large dose of oversimplification and distortion. It is true that for most voters the salience of foreign policy issues has declined relative to that of domestic issues since the end of the Cold War. There has been almost no change since the end of the Cold War, however, in the public's internationalist and multilateralist foreign policy instincts. Rather than becoming isolationist, the public has become, in James Lindsay's phrase, "apathetic internationalists": generally inattentive to and unwilling to make sacrifices for foreign policy, but still supportive of an active U.S. role in world affairs.[2] Moreover, the public becomes interested and informed and often exercises good judgment when particular crises arise.[3] The public is also attentive to the "intermestic" issues (international issues with a large domestic component) that affect daily life in the United States, including immigration, drug smuggling, and international trade and finance.[4] In addition, the American public, while currently suffering from "compassion fatigue" with regard to peacekeeping in ethnic conflicts and failed states, is still willing to use force and risk casualties if important U.S. interests are at stake, as was evident in its support of the Gulf War despite prewar estimates of high casualties.

Moreover, a variety of foreign policy interest groups—ideological party and issue activists, ethnic groups, economic groups, and even the increasingly partisan members of the armed forces—are highly focused upon foreign policy. This is especially true in an era in which globalization has raised the economic and political stakes of these groups with regard to foreign policy. These groups are influential during presidential campaigns, especially during the primaries, through financial contributions and grassroots campaigning. The general public's post–Cold War apathy on foreign policy has given these attentive publics a greater role.

These realities explain why the media and the candidates devoted considerable time in the 2000 campaign to foreign and defense policy despite the conventional wisdom that foreign policy doesn't matter,[5] and they may also explain why econometric models that emphasized domestic economic performance failed to predict the correct outcome of the presidential race.[6] The candidates' positions, values, competence, and character (honesty and independence) on foreign policy decision-making and their ability to manage crises matter even to "apathetic internationalist" voters. The candidates know that in addressing foreign policy they are not merely "waltzing before a blind audience."[7] Thus, foreign policy mattered at least enough to be one of the many factors that could have affected the outcome of such a close election. It mattered in the primaries, when interest groups were attentive and both Al Gore and George W. Bush espoused internationalist foreign policies. It mattered throughout the campaign in the race for funding and grassroots organizational muscle. And it mattered in the general election, when voters' overall judgments of the candidates were affected by how they handled foreign policy, from the ability to name foreign leaders to the handling of the case of Elian Gonzalez.

This chapter lends weight to these conclusions by first briefly reviewing the effect on foreign policy in previous campaigns. It then looks at the roles and attitudes of four "attentive publics" in the campaign: ideological activists and their sympathetic media outlets, ethnic groups, the military, and economic interest groups. Next, it analyzes polling data and media coverage on foreign policy during the general election campaign, and the ways in which candidates' mistakes on foreign policy entered into the public's evaluation of these candidates. It concludes that Bush would have won more votes if he had convinced the public of his personal ability to manage foreign policy and that Gore might have won the election if his apparent policy reversal on Elian Gonzalez had not reinforced the impression among voters that he would say anything to get elected.

Foreign Policy and the Public in Presidential Elections After World War II

Most arguments that "foreign policy doesn't matter" in U.S. presidential elections focus on the "salience" of foreign policy issues, or the relative importance the public places on these issues in polls. The salience of foreign policy is indeed one key factor in judging its impact on elections, but other factors are important as well, including perceived differences in candidates' positions, values, and competence on foreign policy issues. While the salience of foreign policy has dropped sharply since the end of the Cold War, these other factors remain important. Put in other terms, attitudes on candidates' handling of foreign policy may be accessible, or easy for voters to call to mind, thereby influencing voting decisions, even if these attitudes have reduced salience.[8]

In almost every poll from the end of World War II through the early 1970s, the public rated foreign policy as one of the top three most important issues facing the United States, often the very top issue.[9] The Cold

War was generally a top concern, and in addition specific issues mattered greatly in particular elections: the Korean War in 1952, the alleged "missile gap" in 1960, the Vietnam War in 1968 and 1972, the Soviet intervention in Afghanistan and the hostage crisis in Iran in 1980, and the dramatic changes in the Soviet Union in 1988. The salience of foreign policy issues changed dramatically with the end of the Cold War, however. Since 1992, foreign policy has barely ranked in the top dozen of the issues the public deems most important. In a January 2000 Gallup poll asking voters which issues were important to them, for example, military spending ranked only twentieth and the U.S. role in world affairs ranked twenty-second in importance.[10]

As noted above, many observers point to the 1992 election as a watershed event that demonstrated the limited importance of foreign policy after the Cold War. Foreign policy was indeed lower than domestic issues on the list of voters' priorities in 1992. Yet this interpretation overlooks that Bush's loss was also a consequence of setbacks and missed opportunities in foreign policy. Despite Bush's largely successful management of the end of the Cold War and the military and diplomatic conduct of the Gulf War, Saddam Hussein remained in power after the Gulf War, critics complained of Bush's lack of foreign policy "vision," and the president did not take effective action on Somalia (until after the election) or Bosnia.[11] In addition, the more isolationist candidates in both parties in 1992—Patrick Buchanan, Senator Tom Harkin, and former California governor Jerry Brown—did not win their parties' nominations.

Thus, candidates' positions and competence on foreign policy matter in addition to the overall salience of foreign policy issues. Through most of the Cold War, Republican candidates benefited from a reputation for being tougher on the Soviet Union than the Democrats, but with the end of the Cold War positional differences have diminished. Despite some differences in symbolism in the 1996 elections, such as Senator Robert Dole's criticisms of U.N. Secretary-General Boutros Boutros Gali, Dole and Clinton essentially agreed on most foreign policy issues, including the need for continuing the U.S. peacekeeping deployment in Bosnia. Perhaps the clearest generalization on foreign policy positions is that the candidate or the party holding the White House tends to be more internationalist than the opposition candidate or party. President Clinton, for example, focused on his domestic agenda in the 1992 campaign, but as president he was on the internationalist side of issues like U.N. funding, peacekeeping, fast-track trade negotiating authority, and funding of the International Monetary Fund (IMF). Meanwhile, the Republicans in Congress were on the isolationist side of these issues, especially after 1994.

Foreign policy experience matters as well as specific policy positions, but it is not overwhelmingly important: the candidate with less foreign policy experience won in 1992 (Bush–Clinton), 1980 (Carter–Reagan), and 1976 (Carter–Ford). More important than direct foreign policy experience is the voters' sense of the candidates' overall judgment, competence, and character on foreign policy issues. In particular, crisis management ability is a kind of litmus test for voters when they decide whom to vote for as president. Voters judge crisis management skills in a variety of contexts during the campaign, including those not directly related to foreign policy. Clinton's crisis management skills were on display, for example, when he survived the New Hampshire primary in 1992 despite a media feeding frenzy over an alleged extramarital affair. In this regard, George W. Bush's ability to survive a strong primary challenge by Senator John McCain probably helped convince voters of his crisis management skills. Exit polls from the 2000 presidential election support the idea that crisis management skills are important to voters. Of the 64 percent of voters who thought Gore could handle a world crisis, Gore won by 69 percent to 28 percent, and of the 34 percent who thought he could not do so, he lost by 11 percent to 84 percent. Similarly, Bush won by 75 percent to 23 percent among the 55 percent of voters who thought he could handle a crisis, and he lost by 12 percent to 83 percent among the 42 percent of voters who thought he could not.[12]

Foreign Policy and the Attentive Publics in 2000: Primaries, Funds, People Power

The attentive publics, or more specifically the interest groups, on foreign policy issues have a greater impact on the presidential campaigns than the numbers of their members would imply. As collective action theory indicates, because of the intensity of their members' interest in foreign policy issues, these groups are more active, organized, and willing to donate to campaigns than are most voters. The intensity of their views, especially if it reaches the point at which the group becomes a "single issue group" that will vote for or against candidates based on one issue alone, can also allow groups to seize the agenda on an issue even if their views on it are substantially different from those of the public at large.[13] We focus here on four categories of interest groups in the 2000 campaign: ideological partisans and their media allies, ethnic lobbies, the military, and economic groups.

Ideological and Partisan Attentive Publics: Issue Entrepreneurs

With the exception of international crises, key themes, major issues, and critical differences rarely just "emerge" in the conduct of campaigns for national-level office—the stakes for the candidates and their parties are far too high to permit much unscripted spontaneity in the messages delivered to the prospective electorate. Given the drop in the salience of foreign policy since the end of the Cold War, the issues that rise even momentarily in the public's view are even more likely to be the products of the carefully orchestrated efforts of either the political parties or their effective surrogates, particularly sympathetic media organizations. Many media organizations are ideologically aligned with a particular political party, both reflecting and influencing each party's attentive political base. Although issues do not always originate within these media, they are the mechanism by which initial ideas for issues are packaged and delivered for the primary consumption of the party faithful who serve as the first litmus test for an issue's salience. During the primary campaigns, candidates focus on these party activists, who are most likely to vote in the primaries. In the general election activists can compel enough mainstream media interest to propel an issue into the national limelight. Thus, ideologically aligned media outlets function in the public market of campaign issues in a manner similar to that in which business entrepreneurs operate in the market of goods and services—they are issue entrepreneurs.

During the 2000 election cycle, the contrasting foreign policy credentials of the leading Republican and Democratic presidential candidates may have precipitated the differing levels of foreign affairs debate found in the pages of their sympathetic print media outlets. While the *Wall Street Journal* and the *Washington Times* were considered to be more supportive of the Bush campaign agenda, and the *New York Times* and the *Washington Post* formally endorsed the Gore candidacy, a comparison of the foreign policy topics discussed in the more starkly partisan pages of the *Weekly Standard* (a more conservative political magazine ideologically aligned with the Republican Party) and the *New Republic* (a more liberal political magazine that strongly endorsed Al Gore) proves particularly illustrative.

With the aggressive assistance of the *Weekly Standard*, the Bush campaign was able to turn an issue which initially appeared to be an area of considerable weakness into a source of considerable strength, while the Gore campaign and the *New Republic* were often relegated to counterpunching responses. The *Weekly Standard* was an active proponent of Republican foreign policy issues and concerns throughout the presidential campaign. Early in the campaign, the *Standard* highlighted what would eventually become the first major foreign policy topic of the presidential campaign in a March 1999 editorial titled "The Kosovo Debacle."[14] Senator John McCain's campaign soon used this topic as a vehicle to accentuate his disagreements with prevailing U.S. foreign policy, lifting the issue into the main media spotlight, and as noted below, riding it to a favorable bounce in the public opinion polls. In the same month, and at several points throughout the campaign, the *Standard* also published articles and editorials favoring tougher U.S. foreign policy efforts regarding China, which became another major campaign issue.[15] By the end of 1999, the *Standard* was contributing to the development of the Republican Party platform with commentaries championing the rejection of isolationist ideals.[16] The *Standard* also rebutted issues that became problems for Bush, such as his poor performance on an international relations "pop quiz" in November 1999. The magazine countered the poor publicity from this incident by running a short summary of a prior foreign affairs gaffe by President Clinton.[17]

However, the *Standard* remained mostly on the offensive, capturing the foreign policy issues in the final months of the campaign in ways that were quickly reinforced by the Bush campaign itself. *Standard* articles and opinion pieces on missile defense in June 2000 were followed by a large Bush campaign media push on the same topic in July 2000.[18] An article on continued U.S. involvement in Kosovo in August 2000 presaged the Bush campaign's focus on U.S. military readiness (or the lack thereof) in September 2000.[19] In addition, the *Standard* provided the public with a framework for understanding the essence of the Bush foreign policy outlook at important moments during the campaign: "A Distinctly American Internationalism" was published after Bush's November 1999 foreign policy keynote address, "The Candidates' Foreign Policies: It's Bush's American Exceptionalism Versus Gore's Liberal Multilateralism," appeared in June 2000 during the summertime buildup to the conventions, and "A Compassionate Foreign Policy: Bush's Principle Works Surprisingly Well Abroad" ran during the September 2000 postconvention season Democratic surge.[20] Finally, the *Standard* offered a stretch-run foreign policy game plan for the Bush campaign in editorials that outlined "The High Road to High Office" and preached caution regarding "Gore's Last Stand?"[21]

On the other hand, the *New Republic* was somewhat less active on the foreign policy front. While the *Republic* did publish a forward-looking article on the similarities between the foreign policy teams and tenets of the George H. W. Bush administration and the George W. Bush campaign,[22] the *Republic* spent most of the campaign countering Republican attacks. Republican attempts to capitalize on the Elian Gonzalez incident (discussed further below) were derided in a May 2000 article titled "There They Go Again."[23] After Al Gore's Russia dealings and overall foreign policy perspectives were called into question, the *Republic* responded with pieces in August 2000 on Dick Cheney's Russia connections and the Bush foreign policy's lack of vision.[24] When the Clinton/Gore administration's commitment to military readiness came under fire, the *Republic* provided counterpoints in articles titled "Apocryphal Now" in September 2000 and "How the Democrats Became Hawks" in October 2000.[25] For both the Democratic and Republican parties, sympathetic media shaped and articulated the foreign policy talking points of the campaigns and the related views of party loyalists.

Ethnic Lobbies: Intermestic Issue Agents

In many ways, the 2000 presidential campaign cycle marked the beginning of a new calculus in the political battle for the patronage of the major ethnic minority groups in the United States. The key new development was that the votes of many of these groups could no longer be taken for granted or disregarded by either party. While African Americans have traditionally been the largest minority group in the national voting bloc and continued to support the Democratic Party candidate in an overwhelming fashion (see chapter 3 and 7 for more insights on this topic), some other growing ethnic minorities compelled increased attention from both political parties during the 2000 election campaign.

The impetus for this new dynamic can most likely be traced to both the changing demographics of the U.S. electorate and a calculated attempt by the Bush wing of the Republican party to broaden its political base. U.S. Census Bureau statistics show that Hispanics (also referred to as Latinos in the census) and Asians have been the fastest-growing major ethnic groups in the United States since the national elections of 1996, and 2000 census data indicate that the Latino population is currently roughly the same size as the African American population. The 2000 census data also reflect a widening geographic distribution of the Latino and Asian populaces; indeed, by 2000 eleven states' populations included double-digit percentages of either Latino or Asian minorities. The Census Bureau forecasts that the Latino and Asian populations will continue to grow (and presumably spread) faster than any of the other ethnic groups in the United States.[26] The aforementioned eleven states alone accounted for a total of 210 electoral votes for president (of a requisite 270) in 2000, and the number of significantly affected states and related electoral votes is almost certain to rise by the next presidential election cycle. In a strategic move, which may have long-term implications for the Republican party, the Bush campaign capitalized on its familiarity with campaigning among the large Latino contingents in Texas and Florida (two states that account for a total of 59 electoral votes) to court ethnic minority votes actively nationwide. The battle over minority votes became one of the enduring themes of this campaign, and intermestic foreign policy issues became significant points of contention on the campaign trail.[27]

Although Asians account for only 2 percent of the national electorate according to exit polls, they constitute an 11 percent share of the electorate in California, which was the state with the largest number of electoral votes, 54 in 2000. Asians are also the majority group in Hawaii (at 45 percent of the state voting-age population), but, with only 4 electoral votes, Hawaii often occupies a less prominent role in presidential election campaign politics.[28] Nationally, the Asian voting bloc appears to be the least likely ethnic minority group to side with the Democrats; exit polls indicate that Asian voters produced the slimmest Democratic majority among ethnic minority groups polled in 2000, with 55 percent of their votes going to Gore and 41 percent of their votes going to Bush. Furthermore, while the Asian majority in Hawaii delivered 61 percent of its votes to the Gore camp and only 35 percent of its votes to Bush, the Republicans were able to draw roughly even among Asian voters in California, where the Asian voting bloc split their vote 48 percent to 47 percent, Gore to Bush, according to the VNS exit poll.[29] Based on these figures, it appears that the Republican Party may already be making significant inroads into the Asian American electorate, with the potential for further expansion as the Asian minority grows within the United States.

Republican views regarding U.S. foreign policy in Asia, while in many ways consistent with the policies of the Democrats, may have inspired greater confidence among Asian Americans due to differences in both tone and implied prioritization. Throughout 1999, while U.S. entanglements in Kosovo and the Middle East peace process continued to dominate the news, concerns about Clinton administration policies in Asia, particularly regarding China, began to manifest themselves in the print media.[30] By June 1999, Republican presidential candidate Gary Bauer was "blasting" Gore on China policy, and in August Dan Quayle proposed a U.S. "foreign policy shift toward Asia."[31] After George W. Bush placed security concerns regarding China at the top of his list of foreign policy challenges (equal to, or higher than, problems in the Middle East and Europe), U.S. foreign policy in Asia remained a hot-button issue for the remainder of the campaign. While it is doubtful that the highlighting of potential U.S. difficulties in Asia was inspired significantly by anything other than the Republicans' interest in identifying weaknesses in the policies of a Democratic president, the vocal reassurances of the Bush campaign to Asian allies issued during campaign swings through California probably reflected somewhat the tailoring of the Bush message to fit the audience.[32] As the Asian presence increases in the United States, the Republican Party can be expected to focus such messages for Asian American audiences in a broader number of states.

A prime example of this trend can be found in the efforts of the Republican Party to court Latino voters. Similar to Asian Americans, Hispanic Americans have been voting in greater numbers since 1996, composing 7 percent of the total national vote in 2000 according to the exit poll. Ten states that account for 206 electoral votes have electorates with double-digit percentages of Latino voters. While nationally voters identifying themselves as Hispanic in the VNS exit poll tended to favor Gore over Bush at a rate just below 2 to 1 (62 percent for Gore and 35 percent for Bush), the group's vote has varied from 55 percent for Clinton in 1992 to 71 percent for Clinton in 1996, indicating that its votes can go to either party and that there were states where the Republicans were able to make inroads in 2000.[33] According to the same exit poll, the Hispanic vote in Florida slightly favored Bush over Gore, at a rate of 49 percent to 48 percent, and Hispanic voters in Texas and New Jersey favored Gore over Bush by margins of only 9 percent and 13 percent, respectively. While the status of George W. Bush and Jeb Bush as governors in Texas and Florida may have facilitated increases in the Republican share of the vote, it is possible that the Hispanic votes in Florida and New Jersey may have been at least partially influenced by the Elian Gonzalez case.

In addition to that case, a number of other foreign policy issues related to Latin America were raised during the campaign. During campaign swings through the states of the South and the West, the Bush camp made several commitments to increase the priority of U.S. ties with Latin America. Building upon Bush's gubernatorial experiences dealing with Mexico, in April 2000 his campaign team even considered a trip to Latin America as a means of indicating his foreign policy expertise.[34] By July 2000, Bush was showing interest in making Latin America a focal point of U.S. foreign policy, including proposals to make it easier for foreign nationals to join their immigrant families in the United States.[35] At the end of the summer, Bush accused the Clinton administration of neglecting Latin America and pledged to put the region at the center of his foreign policy agenda, to include a more active relationship with Mexico and broader economic, trade, and development programs for the hemisphere. While the Gore campaign did provide some counter proposals regarding the immigration issue and mounted a late effort to win over Cuban Americans during the Elian Gonzalez impasse, the overall Democratic agenda for Latin America seemed far less aggressive than its Republican counterpart. Given the relative success of the Republicans in Florida and Texas, and the projections for a large increase in the size of the Latino populace in the coming years, one can expect that the Republican Party will continue to court this growing ethnic group.

While smaller ethnic minorities received additional attention in some battleground states (particularly Arab and Central/Eastern European minorities in the Midwest),[36] with the Democratic nomination of Senator Joseph Lieberman for vice president the national Jewish electorate uniformly received far more media attention than in previous presidential election campaigns. However, the Republicans were actively courting this voting bloc as well, despite the traditionally high correlation of Jewish voters with the Democratic Party. As the Arab-Israeli peace talks faltered in late 1999 and early 2000, the Republican Party began to give more attention to Jewish voters,[37] and George W. Bush, in speeches before Jewish groups, promised he would "stand by Israel" and move the U.S. embassy to Jerusalem.[38] As the battleground states became more clear and Florida became a focal point for both campaigns' efforts, the Democrats began to vie for a large turnout in absentee ballots from the estimated 120,000 U.S. citizens living in Israel, in the expectation that the Lieberman nomination would reinforce the traditionally strong support that they regularly received from the Jewish American electorate.[39] While the support of the Jewish vote for the Democrats was not in doubt by the end of the campaign (the exit poll indicates that 79 percent of Jewish Americans voted for Gore and 19 percent voted for Bush),[40] the more hawkish views of the Republican Party regarding the terms of Middle East peace may influence future elections if the Lieberman factor does not reemerge in future presidential election contests.

Military Personnel—An Increasingly Partisan Public

For a number of years, the members of the U.S. armed forces were perceived to be above the fray of partisan politics. Part of this belief was based on a military culture which produced a president (Dwight Eisenhower) who cast his first vote in a national election only when he himself was campaigning for the Republican ticket.[41] However, this view has changed greatly since the end of the Vietnam War, as survey and other data have indicated that the military has changed from a largely nonpartisan group to a largely partisan one. Over half of the military officers responding to a survey in 1976 indicated that they were either nonpartisan or independents, and roughly one-third of respondents stated that they were Republicans. In 1996, the number of nonpartisan/independent responses decreased to just over one-fourth of those surveyed, and two-thirds of the survey group identified themselves as Republicans. The Democratic contingent in these surveys dropped from 12 percent in 1976 to 7 percent in 1996. The political self-identification of military personnel shifted from significantly conservative (at a level of 4 to 1, conservative to liberal) to overwhelmingly conservative (running as high as 24 to 1, conservative to liberal) over the same period.[42] Since military members tend to vote at a rate higher than that of the average U.S. citizen, and since several military veterans are involved in the leadership and management structures of defense industry, the military is an audience whose support is coveted by both Democrats and Republicans alike, despite the declining size of the military component of the overall electorate.[43] Yet the military absentee ballot maneuvering by the Democrats in Florida and the quick Republican response indicate a clear expectation that military votes are often Republican ones. The 2000 election campaign provides some indications that the widening gap between the military and the Democratic Party is not merely a function of foreign and defense policy differences.

Throughout the campaign, Bush questioned the wisdom and effectiveness of the Clinton administration's policies for the use and support of the military. He claimed that the U.S. armed forces were overworked, underpaid, and underresourced, and therefore less ready to protect U.S. interests. Bush argued that the primary cause of these difficulties was the overextension of the U.S. military through multiple peacekeeping deployments with unclear missions in areas of questionable U.S. interest. He pledged to rebuild the military, infuse it with the best equipment available, increase its pay, and employ it less often, and then only in direct support of clear U.S. interests.[44] His efforts appeared to resonate with both the leadership of the U.S. armed forces, which produced several retiring admirals and generals who quickly endorsed the Bush campaign,[45] and the U.S. public at large, which polls indicate was convinced that Bush would "improve military security for the country."[46]

However, some evidence suggests that the growing identification of the military with the Republican Party versus the Democratic Party is linked to a combination of differences regarding U.S. foreign, defense, and social policies. While the increased number of deployments may be affecting military morale, Department of Defense reenlistment data suggest that deployed members of the U.S. armed forces look favorably upon their efforts in many of the operations that the Republicans criticized (such as U.S. operations in Bosnia and Kosovo).[47] Several distinguished former military leaders have also asserted that these types of deployments can actually be beneficial for unit readiness and training.[48] Additionally, a comparison of the budget proposals of the two major campaigns indicates that Gore's proposed increase for the Defense Department budget was over twice the size of the increase proposed by Bush ($100 billion vs. $45 billion).[49] The Gore campaign may have paid the price for a perceived Democratic attack on military culture stemming back to the Vietnam era, extending through the Navy Tailhook scandal to the Clinton/Gore position on homosexuals serving in the military.[50] Military personnel have also indicated an interest in having a president with a greater moral imperative than President Clinton, whose credibility was undercut even before he entered office by assertions that he dodged the draft during Vietnam. Yet similar assertions regarding Bush's Air National Guard service during the Vietnam War apparently did not greatly affect his credibility, despite the contrasts provided by McCain's POW experience and Gore's U.S. Army service in Vietnam. Based on these observations, the evolving largely Republican partisanship of the U.S. military is probably a product of both a clash of cultures and differences in foreign and defense policy ideals.

Economic Interest Groups: The Defense Industries and Labor Unions

One of the big stories of the 2000 campaign was the surge in campaign funding. Campaign contributions by groups with foreign policy interests, particularly the defense industry and labor groups, were a substantial part of the fund-raising story.

Missile defense was one of the clearest foreign policy issue contrasts between the two candidates. Missile defense contracts are scheduled to total $12 billion or higher over the next six years, but campaign contributions by missile defense contractors were surprisingly limited. The top four missile defense contractors, Boeing, Raytheon, Lockheed Martin, and TRW, gave about $3.75 million in campaign contributions in 2000, but less than $200,000 of the nearly $13 million total of *all* defense sector contributions went to the presidential candidates. Bush received the lion's share—$150,000 to Gore's $40,000—as their respective positions on defense issues would lead us to expect. The direct contributions of defense businesses to the presidential campaigns were dwarfed by the overall funds raised by Bush and Gore.[51] A key caveat to these figures, however, is that they capture only contributions by political action committees (PACs), not those by individuals working in the defense or other industries, and individuals contributed roughly 80 percent of the nonfederal funds for the Bush campaign and more than 90 percent of such funds for the Gore campaign.[52] Thus, the PAC contribution figures may be more useful as a rough guide to the proportion of their monies that groups gave to each campaign than they are an accurate measure of the total funds given by any economic sector.[53]

The direct financial contributions of labor groups to the two campaigns were even smaller—$38,000 in organizational contributions to Bush and $99,000 to Gore—and probably also understated due to the limited data on individual contributions. More significant was the $30 million in soft money that labor groups contributed, primarily to causes favored by Democrats. Labor groups constituted six of the top ten soft money contributors.[54] Perhaps equally important was the contribution that labor groups made in organizational skills and grassroots campaigning, especially to the Gore campaign, which won 59 percent to Bush's 37 percent among the one-fourth of households in the nation that included union members. Labor interests of course did not focus only or even primarily on international issues like trade—the Gore campaign won the labor vote despite Gore's support for free trade with Mexico and China. In view of labor groups' importance to the Democratic party in the 2000 campaign, however, these groups are likely to carry added weight in trade issues before the Congress.

Foreign Policy and the General Public

The presidential candidates' campaign strategies and the results of voter exit polls were broadly consistent with the results of foreign policy polls through the 1990s. These results include the decreased salience of foreign policy after the Cold War and the public's continuing internationalism, multilateralism focus on intermestic issues, and reluctance to make foreign policy sacrifices but willingness to risk casualties when important national interests were at stake. Regarding the salience of foreign policy, the number of foreign policy issues mentioned as among the most important problems facing the country dropped by 50 percent in comparable polls from 1994 to 1999.[55] Foreign policy remained at or near the bottom of the public's priorities through the election year, and in national exit polls only 12 percent of voters said foreign policy mattered most to them, less than the proportion citing the economy, taxes, education, and social security. Yet the proportion of voters who agreed that the United States should take an active role in world affairs remained between 61 percent and 69 percent in polls throughout the 1990s, levels not markedly different from those during the Cold War, when public responses to this same question ranged between 54 percent (in 1982) and

71 percent (in 1956).[56] At the same time, elites, in the leading poll that samples them, were far more internationalist than the public, with a remarkable 97 percent agreeing that the United States should take an active role in world affairs.[57] With regard to multilateralism, 77 percent of the public agreed in a 1999 poll that in international crises the United States should not act alone without the support of U.S. allies, and in various other polls similarly high proportions of the public agreed that it was at least somewhat important to work through the U.N. to build support for U.S. policies.[58] When asked about the foreign policy issues it considered the most important, the public in the 1990s focused on intermestic issues: solid majorities listed immigration, terrorism, drug smuggling, and protection of manufacturing jobs from international competition as important issues.[59] Lastly, while the public had mixed views on peacekeeping and humanitarian intervention in the 1990s, and while it was generally more reluctant than elites to use force, the public was willing to risk casualties if important national interests were at stake.[60]

The presidential candidates in 2000 thus faced an electorate that placed low priority on foreign policy but that remained internationalist and wanted a president able to manage foreign policy crises. The candidates responded with foreign policies that were similar in their broad outlines but different in details, symbolism, and presentation. In the end, despite the low salience of foreign policy and the limited positional differences between the candidates, the evidence from polling data, while limited, suggests that the public's perceptions of foreign policy mistakes in the campaigns affected the outcome in the extremely close presidential race.

Reflecting the low salience of foreign policy, neither Gore nor Bush placed much emphasis on foreign policy in public statements. Both candidates articulated their foreign policies in a few key speeches early in their campaigns, adopting generally internationalist policies.[61] Bush's foreign policy advisers and supporters, including Condoleeza Rice, Colin Powell, Henry Kissinger, and Norman Schwarzkopf as well as vice presidential candidate Richard Cheney, played a prominent role in Bush's campaign, often appearing with him on the stage at important foreign policy speeches to allay concerns over Bush's lack of foreign policy experience. Due to Gore's long foreign policy experience and his hands-on managerial style, his foreign policy advisers had a less prominent and public role.

Both candidates made very little reference to foreign policy in their convention speeches. Bush drew attention to the issue of defense readiness in his convention speech and in the weeks that followed, which helped him gain an edge in polls on the defense issue. Similarly, Bush attempted to gain advantage from his emphasis on building ballistic missile defenses, but this won him limited support in the face of Gore's similar support for research on missile defenses. As for the Democratic convention, Gore discussed foreign policy in a few paragraphs, overriding the suggestions of some of his advisers to cut out any mention of foreign policy.[62] The candidates' policy differences on other highly visible issues were limited: both supported the establishment of permanent normal trading relations with China, and both opposed a bill proposed in Congress to set a summer deadline for the withdrawal of U.S. troops from Kosovo.

Perhaps due to the limited differences in the candidates' foreign policy positions and the low salience of foreign policy, polls in spring 2000 showed that the public was evenly divided on whether Gore (42 percent) or Bush (43 percent) would handle foreign affairs better.[63] This actually represented a comeback of sorts for Gore—in June 1999 Bush began with a substantial advantage of 53 percent to Gore's 36 percent on the question of who could better handle foreign policy, but this margin eroded over time.[64] Some of this shift was no doubt due to the typical rise in a vice president's stature upon becoming the nominee. More detailed polling results, however, suggest that Bush's mistakes and gaffes on foreign policy—lack of leadership on Kosovo and lack of facility with the names of foreign leaders and peoples—reduced his support. At the same time, Gore's abrupt policy change regarding Elian Gonzalez may have cost him support in Florida, which proved crucial to the election outcome. In general, foreign policy issues reinforced the overall perceptions that voters had of the candidates: Gore won points on his experience and his positions on the issues, while Bush won among those who emphasized trustworthiness and other personal qualities. As with many of the exit poll results, these numbers should be treated with caution, as they could indicate either that Bush voters were more likely to find foreign policy important or that voters who emphasized foreign policy were more likely to support Bush.

Bush's Hesitation on Kosovo

Bush's hesitation in stating a clear policy on the crisis in Kosovo was arguably his most costly foreign policy mistake in the campaign. When the crisis erupted in late March 1999, Senator John McCain immediately stated that if the United States used force, it should use it to win, and it should not rule out the use of ground forces. This stand, together with McCain's reputation as a Vietnam War hero, gave him tremendous national exposure and credibility on television news and talk shows. In contrast, Bush avoided making a clear policy statement on the crisis for several weeks before finally echoing McCain's policy position. This delay may have resulted in part from Bush's caution as a front-runner, but it also reportedly reflected divisions among Bush's foreign policy advisers.[65] Whatever the reason for Bush's indecisiveness, this episode clearly marked the start of McCain's rise over the other candidates for the Republican nomination, which forced Bush into a longer, more expensive, and more politically damaging nomination fight than previously anticipated by several party members. Polls in New Hampshire in April and May 1999 showed McCain rising to third place in the Republican race, behind Bush and Elizabeth Dole, and in national polls McCain rose from 3 percent in March to 6 percent in May.[66] When McCain jolted the Bush campaign by winning the New Hampshire primary in February 2000, the exit poll showed voters strongly favored McCain on foreign policy issues and decisive leadership.[67] By summer 2000, however, as Bush won his party's nomination, he also stayed even with or slightly ahead of Gore in polls asking which candidate could handle foreign policy better.[68] By November, among the 12 percent of voters nationally who said foreign policy was the most important issue, Bush won over Gore by 54 percent to 40 percent.

Bush's Failure on the "Pop Quiz"

Bush's better-known mistakes concern his ability to name only one of four foreign leaders in response to a reporter's "pop quiz" in November 1999 and his frequent misnaming of foreign peoples (such as calling the Greeks "Grecians"). These mistakes did not cause any immediate or marked drop in Bush's standing in the polls. Public attention to the campaign at the time was limited, and the public distinguishes between substantive knowledge of policy details and judgment in a crisis. The defensive manner of Bush's response to the pop quiz, however, gave the story a long lease on life and reduced the public's confidence in Bush's knowledge of foreign affairs. The Lexis-Nexis database of newspaper stories shows 96 stories with the keywords "Bush" and "quiz" in the first week after the quiz, and 236 stories with these terms through the end of December 1999. Meanwhile, confidence that Bush would do a "good job" on foreign policy fell from 61 percent in mid-September 1999 to 55 percent in mid-January 2000. A December 1999 poll showed that 58 percent of the public thought Gore knew enough about foreign affairs to be a good president, versus only 44 percent who thought this of Bush. In contrast, the public's assessments of the two candidates' knowledge of economic and education policy differed by only 1 to 2 percent.

These differences in the public's views of the foreign policy knowledge of the two candidates persisted through the November election. Among the 13 percent of voters who said that an understanding of the issues was a candidate's most important quality, Gore won by 75 percent to 19 percent, and he similarly won by 82 percent to 17 percent among the 15 percent of voters who said experience mattered most. In addition, more than one-third of voters said that only Gore had sufficient knowledge to be president, while slightly less than one-fourth of voters said that only Bush had such knowledge. Perhaps most striking, of the 30 percent of voters who said both candidates knew enough to be president, Bush won 71 percent of the vote. While the exit poll did not specifically ask whether either candidate knew enough about "foreign policy" to be president, when combined with the poll cited above indicating a perceived "knowledge" gap of 14 percent on foreign affairs and only 1 to 2 percent on other issues, the data suggest that if more voters had been convinced of Bush's knowledge of world affairs, he could have garnered a significantly higher number of votes.

Gore's Policy Shift on Elian Gonzalez

Gore's foreign policy standing suffered when, breaking from a Clinton administration policy that he had tacitly supported, Gore abruptly endorsed proposed legislation in late March 2000 to grant permanent resident status to Elian Gonzalez, a Cuban boy who had barely survived a raft trip to the United States. This position put Gore at odds with the strong majority of the public, who felt that Elian should be reunited with his father in Cuba. More important, Gore's decision raised concerns that he was conceding in a self-serving way to pressure from Cuban Americans. Consequently, a USA Today poll on April 24 showed that 37 percent disapproved of Gore's handling of Elian's case and only 25 percent approved of his actions, and between March 30 and April 7 Gore dropped from 45 percent to 41 percent among likely voters in polls pitting him against Bush. The VNS poll from November showed that Gore suffered from a feeling among voters that he would "say anything" to be elected, and Gore's handling of the Elian Gonzalez incident probably contributed to this perception. One-third of voters nationally said only Gore would "say anything" to get elected, and he lost by more than a 5 to 1 margin among this group. Of those who said both candidates or neither candidate would say anything, Gore won by about 57 percent to 38 percent (only 17 percent of voters said only Bush would say anything and this group voted for Gore by a 5 to 1 margin). Among the one-quarter of voters who said trustworthiness was the most important quality, Bush won by 80 percent to 15 percent, and of those emphasizing strong leadership, he won by 64 percent to 34 percent. As Carter Eskew, one of Gore's top campaign strategists, later bluntly remarked, Gore's break with the Clinton administration on the status of Elian "made us look unprincipled and stupid."[69]

Gore's policy shift regarding Elian may in fact have cost him votes among non-Cuban Latino voters in Florida, some of whom may have been upset that Gore would make an exception for one boy attempting to immigrate from Cuba while thousands of other Latinos were being turned away at U.S. borders every day.[70] Although Gore won among Latino voters nationally by 62 percent to 35 percent, he lost by 48 percent to 49 percent among Latino voters in Florida, where 80 percent of the Latinos who voted were non-Cubans and Latinos as a whole made up 11 percent of those who voted.

Conclusions

In an increasingly globalized world in which domestic and foreign policy are ever more closely intertwined, foreign policy will continue to matter to the presidential preferences of the American public. The generally low salience of foreign policy after the Cold War does not make candidates' foreign policy credentials and their ability to manage crises unimportant to voting decisions, and international economic and security crises retain the potential to vault foreign policy to the top of the agenda. The low salience of foreign policy does, however, heighten the importance of foreign policy interest groups in the absence of headline-grabbing crises. Presidential candidates will have to continue to steer a delicate course between the public which is generally internationalist and multilateralist but reluctant to make sacrifices for less than vital goals, and interest groups that are deeply committed to policies that are variously more internationalist or more isolationist than the public desires. Any mistakes or gaffes that candidates make in either direction—alienating the apathetic internationalist public through a display of incompetence, indecisiveness, or unprincipled concessions to interest groups, or losing the financial and organizational support of foreign policy interest groups through insufficient attentiveness to their concerns—can cost an election. When it comes to foreign policy, presidential candidates waltz not before a blind audience, but before an audience filled with raucous partisans in the front rows and theater critics in the back who want to see whether the dancers on stage can keep the hecklers in check without missing a beat.

Notes

1. Steven Kull, I. M. Destler, and Clay Ramsey, *The Foreign Policy Gap: How Policymakers Misread the Public*, iii–iv.
2. James M. Lindsay, "From Containment to Apathy," 2–9.
3. Bruce Jentleson, "The Pretty Prudent Public: Post-Vietnam American Opinion on the Use of Military Force," 49–73.
4. John E. Reilly, ed., *American Public Opinion and U.S. Foreign Policy 1999*.
5. Foreign policy was a prominent issue in the candidate debates, and Gore and Bush each made at least a half-dozen campaign speeches devoted mostly or solely to foreign policy. The media also devoted attention to foreign policy; a search of Lexis-Nexus from October 15 to November 7, 2000, returned eighteen records for the search terms "foreign policy" and "campaign."
6. On this issue, see Robert Kaiser, "Political Scientists Offer Mea Culpas for Predicting Gore Win," A10.
7. John Aldrich, John Sullivan, and Eugene Borgida, "Foreign Affairs and Issue Voting: Do Presidential Candidates 'Waltz Before a Blind Audience'?" 123–141. For additional evidence that the presidential candidates' handling of foreign policy affects voters' overall perceptions of these candidates, see Miroslav Nincic and Barbara Hinckley, "Foreign Policy and the Evaluation of Presidential Candidates," 333–355.
8. Aldrich et al., "Foreign Affairs and Issue Voting," 125.
9. Ibid., 131.
10. *Gallup Poll Monthly* from January 2000. Subsequent polling numbers cited herein, unless otherwise noted, are also from the *Gallup Poll Monthly* of the relevant dates.
11. Thomas Omestad, "Why Bush Lost," 70–81.
12. "Exit Polls," CNN Election 2000.
13. Robert Putnam, "Diplomacy and Domestic Politics: The Logic of Two-Level Games," 427–460.
14. Robert Kagan, "The Kosovo Debacle," 8.
15. See Matthew Rees, "Congress's China Challenge," 10; William Kristol and Robert Kagan, "Call Off the Engagement," 9; William Kristol and Robert Kagan, "Free Taiwan," 11; William Kristol and Robert Kagan, "Pressuring Taiwan, Appeasing Beijing," 5; Greg Mastel, "Let's Not Make a Deal," 16; "Bush vs. Forbes on China," 2; "Democracy Makes All the Difference: China Mavens Are in Denial about the Meaning of the Taiwan Election," 16; Robert Kagan, "China, Taiwan, and a Load of Fertilizer," 11; and John R. Bolton, "Beijing's WTO Double-Cross: Surprise! China Is Trying to Keep Taiwan Out of the World Trade Organization," 19.
16. See William Kristol and Robert Kagan, "Time to Pay Our Dues," 9; and Lawrence F. Kaplan, "The Lessons of 1952: Will the GOP Presidential Nominee Shape His Party's Foreign Policy?" 17.
17. "The President and His Marbles," 2.
18. See Alexander Rose, "Al's Risky Scheme: Why Gore Prefers Outdated Arms Control to a National Missile Defense," 21; "The Bush-Clinton Missile Defense," 2; and Robert Kagan, "Bush's Missile Defense Triumph," 11.
19. Tom Donnelly and Gary Schmitt, "What Winning Means: In Kosovo to Stay?" 38.
20. See William Kristol and Robert Kagan, "A Distinctly American Internationalism," 7; Marc A. Thiessen, "The Candidates' Foreign Policies: It's Bush's American Exceptionalism Versus Gore's Liberal Multilateralism," 16; and Peter Feaver and Ed-

mund Malesky, "A Compassionate Foreign Policy: Bush's Principle Works Surprisingly Well Abroad," 17.

21. See David Brooks and William Kristol, "The High Road to High Office," 11; and William Kristol, "Gore's Last Stand?" 9.

22. Jacob Heilbrunn, "Team W," 22.

23. Ryan Lizza, "There They Go Again," 15.

24. See Lawrence Kaplan, "From Russia with Loans," 22; and "Unwelcome Back," 9.

25. See Gregg Easterbrook, "Apocryphal Now," 22; and "How the Democrats Became Hawks," 23.

26. See Gregory Rodriguez, "The Future Americans," M1; and "Census 2000 Briefs" and "Census 2000 Redistricting Data Summary File," U.S. Census Bureau. It should be noted that although African Americans, Asians, and Hispanics/Latinos are referred to as ethnic minorities in this article, the U.S. Census Bureau now considers the Hispanic/Latino minority group to represent a separate ethnic origin and lists the African American and Asian minorities as races.

27. Jonathan Tilove, "Diversity Debate Changing American Politics: Parties Strive to Prove Their Inclusiveness," 17.

28. "Census 2000 Redistricting Data," U.S. Census Bureau.

29. "Exit Polls," CNN Election 2000.

30. See James Kitfield, "Indispensable, Yet Uncertain," 1010; Stan Crock, "The New China Syndrome," 30; and Deb Price, "Al, Voters, Keep Eye on World: Foreign Affairs Emerge as Key Issue in 2000 Election," A1.

31. See "Bauer Blasts Gore on China Policy in VP's Home State," *U.S. Newswire;* and "Quayle Suggests Foreign Policy Shift Toward Asia," *The Bulletin's Frontrunner.*

32. For example, see Tom Zoellner, "Ex-President Bush Stumps for Son in S. F.'s Chinatown," A3.

33. Patrick McDonnell and George Ramos, "Latinos Make Strong Showing at the Polls," *Los Angeles Times*, November 8, 1996, A1.

34. Danielle Decker, "Hotline Extra for April 29, 2000," 1378.

35. See Jim Hoagland, "Mexico: Fox Victory Shows Political Globalization Has Crossed the Rio Grande," 21A; and Stewart M. Powell, "Bush Makes Pitch for Immigrant Families: He'd Make It Easier for Foreign Nationals to Join Their Kin," A-6.

36. Matthew Rees, "Arabs, Poles, and Other Key Voters: Ethnic 'Outreach' Could Decide Who Makes It to the White House," 22.

37. Michael Shapiro, "Republican Presidential Hopefuls Gather to Woo GOP Jewish Group," 4.

38. Barbara Slavin, "Bush Says He'll Stand By Israel, Vows to Move U.S. Embassy to Jerusalem," 22A.

39. Bob Davis and Greg Jaffe, "Parties Estimate Critical Role of Overseas Voters," A20.

40. "Exit Polls," CNN Election 2000.

41. Thomas E. Ricks, " 'I Think We're Pretty Disgusted': Challenging of Overseas Ballots Widens Divide Between Military, Democrats," A18.

42. Ole R. Holsti, "A Widening Gap between the U.S. Military and Civilian Society? Some Evidence, 1976–96," 11–13.

43. Catherine Edwards, "Overseas Ballots Don't Reach Home," 23–25.

44. See Terry M. Neal, "Bush Outlines Defense Plan in Address at the Citadel: GOP Front-Runner Pushes Pay Hikes, High-Tech Weapons," A3; and Otto Kreisher and Stephen Green, "Rebuilding Military Takes Spotlight as Bush, Gore Joust: Candidates Would Spend Millions on Different Priorities," A17.

45. Richard H. Kohn, "General Elections: The Brass Shouldn't Do Endorsements," A23.

46. "Public Opinion Uneasy About Economy, Polls Find; Opinion: As Bush Takes Office, About Twice as Many People Are Optimistic about the Next Four Years as Are Pessimistic. Most Think He Will Improve the Military," A16.

47. William S. Cohen, "No Shortchanging Defense," A27.

48. "Warriors and Peacemakers," A14.

49. Kreisher and Green, "Rebuilding Military Takes Spotlight," A17.

50. See Tom Donnelly, "Why Soldiers Dislike Democrats," 14–15; Mackubin Thomas Owens, "The Democratic Party's War on the Military," A22; and Ricks, " 'I Think We're Pretty Disgusted,' " A18.

51. "Who's Getting: 2000 Presidential Race," Center for Responsive Politics.

52. Ibid.

53. Missile defense contractors were also unusually quiet in their lobbying efforts because they felt support for missile defense was so strong that additional lobbying would be unnecessary or even counterproductive. In addition, missile defense contracts, while large, are only a small part of the top defense contractors' business (for example, current contracts are roughly 1 percent of overall revenues for both Boeing and Lockheed Martin). See Greg Schneider, "A Strategy of Silence on Missile Defense," H1; and Lesley Wayne, "After High-Pressure Years, Contractors Tone Down on Missile Defense Lobbying," A6.

54. Brody Mullins and Charlie Mitchell, "Soft Money Unleashed," 500–501.

55. Reilly, *American Public Opinion*, 7

56. "Gallup/CNN/USA Today Poll," The Polling Report.

57. Reilly, *American Public Opinion*, 38.

58. Ibid, 38; and Kull, Destler, and Ramsay, *Foreign Policy Gap*, 49–50.

59. Reilly, *American Public Opinion*, 38.

60. Ole R. Holsti, "Public Opinion and Foreign Policy," in Robert J. Lieber, ed., *Eagle Rules? Foreign Policy and American Primacy in the 21st Century*, forthcoming.

61. The foreign policy speeches that received the widest coverage included Bush's speech of October 19, 1999 (see Dan Balz, "Bush Favors Internationalism: Candidate Calls China a 'Competitor,' Opposes Test Ban Treaty," A1), and Gore's speech of April 30, 2000 (see Edwin Chen, "Campaign 2000; Gore Touts Foreign Policy Experience; Politics: Vice-President Outlines an Agenda that Focuses on Issues 'Before They Become Crises'," 12).

62. Melinda Henneberger, "In Reversal of Speech Process, Gore Wrote and His Aides Then Whittled," 17.

63. *Gallup Poll Monthly* for May 2000, 11.

64. Ibid.

65. See John Lancaster and Terry M. Neal, "Heavyweight 'Vulcans' Help Bush Forge a Foreign Policy," A2, which indicates that Bush adviser Dov Zakheim was against taking military action to stop ethnic cleansing in Kosovo, while Paul Wolfowitz was for it, contributing to Bush's indecisiveness on the issue.

66. See Ronald Brownstein, "Crisis in Kosovo Gives McCain's Presidential Bid a Boost," 8; and *Gallup Poll Monthly* for March–May 1999.

67. Robert Kagan, "The Biggest Issue of All," A23.

68. Polls from April to July showed a modest increase in the belief that Bush could handle foreign policy better than Gore, yielding a 45 percent to 40 percent advantage for Bush on this question by July. See "Bloomberg, ABC News and Washington Post Polls" and "CNN/USA Today Polls," The Polling Report.

69. Richard Berke, "Gore and Bush Strategists Analyze Their Campaigns," A19.

70. Philip Pan and Michael Fletcher, "Other Latinos More Divided over Fate of Cuban Boy," A2.

Bibliography

Aldrich, John, John Sullivan, and Eugene Borgida. "Foreign Affairs and Issue Voting: Do Presidential Candidates 'Waltz Before a Blind Audience'?" *American Political Science Review* 83, no. 1 (March 1989): 123–141.

Balz, Dan. "Bush Favors Internationalism: Candidate Calls China a 'Competitor,' Opposes Test Ban Treaty." *Washington Post* (November 20, 1999): A1.

"Bauer Blasts Gore on China Policy in VP's Home State." *U.S. Newswire*, June 16, 1999.

Berke, Richard. "Gore and Bush Strategists Analyze Their Campaigns." *New York Times* (February 12, 2001): A19.

"Bloomberg, ABC News and Washington Post Polls." The Polling Report. July 2000. <www.pollingreport.com/defense/htm>.

Bolton, John R. "Beijing's WTO Double-Cross: Surprise! China Is Trying to Keep Taiwan Out of the World Trade Organization." *Weekly Standard* (August 14, 2000): 19.

Brooks, David, and William Kristol. "The High Road to High Office." *Weekly Standard* (September 25, 2000): 11.

Brownstein, Ronald. "Crisis in Kosovo Gives McCain's Presidential Bid a Boost." *Los Angeles Times* (April 22, 1999): 8.

"The Bush-Clinton Missile Defense." *Weekly Standard* (June 12, 2000): 2

"Bush vs. Forbes on China." *Weekly Standard* (November 22, 1999): 2.

"Census 2000 Briefs." U.S. Census Bureau. March 13, 2001. <www.census.gov>.

"Census 2000 Redistricting Data Summary File." U.S. Census Bureau. March 13, 2001. <www.census.gov>.

Chen, Edwin. "Campaign 2000; Gore Touts Foreign Policy Experience; Politics: Vice-President Outlines an Agenda that Focuses on Issues " 'Before They Become Crises'." *Los Angeles Times* (May 1, 2000): 12.

"CNN/USA Today Polls." The Polling Report, July 2000. <www.pollingreport.com/defense/htm>.

Cohen, William S. "No Shortchanging Defense." *Washington Post* (January 27, 2000): A27.

Crock, Stan. "The New China Syndrome." *Business Week*, no. 3632 (June 7, 1999): 30.

Davis, Bob, and Greg Jaffe. "Parties Estimate Critical Role of Overseas Voters." *Wall Street Journal* (November 10, 2000): A20.

Decker, Danielle. "Hotline Extra for April 29, 2000." *National Journal* 32, no. 18 (April 29, 2000): 1378.

"Democracy Makes All the Difference: China Mavens Are in Denial About the Meaning of the Taiwan Election." *Weekly Standard* (April 3, 2000): 16.

Donnelly, Tom. "Why Soldiers Dislike Democrats." *Weekly Standard* (December 4, 2000): 14–15.

Donnelly, Tom, and Gary Schmitt. "What Winning Means: In Kosovo to Stay?" *Weekly Standard* (August 28, 2000): 38.

Easterbrook, Gregg. "Apocryphal Now." *New Republic* (September 11, 2000): 22.

Edwards, Catherine. "Overseas Ballots Don't Reach Home." *Insight on the News* 17, no. 2 (January 8, 2001): 23–25.

"Exit Polls." CNN Election 2000. December 29, 2000. <http://www.cnn.com/ ELECTION/2000/>.
Feaver, Peter, and Edmund Malesky. "A Compassionate Foreign Policy: Bush's Principle Works Surprisingly Well Abroad." *Weekly Standard* (September 25, 2000): 17.
"Gallup/CNN/USA Today Poll." The Polling Report. July 2000. <www.pollingreport. com/defense/htm>.
Gallup Poll Monthly 1999–2000. <www.gallup.com>.
Heilbrunn, Jacob. "Team W." *New Republic* (September 27, 1999): 22.
Henneberger, Melinda. "In Reversal of Speech Process, Gore Wrote and His Aides Then Whittled." *New York Times* (August 18, 2000): 17.
Hoagland, Jim. "Mexico: Fox Victory Shows Political Globalization Has Crossed the Rio Grande." *Dallas Morning News* (July 6, 2000): 21A.
Holsti, Ole R. "Public Opinion and Foreign Policy." In Robert J. Lieber, ed., *Eagle Rules? Foreign Policy and American Primacy in the 21st Century*. Englewood Cliffs, NJ: Prentice-Hall, 2001.
———. "A Widening Gap between the U.S. Military and Civilian Society? Some Evidence, 1976–96." *International Security* 23, no. 3 (Winter 1998/1999): 11–13.
"How the Democrats Became Hawks." *New Republic* (October 23, 2000): 23.
Jentleson, Bruce. "The Pretty Prudent Public: Post-Vietnam American Opinion on the Use of Military Force." *International Studies Quarterly* 36 (March 1992): 49–73.
Kagan, Robert. "The Biggest Issue of All." *Washington Post* (February 15, 2000): A23.
———. "Bush's Missile Defense Triumph." *Weekly Standard* (June 26, 2000): 11.
———. "China, Taiwan, and a Load of Fertilizer." *Weekly Standard* (April 3, 2000): 11.
———. "The Kosovo Debacle." *Weekly Standard* (March 8, 1999): 8.
Kaiser, Robert. "Political Scientists Offer Mea Culpas for Predicting Gore Win." *Washington Post* (February 9, 2001): A10.
Kaplan, Lawrence F. "From Russia with Loans." *New Republic* (August 7, 2000): 22.
———. "The Lessons of 1952: Will the GOP Presidential Nominee Shape His Party's Foreign Policy?" *Weekly Standard* (December 27, 1999): 17.
Kitfield, James. "Indispensable, Yet Uncertain." *National Journal* 31, no. 16 (April 17, 1999): 1010.
Kohn, Richard H. "General Elections: The Brass Shouldn't Do Endorsements," *Washington Post* (September 19, 2000): A23.
Kreisher, Otto, and Stephen Green. "Rebuilding Military Takes Spotlight as Bush, Gore Joust: Candidates Would Spend Millions on Different Priorities." *San Diego Union-Tribune* (November 4, 2000): A17.
Kristol, William. "Gore's Last Stand?" *Weekly Standard* (October 23, 2000): 9.
Kristol, William, and Robert Kagan. "Call Off the Engagement." *Weekly Standard* (May 24, 1999): 9.
———. "A Distinctly American Internationalism." *Weekly Standard* (November 29, 1999): 7.
———. "Free Taiwan." *Weekly Standard* (July 26, 1999): 11.
———. "Pressuring Taiwan, Appeasing Beijing." *Weekly Standard* (August 2, 1999): 5.
———. "Time to Pay Our Dues." *Weekly Standard* (November 8, 1999): 9.
Kull, Steven, I. M. Destler, and Clay Ramsey. *The Foreign Policy Gap: How Policymakers Misread the Public*. College Park, MD: Center for International and Security Studies, 1997.
Lancaster, John, and Terry M. Neal. "Heavyweight 'Vulcans' Help Bush Forge a Foreign Policy." *Washington Post* (November 19, 1999): A2

Lieber, Robert J., ed. *Eagle Rules? Foreign Policy and American Primacy in the 21st Century.* Englewood Cliffs, NJ: Prentice-Hall, 2001.

Lindsay, James M. "From Containment to Apathy." *Foreign Affairs* 79 (September/ October 2000): 2–9.

Lizza, Ryan. "There They Go Again." *New Republic* (May 8, 2000): 15.

Mastel, Greg. "Let's Not Make a Deal." *Weekly Standard* (September 13, 1999): 16.

McDonnell, Patrick, and George Ramos. "Latinos Make Strong Showing at the Polls." *Los Angeles Times* (November 8, 1996): A1.

Mullins, Brody, and Charlie Mitchell. "Soft Money Unleashed." *National Journal* 33, no. 7 (February 17, 2001): 500–501.

Neal, Terry M. "Bush Outlines Defense Plan in Address at the Citadel: GOP Front-Runner Pushes Pay Hikes, High-Tech Weapons." *Washington Post* (September 24, 1999): A3.

Nincic, Miroslav, and Barbara Hinckley. "Foreign Policy and the Evaluation of Presidential Candidates." *Journal of Conflict Resolution* 35, no. 2 (June 1991): 333–355.

Omestad, Thomas. "Why Bush Lost." *Foreign Policy*, no. 89 (Winter 1992–93): 70–81.

Owens, Mackubin Thomas. "The Democratic Party's War on the Military." *Wall Street Journal* (November 22, 2000): A22.

Pan, Philip, and Michael Fletcher. "Other Latinos More Divided over Fate of Cuban Boy." *Washington Post* (April 10, 2000): A2.

Powell, Stewart M. "Bush Makes Pitch for Immigrant Families: He'd Make It Easier for Foreign Nationals to Join Their Kin." *Pittsburgh Post-Gazette* (June 27, 2000): A6.

"The President and His Marbles." *Weekly Standard* (December 6, 1999): 2.

Price, Deb. "Al, Voters, Keep Eye on World: Foreign Affairs Emerge as Key Issue in 2000 Election." *Detroit News* (July 12, 1999): A1.

"Public Opinion Uneasy About Economy, Polls Find; Opinion: As Bush Takes Office, About Twice as Many People Are Optimistic about the Next Four Years as Are Pessimistic. Most Think He Will Improve the Military." *Los Angeles Times* (January 21, 2001): A16.

Putnam, Robert. "Diplomacy and Domestic Politics: The Logic of Two-Level Games." *International Organization* 42, no. 3 (Summer 1988): 427–460.

"Quayle Suggests Foreign Policy Shift Toward Asia." *Bulletin's Frontrunner.* August 4, 1999.

Rees, Matthew. "Arabs, Poles, and Other Key Voters: Ethnic 'Outreach' Could Decide Who Makes It to the White House." *Weekly Standard* (October 30, 2000): 22.

———. "Congress's China Challenge." *Weekly Standard* (March 22, 1999): 10.

Reilly, John E., ed. *American Public Opinion and U.S. Foreign Policy 1999.* Chicago: Chicago Council on Foreign Relations, 1999.

Ricks, Thomas E. " 'I Think We're Pretty Disgusted': Challenging of Overseas Ballots Widens Divide Between Military, Democrats." *Washington Post* (November 21, 2000): A18.

Rodriguez, Gregory. "The Future Americans." *Los Angeles Times* (March 18, 2001): M1.

Rose, Alexander. "Al's Risky Scheme: Why Gore Prefers Outdated Arms Control to a National Missile Defense." *Weekly Standard* (June 5, 2000): 21.

Schneider, Greg. "A Strategy of Silence on Missile Defense." *Washington Post* (June 4, 2000): H1.

Shapiro, Michael. "Republican Presidential Hopefuls Gather to Woo GOP Jewish Group." *Ethnic News Watch* (December 2, 1999): 4.

Slavin, Barbara. "Bush Says He'll Stand By Israel, Vows to Move U.S. Embassy to Jerusalem." *USA Today* (May 23, 2000): 22A.

Thiessen, Marc A. "The Candidates' Foreign Policies: It's Bush's American Exceptionalism Versus Gore's Liberal Multilateralism." *Weekly Standard* (June 12, 2000): 16.

Tilove, Jonathan. "Diversity Debate Changing American Politics: Parties Strive to Prove Their Inclusiveness." *New Orleans Times-Picayune* (August 19, 2000): 17.

"Unwelcome Back." *New Republic* (August 14, 2000): 9.

"Warriors and Peacemakers." *Washington Post* (July 12, 1999): A14.

Wayne, Lesley. "After High-Pressure Years, Contractors Tone Down on Missile Defense Lobbying." *New York Times* (June 13, 2000): A6

"Who's Getting: 2000 Presidential Race." Center for Responsive Politics. January 2001. <http://www.opensecrets.org>.

Zoellner, Tom. "Ex-President Bush Stumps for Son in S. F.'s Chinatown." *San Francisco Chronicle* (February 14, 2000): A3.

3

The Incorrigibly White Republican Party
Racial Politics in the Presidential Race

Jeremy D. Mayer

Race and the shifting array of issues surrounding it have been a fundamental structuring force in elections for much of American history.[1] In modern times, race was one of the crucial issues responsible for the decomposition of the New Deal coalition and the string of Republican successes in presidential elections from 1968 to 1992.[2] For example, in 1988, George Bush effectively exploited white fears of black crime to maintain the loyalty of Reagan Democrats. In 1992, by contrast, Bill Clinton found a way to appeal to white Reagan Democrats while maintaining fervent support among African Americans. Clinton's strategic brilliance allowed him, in the words of political scientist Lucius Barker, to "deracialize" the presidential election.[3] Much the same could be said of the Dole–Clinton race of 1996, in which racial issues seldom surfaced. Yet throughout the period 1964–1996, as issues shifted and blacks gained in electoral power, two things remained constant. The Democrats received an overwhelming majority of the black vote, and the Republicans received more white votes than the Democrats did, sometimes by landslide margins (as in 1984). At the same time, Republicans also had been losing support among other racial groups, particularly Hispanics and Asians. In the wake of the anti-immigrant rhetoric and actions by Republicans in the early 1990s, many racial minorities began voting Democratic at even higher rates than before. Thus, every Republican presidential campaign was premised on winning enough white votes to beat the Democratic advantage among nonwhites.

As the 2000 presidential election season loomed, however, it seemed that the Republican Party had resolved to challenge the racial status quo of American politics. Their presumptive nominee, Texan George W. Bush, had received a relatively high level of black support in his gubernatorial race of 1998 (28 percent). By contrast, it appeared that the Democrats would nominate Vice President Al Gore, a New Democrat whose record in the black community was spotty. Would 2000 be the year in which black bipartisanship at the presidential level became a reality for the first time since 1956? Would the Republicans also be able to overcome the negative image of their party in the Hispanic and Asian communities?

A Not-So-New Kind of Republican: The GOP Primaries

As in every presidential primary since 1980, the preprimary campaign of fundraising and name-recognition proved vital to success in 2000.[4] In their efforts to gain advantage during that period, some of the dark horses in the Republican race tried to use affirmative action to rally white conservatives to their campaign. For example, Lamar Alexander of Tennessee stated flatly, "Government should stop making distinctions based on race. No discrimination, no preferences." Similarly, publisher Malcolm "Steve" Forbes and former vice president Dan Quayle took strong positions against affirmative action.[5] By contrast, Bush, the front runner, downplayed his opposition to affirmative action, refusing to even comment on anti–affirmative action referenda.[6] Bush's brother, the governor of Florida, joined with other national leaders to keep affirmative action off the Florida ballot in 2000, as did Republicans in Michigan. The fear articulated by many Republicans was that this issue would hurt in the general election. If it were on the ballot in November, or the focus of the Republican general campaign, it would do little to move white voters but might incite minority voters against Republicans.[7] It would also hurt Bush's effort to portray himself as a "new kind of Republican" who would finally reach out to the minority community in a way that no Republican had done since Nixon in 1960. Indeed, Bush supporters touted his appeal to Hispanics and blacks in Texas as strong reasons for Republicans to nominate him: A Republican who could take 28 percent of the black vote while winning half the Hispanic vote would cakewalk to the White House.

First, though, Bush had to win the Republican nomination, and thanks to Arizona senator John McCain, that was no cakewalk. McCain, running as a populist outsider, won New Hampshire by a strong margin, stunning the establishment Bush forces. Reeling, Bush's campaign now faced the next contest, in South Carolina. At this juncture, the "new kind of Republican" showed that he could appeal to, or at least appease, white racial conservatives. Two symbolic racial issues unexpectedly became part of the campaign discourse: the Confederate flag and interracial dating. South Carolina's state politics had been roiled for more than five years by the flying of the Confederate flag over the state capitol building. Blacks perceived it as a direct attack on the civil rights movement. Many whites saw it as a tribute to the honor and valor of the Confederate South. The fact that it first appeared atop the statehouse during the acme of white Southern resistance to black equality (1962) and had been a direct attack on the civil rights movement did not matter to many white Carolinians. The debate became extremely bitter in the midst of the presidential primary. A local Bush supporter, Arthur Ravenal, attacked the National Association for the Advancement of Colored People (NAACP), which had been leading a national boycott of the state over the issue. Ravenal labeled the group the "National Association for Retarded People" and then apologized the next day for offending retarded people by associating them with the NAACP. Bush labeled the remarks "unfortunate" but did not immediately apologize for Ravenal's extraordinary linkage of blacks and mental retardation.[8] Bush also refused to give his opinion on the flag controversy, saying it was a decision for South Carolinians. McCain, who stated that the flag was a symbol of "racism and slavery" when first asked, the next day reverted to echoing Bush's stance that the flag was a states rights question and that it was also "a symbol of heritage."

Also in the week before the crucial South Carolina voting, Bush made a trip laden with racial symbolism when he agreed to speak at Bob Jones University. The school, founded by men who fervently believed in divine white superiority, segregation, and the evils of Catholicism and Mormonism, had a long record of opposition to civil rights. More recently, it had admitted blacks, but still maintained that interracial dating was against God's will. While Bush's speech at Bob Jones did not contain any explicit or implicit references to racial issues, the visit was widely interpreted as an appeal to cultural conservatives in the South Carolina primary. McCain's record on race also came under its tightest scrutiny in South Carolina, as the media scoured his record. A liberal interest group chose this moment to attack McCain for hiring Richard Quinn as a campaign adviser. Criticized as the editor of *Southern Partisan,* a little-known magazine that lamented the defeat of the South in the Civil War and argued that slavery had not been so bad for blacks, Quinn himself had called Nelson Mandela a "terrorist," attacked Martin Luther King as a fraud, and advocated protest voting for former Ku Klux Klansman David Duke. McCain refused to fire Quinn, though Bush's campaign joined the media in criticizing the decision. So salient was race during the South Carolina campaign that McCain, a former prisoner of war in Vietnam, was attacked for using the word "gook" to refer to his captors.[9] By the time of the balloting, both Bush and McCain had shown a surprising tolerance of modern racism, as manifested in their supporters Ravenal and Quinn, as well as great deference to the Confederate flag.[10] Bush won a strong victory in South Carolina, now running as a true conservative, not a new kind of Republican.

The swing to the racial right did not come without its costs. Bush's appearance at Bob Jones caused a moderate New York congressman to switch to McCain (more because of the school's record of strident anti-Catholic rhetoric than its record of racism).[11] Later, Faye Anderson, a long-time black GOP activist, resigned from the party in bitter anger over Bush's appearance at the school. Anderson, whose resignation attracted national media attention, was also offended that Bush apologized to Catholics, but not to blacks.[12] In Michigan, black voters organized to vote in the Republican primary for McCain, although probably not because they perceived McCain as more friendly to black interests.[13] Following South Carolina, indeed, race almost disappeared from the Republican primaries as an issue. However, during those few days when race dominated the campaign coverage, Bush had shown a great dexterity with racial politics and a willingness to appeal to white backlash voters when necessary.

Bradley Fumbles the Race Card: The Democratic Primaries

African Americans are vital components of the Democratic Party, playing an increasingly large role in the primaries and caucuses. The only two successful Democratic presidential candidates in the modern era, Jimmy Carter and Clinton, owed their nominations in part to their ability to rally black voters in the primaries.[14] The 2000 contest would also demonstrate the power of the black vote. Gore, the presumptive nominee, had worked hard during the eight years of the Clinton presidency to woo black leaders to his cause. Gore was far from the first choice for blacks at the start of the Clinton presidency. In his 1988 run for the nomination, Gore had made little secret of his desire to reach out to conservative whites. Gore had made the sharpest attacks of any Democrat in history on Jesse Jackson in the New York primaries, attacks so strident that they eliminated Gore from contention for the vice presidential slot that year. Gore was also the first candidate to attempt to use the case of Willie Horton, a black criminal, against Michael Dukakis, a tactic that George H. W. Bush's campaign later exploited to devastating effect. Gore, like Clinton, was a New Democrat, but unlike Clinton, Gore never had a reservoir of good feeling in the black community. His speaking style was hardly one that would resonate with those raised in the tradition of the black church, for example. Ideologically, Gore was not the kind of white liberal likely to attract the affection of the Congressional Black Caucus or other national black leaders. At one point during Clinton's presidency, Gore advocated gutting affirmative action, and he was later criticized for the effect of his "reinventing government" initiative on black employees. Yet Gore's careful fence-mending on affirmative action, as well as his personal outreach to black mayors, produced numerous endorsements in the months leading up to the primaries. Gore's strong black support was a key part of his perceived "inevitability."

Gore's only challenger for the nomination was former New Jersey senator Bill Bradley. Bradley, a northeastern liberal, made racial equality a fundamental part of his campaign from the very start. He talked about racial issues, such as racial profiling and preserving affirmative action, far more frequently than Gore. This was part of Bradley's attempt to run to Gore's left and appeal to the Democratic base. However, Bradley was singularly unsuccessful. Every prominent black elected official in the party endorsed Gore, while Bradley could boast only of the support of a number of black basketball stars, including Michael Jordan. Much of Gore's pre-primary lead in states such as Maryland was a product of his huge advantage among blacks. Even when Bradley beat Gore among whites, black preferences put Gore ahead.[15] Still, Bradley continued to press Gore substantively and symbolically on race. Bradley publicly met with the Reverend Al Sharpton and sought his support. Sharpton, whose record included using the fake rape story of Tawana Brawley to inflame racial tensions in New York, as well as ugly comments against Koreans and Jews, was now "mainstreamed" by Bradley's outreach. Gore, who had avoided Sharpton up to this point, now was forced to meet with the controversial leader. Gore at first tried to confer with Sharpton in secret, and his campaign dissembled about the meeting.[16] Bradley met again with Sharpton and even hired his former campaign manager as a top deputy. Bradley and Gore both recognized the importance of the black vote when, for the first time, a Democratic primary debate was held before a largely black audience designed to address black concerns. When the first question at the debate was thrown out by Sharpton, McCain attacked Gore and Bradley for their cozy relationship with one of the nation's "agents of intolerance."[17]

As Bradley's campaign floundered, he put even more emphasis on race, flying to Florida to defend affirmative action and to South Carolina to attack the Confederate flag. He tried to outdo Gore in his indignation at Bush and McCain's silence on the flag issue.[18] But in the end, Gore's black support remained firm, and when Super Tuesday ended with Bradley resoundingly rejected in every state, he withdrew.

Why did Bradley fail to rally black supporters with his strong rhetoric on racial profiling, social justice, and affirmative action? Gore benefited immensely from his strong connection with Clinton, a heroic figure in much of the black community. Furthermore, Bradley was one of the few campaigners who could make Gore seem comparatively exciting. The main effect of the Bradley challenge on race was to deny Gore a "Sister Souljah" moment, an opportunity to demonstrate to conservative white voters that he was not a captive of black "special interests." In forcing Gore to the left on race, Bradley pushed his opponent into the arms of Sharpton, who otherwise might have provided Gore with an opportunity to emulate his mentor, Clinton.[19]

A Republican "Minstrel Show" and Lieberman's Convention Conversion

Conventions remain important parts of the presidential campaign, although they no longer select the nominees, but merely anoint the choices made by the primary electorate.[20] Conventions have also served important roles in modern racial politics. In 1972, George McGovern's unqualified endorsement of busing gave gleeful Republicans a key campaign issue. In the 1980s, the Democratic conventions were closely studied to see how the nominees treated Jesse Jackson. The number of minority speakers and delegates at both conventions is carefully tallied by the media and widely promulgated. The conventions of 2000 were subjected to the same kind of scrutiny.

The Republican convention came under attack for "tokenism," as had the Republican conventions of 1972, 1976, 1980, and 1984.[21] This attack echoed the earlier criticism of Gore campaign manager Donna Brazile, who had said that Republicans "would rather take pictures with black children than feed them."[22] Liberal columnist Bob Kuttner attacked the convention as a cynical "minstrel show" in which "there were more blacks as token entertainers than there were black delegates."[23] A speech by retired general Colin Powell did forthrightly defend affirmative action in terms that offended some Republicans: "Some in our party miss no opportunity to roundly and loudly condemn affirmative action that helped a few thousand black kids get an education, but hardly a whimper is heard from them over lobbyists who load our federal tax codes with preferences for special interests."[24] Still, the Republican platform did not agree with Powell, and the loud cheers that greeted him were probably in spite of his views on affirmative action rather than because of them. Yet it was clear that in giving prominence to Powell, Bush foreign policy adviser Condoleeza Rice, and many other minority Republicans, the party was desperately trying to avoid the exclusionary image projected by the conventions of 1992 and 1996. The media even examined the musical choices of the party, trying to divine whether the inclusion of black and Hispanic musical stars qualified as "outreach." Bush, in his acceptance speech, praised the civil rights movement, saying "racial progress has been steady, if still too slow." However, he did not offer many policy positions likely to appeal to blacks or other minorities.

The Democratic convention in Los Angeles was in many ways a demonstration of black political power. Clinton in his farewell speech to his party took credit for the lowest black unemployment in history. The video of Clinton's achievements featured Clinton with blacks, and the only other politician given a speaking clip in the movie was Jesse Jackson. The irony was palpable: Clinton, who deliberately stiff-armed Jackson in 1992 to aid his quest for the White House, now ended his time in office by embracing the reverend. The burning of black churches, racial profiling, and the need for hate crimes legislation were all highlighted in Clinton's farewell. He even took a dig at the Republican convention, pointing out that his cabinet resembled the Republican stage in Philadelphia, only minorities had real power in his administration. Gore's acceptance speech also made much of black progress under the Clinton administration and promised more. The contrast in podium presence was also vivid. While the Republicans elevated minor black Republicans (such as a state representative) to speaking positions, the list of minority Democratic speakers included very powerful members of Congress, governors, and cabinet officers.

Perhaps the most important function performed by modern conventions is the announcement of the nominee for vice president. The Republicans, in nominating Dick Cheney of Wyoming, had not helped themselves with minorities. Not only had Cheney been one of the only members of Congress to vote against a bill calling for Mandela's freedom, he also had no record of outreach to minorities at all. A number of other Bush choices would have offered dividends with minorities. Rumors abounded throughout the primary season that the nomination was Colin Powell's, if only he would take it. In choosing Cheney, a Republican from one of the whitest states in the country who had never had to campaign among minorities in his life, Bush belied his own rhetoric about outreach.

Gore's nominee for the vice presidency would attract even greater attention: Senator Joseph Lieberman of Connecticut. In choosing a Jewish politician, Gore broke another barrier to ethnic advancement and induced extraordinary excitement in the Jewish community nationwide and, indeed, around the world. At the same time, Lieberman inflamed opposition among some blacks. Black anti-Semitism explained some of the reaction, particularly in the case of the head of the Dallas NAACP, who advocated suspicion toward "any partnerships with Jews at that level," particularly because Jews were only concerned about money.[25] The leader of the Nation of Islam, Louis Farrakhan, suggested that as a Jew, Lieberman was a "dual citizen of Israel" and should be questioned about his loyalty.[26] Still, the uneasiness among most members of the black community had little to do with Lieberman's ethnicity and much more to do with his issue positions.

Lieberman had in the past opposed affirmative action, in language similar to Bush's relatively muted opposition. In 1995 he had said that "you can't defend policies that are based on group preferences as opposed to individual opportunity" and labeled racial preferences "patently unfair."[27] He had spoken out in favor of Proposition 209, a state referendum to eliminate affirmative action in California, although he now said "I wanted to ban quotas, and I think that's basically happened."[28] Unfortunately for Lieberman, both the proposition and the later court decisions were anathema to the leadership of black Democrats. Although Lieberman averred that he now favored affirmative action and had supported Clinton–Gore's "Mend it, don't end it" position on affirmative action, the unease among many black Democrats was obvious. Leading the charge was California congresswoman Maxine Waters. She told reporters that she might not endorse the ticket because of Lieberman's opposition to affirmative action, his support of school vouchers, and his tough stance on crime. In a dull convention's most dramatic moment, Lieberman was called before the Black Caucus to defend his record or, rather, to retreat from it bashfully. He now felt racial preferences were necessary "because history and current reality make it necessary. . . . I was for affirmative action, am for affirmative action, and will be for affirmative action!"[29] Lieberman's retraction of his earlier views on affirmative action and other issues mollified Waters and other Black Caucus members, but analysts expected that Lieberman would depress turnout among blacks. In addition to his other tension points with blacks, Lieberman had been one of the most caustic critics of Clinton's sexual misconduct, a stance offensive to many blacks.

Bush's Record Outreach: The Early General Election

According to former GOP activist Faye Anderson, George W. Bush "would surround himself by black babies, but would not go to speak to black adults, it really tipped his hand to what he is all about—trying to convince white swing voters that he is a different kind of candidate."[30] In response, Bush defended his outreach to blacks: "I haven't had a chance to prove my heart to people."[31]

The 2000 presidential election saw the largest commitment of resources to black outreach in the modern history of the Republican Party. The GOP spent well over a million dollars on radio ads targeted directly at the black community. The radio ads touted Bush's support of school vouchers, an issue that had some appeal in urban black communities. Republicans also formed a New Majority Council in 1997 that hoped to reach out to blacks, Asians, and Hispanics.[32] Perhaps most important, Bush went to the NAACP convention and apologized for the Republican Party's past mistakes on civil rights. In so doing, he became the first Republican candidate to appear at the NAACP since Reagan in 1980. Unlike his father in 1988 and 1992, or Robert Dole in 1996, Bush actually campaigned in black areas. Yet some believed that Bush's campaign was intent not on winning black votes, but rather convincing moderate whites that Republicans were not opposed to black equality.

It is difficult to say how much Bush's silence on the Confederate flag or his speech at Bob Jones University hurt his outreach to blacks, but surely these acts resonated far beyond South Carolina. Bush's image among blacks may also have been damaged by his record as the governor with the most executions to his name since the return of the death penalty in 1976. Black voters are far less supportive of the death penalty than whites, for obvious reasons. Not only was the death penalty used in a blatantly discriminatory fashion during much of American history, but there is also evidence that the current system still places a far higher value on white life than black life. In June, the death penalty entered the campaign over the case of Gary Graham, a convicted murderer on death row in Texas. Graham, a black man, had been convicted on the basis of one eyewitness's shaky testimony. Although Bush did little to publicize this case, the international anti–death penalty movement made it a cause célèbre in May and June. That Bush's Texas had a record of executing blacks and Hispanics whose lawyers were asleep during their trials also did not help his outreach to those communities.

Bush did campaign aggressively in Hispanic areas. He dropped Spanish into some campaign speeches, and the Republicans ran more Spanish language ads than ever, particularly in Florida and New Mexico.[33] The Republican candidate also made it clear that he did not approve of the racialized rhetoric on immigration that had so damaged his party's image among Hispanics and Asians in 1992 and 1996. Bush opposed Proposition

187, a California referendum to deny services to illegal immigrants, and English-only laws, and even favored bilingualism in some circumstances.[34] Opinion polls suggested that Bush's outreach to Hispanics was working, as he cut into the huge margins that the Democrats had won among Hispanics in 1996. However, as the race progressed, both campaigns failed to pay as much attention to Hispanic concerns as activists had anticipated, perhaps because so many of the states with large Hispanic populations were considered noncompetitive (Texas, New York, New Jersey, California, and Illinois).[35] In response to Bush's outreach to Latino voters, Gore tried to attack Bush for visiting only three *colonias* (poor Hispanic towns just across the border from Mexico) during his six years as Texas governor. A Bush supporter and Texas administrator did not do Bush any favors by "defending" Bush with the statement, "You don't have to go to Alaska to know it's cold, and I don't think you have to go to colonias to know what it's like."[36]

Both campaigns also began to target groups who had never played a significant role in American elections, such as Indo-Americans. Clinton issued the first proclamation honoring the Hindu holiday of Diwali. Clinton's visit to India (the first by a U.S. president in more than two decades) allowed the Democrats to reap a harvest of "goodwill and excitement" among Indian voters.[37] The parties also competed for the 5.6 million immigrants who had become citizens since 1991 (almost 2 million since 1999). Many of the new voters lived in crucial battleground states, and they leaned heavily Democratic. Ironically, many of the new citizens had initiated naturalization proceedings because of the tough immigration laws passed in 1995–1996 by the new Republican Congress; surveys suggested that some new immigrant groups favored the Democrats 15 to 1.[38]

Gore's Initial Restraint on Race

Gore was advised early on by black leaders that he needed to campaign hard in the black community. However, the emphasis of the Gore campaign was on keeping centrist whites in the Democratic fold, because they had allowed Clinton to beat the Republicans twice. Some blacks expressed to reporters the belief that they were being ignored, in favor of the white vote and, to a lesser extent, the Hispanic vote.[39] Gore gradually increased his focus on race as the campaign went on. In September, for example, speaking at Howard University, Gore highlighted a local incident that he linked to racial profiling.[40] Still, Gore was not emphasizing racial equality on the scale that Bradley had in his primary campaign. A *Washington Post* article argued that many blacks were supporting Gore as the "lesser of two evils" and compared Gore unfavorably to Clinton.[41]

Yet while Gore was not electrifying black audiences or speaking to their issues with great frequency early in the campaign, some felt that he had not gone far enough to reach out to white voters. Senator John Breaux, a moderate Democrat, went so far as to say that Gore needed "a Sister Souljah moment" to repeat Clinton's calculated insult to Jesse Jackson.[42] Unlike Clinton, or Jimmy Carter (who had opposed busing for integration), Gore made no public stands against symbols of black extremism or against any component of the black agenda. Indeed, Gore quietly endorsed the proposition that blacks should receive some form of reparations for slavery, a very unpopular idea with whites, particularly white racial conservatives.[43]

Gore's reluctance to deal with racial topics was much commented on by African Americans following the first debate with Bush. Black radio host Tom Joyner raised the issue with Gore in a postdebate interview:

> We've got these people registered to vote, we've got people fired up . . . but last night during the debate, neither one of you addressed issues for us, for African Americans. . . . I didn't hear anything about affirmative action . . . we didn't hear about racial profiling, we didn't hear about reparations . . . all these things that affect us we heard nothing about.[44]

Gore blamed the absence of black issues on the moderator and promised to bring up the topic directly in the second debate. However, it was in the third debate when the issue came up most dramatically. While opposing quotas because "they're against the American way," Gore strongly endorsed affirmative action. Bush, aggressively pressed by Gore to state his position, came out in favor of affirmative "access" but opposed to affirmative action if it involved quotas.[45] No Democratic candidate for president had ever been so strident in his endorsement of affirmative action in a presidential debate. This move signaled a shift in Gore's strategy. The last month of his campaign would emphasize race to a much greater degree.

Endgame: The Democrats Turn Up the Heat on Race

The tone of the last month of the presidential race was set by a new force in presidential politics: a bold national ad campaign by the dean of civil rights groups, the NAACP. Under the leadership of former Democratic congressman Kweisi Mfume, the civil rights organization ran radio and television ads of unprecedented emotionalism and partisanship. One radio ad featured an announcer invoking the police dogs and water cannons used

against civil rights demonstrators. While none of these ads could specifically endorse Gore without violating federal election laws, they obviously
were designed to help Democrats. The NACCP ad that received the widest
attention was a television spot featuring the daughter of a black man
lynched during Bush's tenure as governor of Texas. The lynching victim,
James Byrd Jr., had been dragged behind a pickup truck by a chain until
he died. The television ad featured scary black and white footage of a
pickup truck and a chain, while Byrd's daughter drew a direct analogy
between the murder of her father and Bush's failure to support new hate
crimes legislation in Texas:

> I'm Renee Mullins, James Byrd's daughter. On June 7, 1998, in Texas, my father
> was killed. He was beaten, chained and then dragged three miles to his death—all
> because he was black. So when Governor George W. Bush refused to support
> hate crimes legislation, it was like my father was killed all over again. Call
> George W. Bush and tell him to support hate crimes legislation. We won't be
> dragged away from our future.

The NAACP also arranged for Mullins to speak to black audiences across
the country. Republicans cried foul, but the raw emotionalism and the
exploitation of tragedy should rather have reminded Republicans of their
own Willie Horton campaign of 1988. Horton, a black man serving a life
sentence for murder in Massachusetts, escaped during a weekend furlough
and raped a white woman. "Unofficial" groups allegedly unaffiliated with
Bush's campaign had sent Horton's victims on speaking tours and ran
graphic television ads that played on the worst white stereotypes about
blacks. Frantically, Republicans tried to counter the Byrd ads with facts,
such as Bush's support for earlier hate crimes legislation and the death
sentences that two of Byrd's three killers received. But as in 1988, when
Democrats had argued that the Massachusetts furlough was little different
from Reagan's in California or the federal program, the facts were imma-
terial. The NAACP ads allowed Gore to whip up fervor among his black
base. If the radio and television ads stopped just short of calling Bush a
racist, it was not much of a leap of logic for a black voter to make.

While the inflammatory television ad received the most coverage in the
media, the NAACP also launched its largest and most transparently partisan
voter registration drive.[46] At the same time, the Democratic Party began to
run ads on black radio stations touting Gore's record on affirmative action
and his plans for addressing affirmative action. And yet, despite these activities, there remained a distinct lack of enthusiasm for Gore, particularly
when compared to the reverence many blacks felt for Clinton. A community activist in Chicago told a reporter that it seemed as if the Democrats'

focus was on scaring blacks with the idea that if Bush wins "all hell is going to break loose." Similarly, a national black political commentator, Tavis Smiley, said, "As far as I'm concerned Bush . . . is nothing more than a serial killer. But we can't expect that much more from Gore."[47]

Perhaps in response to such attitudes, Gore himself turned up the rhetoric. Gore refused to criticize the NAACP ads that nearly accused Bush of condoning lynching; instead, he emphasized that the lynching had occurred in Bush's home state, as if that somehow made the governor culpable. Then, three days before the election, speaking in a black church, Gore launched the harshest racial rhetoric of his campaign, again linking Bush to the lynching and to the Confederate flag in South Carolina. He accused Bush of employing code words to disguise his intent of turning back the clock on black progress. Gore also alleged that Bush would appoint justices to the Supreme Court with views reminiscent of the days when blacks "were considered three fifths of a human being."[48] Bush personally did not respond to Gore's attacks, although surrogate Republicans continued to insist that the attacks were unfair.[49]

Conclusion: Blacks Refuse to Judge Bush on His "Heart"

> I know the current wisdom, "Well, he's a Republican, a white guy Republican, and therefore he has no chance to get the African American vote." You know they may be right, but that's not going to stop me. So you'll find me in neighborhoods the Republicans normally don't go to.—George W. Bush[50]

When Election Day ended, the outreach to African Americans that Bush had made so much of was a tremendous failure. Nationwide, Bush received 9 percent of the black vote, a stunning rejection. Bush failed to achieve the anemic support levels of his father or even the much disliked Ronald Reagan. In his home state of Texas, Bush did even worse, getting just 5 percent of the black vote, a fifth less than his statewide total two years before. The eventual Bush victory in the electoral college was made possible only through the twelve-point margin Bush won among white voters. As in every election since 1964, the white vote went Republican.[51] Why did the black vote remain so resolutely Democratic?

In part, one explanation was Bill Clinton. Clinton remained the most popular living politician, black or white, among black voters.[52] Moreover, he had presided over a golden age of economic growth for African Americans. Black and Hispanic unemployment in the last year of Clinton's presidency was lower than at any time since records had been kept. The growth in household income among blacks was impressive and sustained during

Table 3.1

Social Groups in the 2000 Presidential Election: Exit Poll Results
(in percent)

Group	Bush	Gore	Buchanan	Nader	Percent of electorate
Whites	54	42	0	3	81
Blacks	9	90	0	1	10
Hispanics	35	62	1	2	7
Asians	41	55	1	3	2
Other	39	55	0	4	1

Source: Data compiled by the author from Voter News Service Exit Poll.

much of Clinton's presidency. Some even suggested that Clinton's problems, which had caused "Clinton fatigue" in many white Americans, actually contributed to his popularity among blacks. So many black leaders,
from Adam Clayton Powell to Martin Luther King Jr. had been investigated
by federal officers and attacked for sexual improprieties that Clinton's
problems were a call to arms, rather than a time for judgment. Even though
Gore limited Clinton's appearances during the campaign, Clinton was
wisely deployed to some black areas in the last month of the campaign.

Another explanation was the NAACP campaign and the hard-biting rhetoric of Gore's last few weeks of campaigning. Just as in 1998, when Democratic radio ads linked Republicans to racist church burnings, the
Republicans were tarred in 2000 with the accusation of racial violence and
racial insensitivity.

Black loyalty and black mobilization were also involved in the riveting
deadlock in Florida that led to the longest wait for a winner since the
presidential election of 1876. Black turnout in Florida rose an astonishing
65 percent from 1996 levels, accounting for 16 percent of the state's electorate, up from 10 percent in 1996. Bush received only 7 percent of that
newly enlarged black vote in Florida.[53] Why did black turnout skyrocket
in Florida? Jesse Jackson, who had campaigned hard for Gore–Lieberman
in Florida, kept tying George Bush to Jeb Bush, his brother, the governor
of Florida, with his simple slogan "Stay Out The Bushes!" But Jackson
had been in Florida long before the campaign season. When Jeb Bush had
presided over a retreat on affirmative action, Jackson and other black leaders had promised to "remember in November." The extraordinary jump in
turnout in Florida, along with higher levels of Democratic voting than even
the beloved Clinton had experienced, demonstrated that blacks in Florida

were particularly motivated against the GOP.[54] Had that not been true, George Bush would have won the state easily.

Just as race was fundamental to Gore's ability to make Florida competitive, it also was widely alleged that there were racial patterns to some of the voting irregularities that occupied the attention of the nation during the month of November. Not only were black voters far more likely than whites to vote at precincts with more error-prone voting machines, but there were also allegations that blacks had been aggressively struck from the voting rolls in the year before the election. Florida had hired an outside vendor with Republican ties, ChoicePoint, to remove felons from its rolls. At least 8,000 names were deleted without cause, disproportionately minorities.[55] Jackson, Sharpton, and the NAACP's Mfume all claimed that even more blatant disenfranchisement of blacks had occurred and called for a federal investigation.

By the time a deeply divided U.S. Supreme Court stopped the counting in Florida and declared Bush the victor, the allegations of large-scale disenfranchisement of blacks were widely believed in the black community. Survey after survey showed a racial divide in acceptance of Bush's legitimacy, with blacks by overwhelming majorities believing that Bush had stolen the election.[56] Thus, the 2000 presidential election, which had at first seemed so promising for Republican outreach to blacks, ended with the party more alienated from African Americans than at any time since the Goldwater campaign of 1964.

One bright spot for the GOP was the rise in Hispanic support that the party experienced in 2000. Bush captured 35 percent of the Hispanic vote, proving that not all outreach to minorities was fruitless for the GOP. Yet Bush memorably failed among Asian Americans, losing to Gore among that group by 55–41, when both his father in 1992 and Bob Dole in 1996 had managed to win the Asian vote handily. Even the director of minority outreach for the Republicans worried that the message for many Republicans might well be that the minority vote was simply unreachable.[57] The last time the Republicans had conducted serious outreach to blacks and been rejected, in 1960, had ended with the leader of the GOP concluding privately, "the hell with them [blacks]."[58] Would Bush take a similar position?

Early signs of his administration have been mixed. The Bush cabinet is quite integrated by race, with blacks occupying far more powerful positions than under Clinton. As Secretary of State, Colin Powell became the first African American to occupy one of the top four Cabinet slots (treasury, state, defense, and justice), while Condoleeza Rice also broke ground as the first African American national security advisor. Bush has also been aggressively visiting black communities and inviting black leaders to the White House. When Jackson was revealed to have had a long-term affair with a staffer, Bush made a warm call to the civil rights leader, who had devoted months to defeating Bush and spoken of him with unmitigated distaste. On the other side, Bush nominated John Ashcroft to be attorney general, a move seen by many black groups as an affront, given Ashcroft's record on the controversial nomination of a black judge. Whether Bush can convince black voters to judge him "on his heart" now that he is in office, as they apparently refused to do in 2000, remains to be seen. There are reasons for Republicans to be optimistic about 2004 if Bush is the nominee. Like many Republican governors, Bush was elected with little black support in his first election for governor, but more than doubled that level in his second run.[59] It is possible that the racial politics of 2004 will emulate this pattern. Yet those who would blithely predict a return to black bipartisanship in the new millennium must be mindful of the daunting nature of the task facing the GOP and must also not forget the ability of Democrats to rally black loyalty with emotional and historic appeals. It probably will take a dramatic and substantive shift in Republican policy, or perhaps the appearance on the Republican ticket of a black candidate for vice president, to truly shake up the enduring status quo of American racial politics.

Notes

1. Edward G. Carmines and James A. Stimson, *Issue Evolution: Race and the Transformation of American Politics* (Princeton: Princeton University Press, 1989); Kenneth O'Reilly, *Nixon's Piano: Presidents and Racial Politics from Washington to Clinton* (New York: Free Press, 1995).

2. Dan T. Carter, *The Politics of Rage* (Baton Rouge: Louisiana University Press, 1995); Thomas B. Edsall and Mary D Edsall, *Chain Reaction: The Impact of Race, Rights and Taxes on American Politics* (New York: Norton, 1992).

3. Lucius J. Barker, "Limits of Political Strategy: A Systemic View of the African American Experience," *American Political Science Review* 88 (1994): 1, 1–13.

4. Sandy Maisel, *The Parties Respond* (Boulder, CO: Westview, 1998).

5. David S. Broder, "For 2000, an Issue of Race: Michigan Targeted in Drive Against Affirmative Action," *Washington Post,* January 23, 1999, A1.

6. Terry M. Neal and David S. Broder, "Affirmative Action Tears at Fla. GOP," *Washington Post,* May 15, 2000, A1.

7. Phone interviews with Republican campaign consultant Doug Bailey, November 14, 2000, and Republican pollster Richard Wirthlin, November 20, 2000.

8. Jesse Jackson, "Pandering to Racism," *Los Angeles Times,* January 19, 2000.

9. Terry M. Neal and Edward Walsh, "Racial Issues Dog GOP Foes," *Washington Post,* February 18, 2000, A1.

10. McCain later expressed profound regret for his failure to attack the Confederate flag as a symbol of racism. Had he done so, he might have received the support of black military veterans, who had been expected to rally to him in South Carolina. It

would have been the first significant role played by blacks in a Republican primary since they provided the narrow margin of victory for Ford over Reagan in the nomination fight of 1976. See Jeremy D. Mayer, *Running on Race: Racial Politics in Presidential Campaigns, 1960–2000* (New York: Random House, forthcoming).

11. Dan Balz and Thomas B. Edsall, "McCain Struggles to Regain Support," *Washington Post,* February 21, 2000, A1.

12. Terry M. Neal, "In Outreach to Blacks, A GOP Credibility Gap," *Washington Post,* June 13, 2000, A1. Bush did say later when asked by reporters that he opposed the school's ban on interracial dating, but his greatest concern was the offense done to Catholics, not blacks.

13. Thomas B. Edsall, "For Governor, Halting McCain in Michigan Is Test of Power," *Washington Post,* February 2, 21, 2000, A8.

14. Mayer, *Running On Race.*

15. Ronald Brownstein, "Bradley's Drive for Minority Vote Is a Raid on Gore's Home Territory," *Los Angeles Times,* February 19, 2000, A14; Jeremy D. Mayer and Alexander Sarapu, "Bradley's Failure and McCain's Michigan Success: The Preprimary Campaigns of 2000," *Political Chronicle* 12 (Fall): 2.

16. Michael Kelly, "Sharpton's Supplicants," *Washington Post,* February 16, 2000, A23.

17. Lynne Duke, "The Mainstreaming of Al Sharpton," *Washington Post,* March 7, 2000, A7.

18. David W. Chen, "Bradley Attacks GOP Over the Confederate Flag," *New York Times,* February 9, 2000, A15.

19. Bradley's challenge, and the surprising strength of it in late 1999, led directly to Gore's selection of a black woman as his campaign manager, the highest office any African American had ever risen to in a national campaign.

20. Nelson Polsby and Aaron Wildavsky, *Presidential Elections,* 8th ed. (New York: Free Press, 1991), 295–302.

21. Mayer, *Running on Race.*

22. Paul Alexander, "Gore Risks Backlash If He Drops Campaign Chief Brazile," *Bloomberg News,* March 28, 2000.

23. Robert Kuttner, "The Lynching of the Black Vote," *Boston Globe,* December 10, 2000.

24. Ralph Z. Hallow, "Powell's Speech Called 'His Views,' Not Party's Line," *Washington Times,* August 2, 2000.

25. Melissa Healy and Jeff Leeds, "NAACP Official Resigns Over Remarks on Jews," *Los Angeles Times,* August 10, 2000, B9; Jesse Jackson, "Gore's Choice Brings the Dream Closer to Reality," *Los Angeles Times,* August 11, 2000, B9. The NAACP immediately attacked the anti-Semitic remarks of its Dallas leader and demanded and received his resignation.

26. Teresa Watanabe, "Nation of Islam Leader Raises the Loyalty Issue," *Los Angeles Times,* August 12, 2000, A15.

27. James Dao and Kevin Sack, "Some Discontent at Centrist Theme of Gore's Ticket," *New York Times,* August 9, 2000, A1.

28. Cathleen Decker, "Lieberman Promises to Stand United With Gore," *Los Angeles Times,* August 14, 2000, A1.

29. Dao and Sack, "Some Discontent."

30. Neal, "In Outreach to Blacks."

31. Ibid.

32. Phone interview with Rene Amoore, national director of the New Majority Council (December 7, 2000).

33. Jeff Leeds, "GOP Courts Traditional Democrats," *Los Angeles Times,* October 11, 2000, A18.

34. Fred Barnes, "The Bush Republicans," *Weekly Standard,* August 21, 2000, 21–22.

35. Hector Tobar, "Latino Votes Pursued in Few Unusual Places," *Los Angeles Times,* October 30, 2000, A17.

36. Students of racial politics with long memories will be reminded of Spiro Agnew's 1968 campaign comment in defense of Republicans who did not visit black areas: "If you've seen one ghetto, you've seen them all."

37. Connie K. Kang, "Indo-Americans Begin to Flex Political Muscle," *Los Angeles Times,* October 30, 2000, A3.

38. Walter V. Robinson, "Immigrant Voter Surge Seen Aiding Gore," *Boston Globe,* November 4, 2000, A1.

39. Terry M. Neal, "Some Black Voters View Gore as the Lesser of Two Evils," *Washington Post,* October 29, 2000, A24.

40. Edwin Chen, "Gore Emphasizes Education Agenda in Speech at Howard University," *Los Angeles Times,* September 16, 2000, A9. The case involved a black officer shooting a black student, a dubious, or at least complicated, example of racial profiling.

41. Neal, "Some Black Voters."

42. Robert L. Borosage, "Gore Doesn't Need Friends Like These," *Washington Post,* May 15, 2000, A23.

43. Gore was disingenuous during his only comment on the reparations question, telling a national black radio talk show host that the proposal for a reparations study was about affirmative action and support for historically black colleges. The legislation, however, called for a study of direct payments to descendants of slaves. (See Tom Joyner's interview with Al Gore, October 4, 2000. Available at <http://www.tomjoyner.com/missed/archive/celebrity_archive.html>). The Democratic platform had also endorsed a study of the reparations issue, and it is a demonstration of the Republicans' restraint on race that they never made an issue of this. Surely, the late Lee Atwater would have found a way to publicize and exploit this unpopular stance.

44. Tom Joyner's interview, October 4, 2000.

45. Tom Ramstack, "Clinton Orders Increase in Hispanic Workers," *Washington Times,* October 20, 2000.

46. Michael A. Fletcher, "NAACP Works to Boost Black Turnout," *Washington Post,* October 21, 2000, A1.

47. Neal, "Some Black Voters."

48. Ceci Connolly and Ellen Nakashima, "Gore Labels Bush Racially Insensitive," *Washington Post,* November 5, 2000, A22.

49. At least one prominent Democrat agreed: Senator Bob Kerrey called on Gore to disavow the NAACP ad as racially divisive.

50. Ariana Huffington, "Florida's Ugly Secret: Nullified African American Votes," *Los Angeles Times,* December 8, 2000, B9.

51. A few surveys of voters in the 1992 and 1996 elections suggest that Clinton won a narrow victory among white voters in one or both of those elections. However, national exit polls give Republicans a very narrow victory in 1992 and a larger one in 1996. See Henry C. Kenski, Carol Chang, and Brooks Aylor, "Explaining the Vote: The Presidential Election of 1996" in *The 1996 Presidential Campaign: A Communication Perspective,* Robert E. Denton, Jr., ed. (Westport: Praeger, 1998).

52. Edwin Chen, "Gore Emphasizes."

53. Neal, "Some Black Voters."

54. Kuttner, "Lynching."

55. Tim Palast, "Florida's Flawed 'Voter Cleansing' Program," *Salon,* December 4, 2000. Another aspect of Florida law with racial implications was that Florida had one of the strictest bans on one-time felons voting. Because 31 percent of black males in Florida had criminal records, this lifetime ban effectively disenfranchised almost a sixth of the black electorate. Florida's Republican-controlled state government repeatedly violated state law by ordering localities to purge voters with felonious records from other states. Many localities did, although court precedent held that they should not.

56. Ronald Brownstein, "Bush Has Legitimacy, But It's Fragile," *Los Angeles Times,* December 17, 2000, A1.

57. Amoore interview.

58. Bryce N. Harlow, "Memorandum for the Record," December 28, 1960, notes of December 15, 1960, meeting, Box 55, Papers of Bryce Harlow, Dwight David Eisenhower Presidential Library, Abilene, Kansas. The Harlow memo records the conversation of Harlow, Eisenhower, Nixon, and GOP chair Thurston Morton.

59. Bailey interview.

II

Voting Groups and Their Choices

4

Gender As a Political Constant

The More Things Change, the More They Stay the Same

Melissa Levitt and Katherine C. Naff

Perhaps Matt Randall, a 22-year-old interviewed by the *Los Angeles Times* shortly before the 2000 election, put it best when he said, "Bush is a guy's guy. He's from Texas, so he's more of a he-man, leatherneck type. . . . Gore, he's sensitive. He's supposed to be for the environment. He's always talking about kids and families."[1] Randall's assessment of the two candidates epitomizes the "gender gap," or the greater likelihood for Democratic candidates to appeal to women, and Republican candidates to appeal to men. That the gap has become a force that helps to shape presidential campaigns can be seen in the two major candidates' efforts during the 2000 campaign to appeal to the gender that was less likely to vote for them: George Bush by campaigning on a platform of "compassionate conservatism" and emphasizing education reform, and Al Gore by highlighting his record as a Vietnam veteran and a tough investigative reporter.

Most scholars agree that the gender gap appeared as early as 1964. The gap gained notable prominence following the 1980 election when women hoped to persuade Democratic Party officials to endorse the ratification of the Equal Rights Amendment (ERA) and a female vice presidential candidate in the 1984 presidential race. Although the ERA was never ratified and the 1984 candidate and his female running mate (Walter Mondale and Geraldine Ferraro) met resounding defeat, the attention paid to the gender gap increased during the 1980s and 1990s. Contributing to this growing awareness was the reality that since 1980 women have comprised the majority of registered voters while also turning out to vote at a greater rate than men.[2] As a result, the "gender gap" has become a standard part of the American political lexicon, and both parties now consider women a voting bloc to be reckoned with.[3]

Yet men and women do not necessarily hold opposing views of candidates. The plurality of both men and women voted for Bill Clinton in 1992 and 1996, but his margin of victory was greater among women than men. The 2000 election is noteworthy, however, because for the first time since 1980, the two groups elected different candidates. That is, a majority of women voted for Gore, while the majority of men voted for Bush.[4]

In this chapter, we begin with a brief review of the considerable literature devoted to understanding the development and effect of the gender gap in presidential elections. In addition to the greater turnout for presidential elections by women, scholars have focused on the ways men and women differ in vote choice, partisanship, and policy preferences. We then turn our attention briefly to the dynamics of the 1992 (known as the Year of the Woman) and 1996 (sometimes called the Revenge of the Soccer Moms) elections. The role that gender played in those two elections then sets the stage for our examination of the 2000 presidential race and the strategies and tactics the candidates undertook to increase support among both men and women.

A Gender Gap is Unearthed

The gender gap in vote choice refers to the fact that in most elections in the last half-century, women and men have differed in the degree to which they support candidates. This concept has been operationalized in several ways. The most common reflects the difference between the men's vote for a particular candidate and the women's vote for the same candidate.[5] In 1984, for example, 62 percent of men voted for Ronald Reagan, compared to 56 percent of women.[6] Reagan won the majority in both cases, but men were more likely than women to vote for him by six points. Another definition of the gender gap views it as the difference between the margin of victory a candidate received between the two groups. That is, in 1984, Reagan's margin of victory among women was 12 points and, among men, 25 points, so under this definition, the gender gap would be 25 minus 12 points, or 13 points.[7] Critics point out that this latter definition inflates the gap, leading some to the conclusion that the gap is really a chasm.[8] In this chapter, we use the former definition.

Regardless of how the gender gap is measured, retrospective studies have revealed a difference in men's and women's voting behavior going back to at least 1952. Until 1964, women were more likely than men to vote for Republican candidates, reflecting their more conservative orientation.[9] That election was the first where over 50 percent of the women stated that they identified with the Democratic Party instead of the Republican Party.[10] Since then, women have been more likely than men to support Democratic candidates. (An exception is the 1976 election, in which about 50 percent of each group voted for Jimmy Carter). Although the conventional wisdom has suggested that this switch is a result of women's more liberal leanings, the reality is that men have become more conservative and Republican. It is changes in the party affiliation and vote choices made by men—rather than women—that result in the gender gap.

Another feature that is often highlighted is the stability of the gender gap. It persists across most demographic groups, including those defined by region, religion, social class, and age.[11] One explanation offered for the uniformity among women is that the gap is based on the growing independence of women, psychologically and economically, as they have moved into professional positions or managing single-parent households.[12] This explanation accounts for the difference between married women who do not work outside the home (and so are less likely to be economically independent) and married women who do. Homemakers tend to support Republican candidates while working women tend to support Democrats.[13] There are also differences between religious and more secular women.[14] For example, among white born-again Christians who voted in the 1992 election, women were slightly less likely than men to vote for Clinton. Among those voters who were 60 or older, women and men, regardless of their religious beliefs, voted for Clinton in equal proportions.[15]

With respect to partisanship, since 1960 an increasingly greater proportion of men have identified themselves as Republicans, while women have continued their Democratic affiliation.[16] This difference in partisanship explained only part of the gender gap during the 1970s and early 1980s, but explained nearly all of the gender gap in the 1988 and 1992 elections.[17] It appears that changes in partisanship lag behind the gender gap in voting such that gender preferences in the voting booth eventually translate into shifts in party identification.[18] The widening gap in vote choice evidenced by the two most recent presidential elections may well presage a further shift of men into the Republican Party.[19]

Men and women's differing preferences with respect to some policy positions also help to explain the gender gap in vote choice.[20] One study concluded that the gender gap with respect to support for Ronald Reagan was centered around political issues rather than partisan or even personal evaluations of that president.[21] Scholars have operationalized these policy preferences in different ways, using varied methodologies to assess the impact of these preferences on voting decisions. However, most would agree with Seltzer, Newman, and Leighton that the gap is based on two fundamental issues: the government's role in ensuring that all Americans enjoy a reasonable standard of living and assessments of the economy.[22]

Women tend to take a more sociotropic view of the economy than men, meaning that women consider how society as a whole is doing, regardless of their own financial straits, and tend to be more pessimistic as to the health of the economy. They support welfare policies and other "compassionate" policy choices and believe that Democrats are more likely than Republicans to support such policies.[23] A gender gap has also shown up over the use of force. Women are more likely than men to oppose the use of force to resolve disputes overseas and to support stricter gun control laws.[24] Although one might think that there would be disagreement between men and women with respect to issues that are of particular importance to women, such as abortion, there is not a division between men and women, once party identification is taken into account.[25] There are some exceptions to this rule especially in regards to "moral" issues, such as pornography, where women have a more conservative view than men.[26]

The Year of the Woman

The 1992 election has been called the Year of the Woman because an unprecedented 119 women stood for election as Republicans or Democrats in Congress and 53 won. Victories by 4 women in the Senate and 47 in the House increased their representation to 10 percent.[27] The way was paved for this focus on women by the hearings to confirm Supreme Court nominee Clarence Thomas. The all-male Senate Judiciary Committee displayed little understanding of the sexual harassment he was accused of by former subordinate Anita Hill.[28] Another contributing factor was a record number of retirements and primary losses by congressional incumbents, which gave well-positioned women a greater opportunity to become officeholders.

The Year of the Woman was also characterized by a gender gap in vote choice. At first, both men and women favored George H. W. Bush over Bill Clinton, although men tended to favor Bush by a wider margin than women. That changed in July when Ross Perot entered the race. He consistently received more support from men than women, but by then Clinton was favored by the plurality of both women and men. By September, the gender gap was beginning to emerge as men's support for Clinton declined. The Bush campaign, aware of the gap, sought to close it by emphasizing family values and claiming that Bush had firsthand knowledge of family issues because his own daughter was divorced and a single mom.[29] Women, however, apparently remained unconvinced. According to Gallup exit poll data, 4 percent more women than men voted for Clinton, while 5 percent more men than women voted for Perot.[30] Women comprised 55 percent of those who voted for Clinton.[31]

Analysts of the gender gap in the 1992 election emphasized that there were some larger differences among groups of women than between women and men. For example, white women were just as likely to vote for each of the two major candidates, while African American women were more than ten times as likely to vote for Clinton as Bush.[32]

There were some differences with respect to the policy positions taken by Bush and Clinton that account for the gap, at least in part. For example, women were more concerned than men with health care and education, while men were more concerned about foreign policy. Women were more supportive of spending on social welfare issues and more pessimistic about the economy than men.[33]

The Revenge of the Soccer Moms

Discussion of the 1996 election in which Clinton ran for reelection against Robert Dole focuses on "soccer moms," who were alienated by the callous policies advocated by then Speaker of the House Newt Gingrich. This term belies the fact that many groups of women supported Clinton, not just the middle-class working mothers that this term implies. However, there is no doubt that it created an appealing backdrop for both candidates' desire to show their concern for women, particularly those with children.[34]

The gender gap was big news in the 1996 election. Kathleen Frankovic writes that eighty-two stories about the gender gap appeared in the *New York Times* in 1996, compared to only ten in 1992.[35] The gap was also wider in the 1996 election than it had been in 1992, as issue positions became more important in men and women's evaluations of the incumbent president. Clinton's positions on issues that traditionally divide men and women, such as jobs, guaranteed incomes, and government services, were reflected in the growing breach.[36] That Dole drew more support among men than Clinton and less support among women should not be surprising given his conservative stance on the role of government and social pro-grams.[37] This is not to say Dole did not try to appeal to women through the "soccer mom" frame. When campaigning, he would sometimes ask if there were any soccer moms in the audience and in speeches mentioned how his policies would benefit, specifically, soccer moms.[38]

Throughout the campaign, the plurality of men and women indicated that Clinton was their choice (except for a brief period in the spring when men were evenly divided between the two candidates). However, while women's support for Clinton remained fairly constant, men's support for him was more volatile.

By May, Dole, aware of the greater reluctance of women to support him, announced his plan to eliminate the gender gap. He highlighted "woman-friendly" legislation he supported, such as the Violence Against Women Act and another provision of the anticrime bill of 1994 that would have made it easier to convict rapists. Journalists were quick to point out, however, that he voted against that bill because it also contained a ban on assault weapons.[39] Dole also brought out his wife Elizabeth to tackle the gender gap. She stressed his commitment to charity, and his commitment to her as a faithful husband. While her effort heightened *her* popularity among women, it did little to strengthen their support for him.[40]

Clinton also went after the women's vote. He targeted suburban mothers, who are traditionally more conservative than those who live in urban areas and hence more likely to support Republicans, with his message of re-sponsibility for children. Clinton's message to these women apparently worked, since he added married women to his already strong support among single women. He was successful in narrowing the so-called mar-riage gap, which had historically favored Republicans. In a June 1996 poll, Clinton led Dole by 29 points among single voters and by 13 points among married voters.[41] During this campaign, Clinton also went out of his way to emphasize women's issues such as the "v-chip," a device that gives parents the ability to block television programs that they consider inappro-priate for their children, an assault weapons ban, and the enforcement of child support payments among "deadbeat dads." This strategy actually lost him male voters while winning larger margins of support among female voters.[42]

After the election, Republican National Committee chairman Haley Bar-bour told GOP governors that the lack of a strong stand on education might have cost them the 1996 presidential election. New Jersey governor Chris-tine Todd Whitman chastened the state executives: "We can't be a national party if we are going to be a party of white males."[43] Polls conducted by the Republicans found an even larger gender gap than revealed by exit polls, causing the GOP leaders to call on their minions to stress that Republicans care about women.

Thus, the gender gap persisted during the 1990s, contributing to the election and reelection of the Democratic candidate. The widening of the breach between 1992 and 1996, and its apparently solid grounding in women's belief in a stronger role for government, made it clear to Republicans that their candidate could not win the election without female support. Conversely, the Democrats were aware that they had lost large percentages of their traditional voting base—working-class and middle-class men—and set about trying to restore their support for the Democratic Party.[44]

The 2000 Election: The Year of Fluctuating Fortunes

Both parties approached the 2000 election with a heightened consciousness about the implications of the gender gap for victory. There was a fear that the gender gap would become a chasm. This fear was not realized.

A Voter.com/Battleground poll in March showed that Gore led Bush among women by just 5 percentage points. Bush was ahead by 12 points among men, however.[45] The gap fluctuated over the course of the 2000 election. By May, women were about evenly divided between the two candidates, while men preferred Bush to Gore by a significant margin.[46] (See Figure 4.1) Over the summer, women's support for Gore briefly subsided. However, a Republican convention designed thematically to galvanize women failed to do so,[47] and by mid-August Gore's lead began to grow. By Election Day, Gore eclipsed Bush's lead among women by 12 points.[48]

Crafting an Image, Maintaining a Balance

Throughout the campaign, Gore endeavored to win the support of men, particularly those Democratic men who had voted for Reagan during the 1980s. Men, as a whole, were not comfortable with Gore. Andrew Kohut of the Pew Center for People and the Press observed, "A lot of men see Gore as the kid who always had his hand up in school, sort of the Eddie Haskell 'I want to please' image."[49] One commentator summarized men's preferences with analogies to cars: Men saw Gore as a Taurus, safe and reliable but not very exciting, while they saw Bush as a zippier, more expensive Maserati.[50] Mary Leonard and Cindy Rodriguez of the *Boston*

Globe put it this way: "Polls show Gore has a big gender gap, and it isn't because women are flocking to support him. It's because men, in big numbers, prefer Texas Governor George W. Bush, who seems manly because he owns a ranch, ran a baseball team, played hard as a college frat boy, and wasn't always at the head of the class."[51]

Additionally, men saw Gore as less honest than Bush. Efforts to overcome this perception were hampered by his close association with President Clinton and by Gore's tendency to exaggerate. Democrats viewed Clinton as a liability among men, particularly the married, middle-class men whom they were trying to reach.[52] For these men, Clinton's marital infidelities disgraced the party, the presidency, and the institution of marriage. The term "yuck factor" was adopted to describe the potential damage Clinton could inflict on the Gore campaign. Gore sought to win over male voters by changing his image from a left-leaning intellectual to more of a "man's man." He did so by changing his wardrobe and emphasizing his service in Vietnam. This effort was designed particularly to swing white men with household incomes of $25,000 to $50,000 back into the fold.[53] The strategy proved effective, since Gore gained 9 percentage points among white men making $20,000 to $50,000 a year.

In contrast, Bush needed to make himself less of a "man's man" and more of a leader of the whole society to win over women. "Compassionate conservatism" became the campaign's battle cry. "The Republican Party must put a compassionate face on a conservative philosophy," George W. Bush told reporters after Dole was defeated in 1996. "The message to women . . . is we care about people."[54]

A March 18 Voter.com/Battleground poll found that voters viewed Bush as the stronger and more trustworthy of the two candidates. The perception of Bush as trustworthy contributed to his success among "soccer moms," who tend to be more values-oriented and more disgusted with the Clinton scandal than single women.[55] At the same time, however, Bush was vulnerable on a powerful issue in this campaign: gun control. In a poll in March, 56 percent of men and 73 percent of women were in favor of stricter gun control laws.[56] While Bush attempted to distance himself from the National Rifle Association and its resolute campaign against gun control, Democrats did not hesitate to point out that he had signed a law allowing Texans to carry concealed weapons.

Los Angeles Times polls from July through the end of September show that on character issues men consistently rated Bush higher than Gore with respect to leadership, likability, and sharing their moral values. Women's perspective fluctuated over this same period, which is noteworthy because character and stands on the issues were more critical to women in this election.[57] Women tended to find Bush more likable than Gore and to rate his leadership ability higher until the end of September, when those ratings flipped in favor of Gore. A July poll showed that women were more likely to say that Bush shared their moral values, but by August, Gore was ahead in this regard.

It seemed that Gore's campaign to woo women into the Democratic fold worked. Two events between mid-August and late September likely contributed to this success. The first was the Democratic National Convention. Democrats took great pains to dispel Gore's image as the wonk "that the voters can't warm up to."[58] The presumably unscripted kiss between Gore and his wife received good reviews. "Even the way he kissed his wife at the convention, whether it was planned or not, it was just really, really nice," stated a Miami voter interviewed by the *Los Angeles Times*.[59] Susan Carroll of the Center for American Women in Politics at Rutgers University had a similar assessment: "The big reservation that voters, and women particularly, had of Gore was . . . 'Is this guy going to be a great leader?' " she told the *Los Angeles Times*. "Since the convention, he's really come through on that and has been able to establish himself and hit hard at issues women care about. That's really moved women strongly."[60]

The second event that may have contributed to Gore's popularity with women occurred the following month when he appeared on the Oprah Winfrey Show, the highest rated show among women aged 25 to 54. Bush also subsequently appeared, it seems that Gore's appearance was more successful, going a long way to warming his taut image in the subsequent reviews of his performance. "Gore was really positive for families and an advocate for education and for people being able to spend more time with their children," a Georgia mother told the *Los Angeles Times*.[61] Throughout the campaign, women viewed Gore as a sympathetic husband and a good listener, in some respects the opposite of Bush.[62] Gore's openly prochoice stance also resonated with many women.

After the convention, Gore also made headway in securing the support of male voters who had been instrumental in the Republicans' takeover of the House and Senate in 1994. He did so, in part, by blaming the corporations and the wealthy for undermining the economic security of working families. Meanwhile, by mid-October, it was clear to the Bush campaign that whatever he had done so far to win female voters was not working, and it was time to bring out the big guns. Notable women like former first lady Barbara Bush, the governor's wife Laura, and vice presidential candidate Richard Cheney's wife Lynne were sent on a "W. stands for women tour."[63] Meanwhile, Cheney was dispatched to shore up the men's vote by going to football games, staging photo opportunities in factories filled with heavy machinery, and talking about military procurement.[64]

The Marriage Gap

Reliable support from married couples was the cornerstone of the GOP coalition that dominated presidential politics from 1968 to 1988. But increasingly that vote has become a crucial swing vote in presidential elections. In the view of pollster Celinda Lake, as told to a *Boston Globe* reporter, "The marriage gap now rivals the gender gap as a hallmark feature of Americans' voting patterns." (See Figures 4.1 and 4.2.) The Clinton campaign narrowed that gap in 1996 by portraying Robert Dole as an "old crank out of touch with soccer moms and dads." That strategy would not work with George W. Bush as an opponent, who is a baby-boomer, married with two teenage daughters, and exudes family values.[65]

To regain the support of moderate swing voters, especially married women whose allegiance Clinton won in 1992 and 1996, Bush adopted education as a centerpiece of his campaign.[66] He advocated an education policy that was very different from that touted in previous Republican campaigns. Bob Dole's 1996 campaign's platform on education included a dismantling of the Department of Education and a return of all control over the schools to the states. In contrast, Bush called for a more aggressive federal role in setting standards and testing and instituting a voucher program, which he hoped would appeal to women, especially mothers.

This strategy apparently met with some success, at least early in the campaign. While Gore had the support of single women, a Voter.com poll in March gave Bush a 14 percentage point lead among married women and a 33 percentage point lead among married mothers.[67] One important reason for the differential in preferences on the basis of marital status is that married women tend to identify more with Republican values and are more likely to be in two-earner households, better able to weather tough economic times and not as likely to require government assistance as are single people.[68]

The Gore campaign responded with a multimillion-dollar advertising campaign designed to stress Gore's image as a "good guy."[69] His tax policies, aimed at working families, included tax credits for college tuition, day care, and after-school programs.[70] Gore also needed to demonstrate that he would do a better job of improving education than Bush. While men consistently favored Bush in this regard, women's views fluctuated. An August poll showed 39 percent of women rated Gore as better able to

Figure 4.1 **Women's Preferences for Candidate 2000 Election**

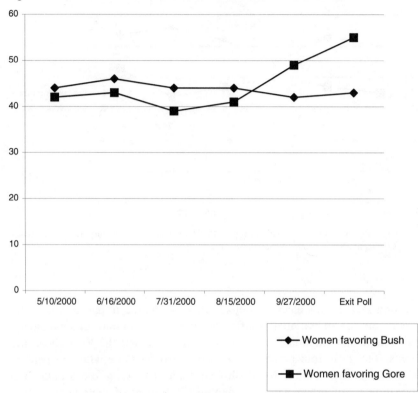

Source: Los Angeles Times Poll Alert, May 10, 2000; *Los Angeles Times* Poll Alert, June 16, 2000; *Los Angeles Times* Poll Alert, August 5, 2000; *Lost Angeles Times* Poll Alert, September 27, 2000; *Los Angeles Times* Poll Alert, November 8, 2000.

improve education compared to 41 percent for Bush. However, Bush's effort to raise his standing among women by highlighting his commitment to education reform was not successful in the long run. By the end of September, women favored Gore by a 17-point margin.[71] By late October, Gore had even closed the gap among married women, leading Bush by one point (43 to 42 percent), according to a CBS/*New York Times* poll.[72]

Who Won the Women's Vote?

Despite fluctuations in women's preferences, and differences between married and single women, ultimately once again the gender gap prevailed on

Figure 4.2 **Men's Preferences for Candidate 2000 Election**

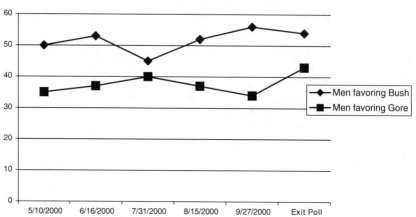

Source: Los Angeles Times Poll Alert May 10, 2000; June 16, 2000; July 31, 2000; August 15, 2000; September 27, 2000; November 8, 2000.

Election Day. In this election, unlike others in the recent past in which the gender gap has shown up as a difference in level of support for a candidate, the Democratic candidate won the women's vote and the Republican the men's vote. Fifty-four percent of women voted for Gore while 53 percent of men cast their ballots for Bush (see Table 4.1). Gore did a better job appealing to suburban women, winning 52 percent of their votes, while Bush won 55 percent of the suburban male vote. The marriage gap was even broader. Bush carried the votes of married men by 20 points while Gore had a 30-point lead among single women. Married women and single men split their votes about evenly between the two candidates.[73] Gore's victory among women, however, is largely attributable to minority women, who, along with minority men, were much more likely to support the Democratic candidate rather than the Republican. White women split their vote between the two candidates, while Gore took nearly 100 percent of black women's votes. Gore did very poorly among white men, ultimately winning the support of only a little more than one-third of them.

With respect to other demographics, the same gender split is apparent. In every age grouping, slightly more than half of women voted for Gore and about the same percentage of men voted for Bush. This is true among those with differing amounts of education, with the exception of those with no high school diploma. These voters were more likely to support Gore regardless of gender.

Table 4.1

Male and Female Constituencies Voting for Gore and Bush (in percent)

	Gore		Bush	
	Men	Women	Men	Women
All	42	54	53	43
Suburban	41	52	55	45
Married	38	48	58	49
Single	48	63	46	32
White	36	48	60	49
Black	85	94	12	6
18–29 years old	41	53	51	42
30–44 years old	42	53	54	45
45–59 years old	41	53	55	44
60 and older	44	56	53	42
Independent	39	51	51	42
No high school diploma	57	60	41	37
High school graduates	43	52	55	45
Some college education	40	50	56	48
College graduates	39	57	57	40

Source: Data compiled by the authors from the Voter News Service Exit Poll.

Concluding Thoughts

The 2000 election was characterized by splits in the electorate between whites and nonwhites, among Protestants, Catholics, and Jews, between suburban and urban residents, and among regions of the country. While these splits are no less important than between men and women, it was the gender gap, and the marriage gap, within the gender gap that, in many ways, helped define the first election of the new millennium. This gap manifested itself through each candidate's tailored message that attempted to appeal to women, while not losing men, and to draw married voters of both genders, but not at the expense of unmarried voters. While Gore clearly lost ground that Clinton had gained with respect to these important swing voters, he ultimately won the popular vote with a coalition that included almost as many married women as sided with Bush. But in this race, winning the popular vote by such a narrow margin was not enough to secure the election.

The gender gap in presidential elections appears to have become a constant; as long as men and women, in general, have differing views and priorities, candidates will make an effort to design their messages to bridge these fault lines. However, this election has also made it clear that the candidate who prevails will be the one who also recognizes the variation within these two categories and adroitly walks the tightrope between them.

Notes

1. Hector Tobar, "For White Males, Bush is Their Guy," *Los Angeles Times*, September 11, 2000, A12.
2. Barbara Norrander, "Is the Gender Gap Narrowing?" in *Reelection 1996: How Americans Voted*, ed. Herbert F. Weisberg and Janet M. Box-Steffensmeier (Chappaqua, NY: Seven Bridges Press, 1999); Richard Seltzer, Judy Newman, and Melissa Leighton. *Sex As a Political Variable* (Boulder, CO: Lynne Rienner Publishers, 1997).
3. See Carol M. Mueller, "The Empowerment of Women," in *The Politics of the Gender Gap*, ed. Carol M. Mueller (Newbury Park, CA: Sage, 1988), for a fuller history of the development of the gender gap as a national news story.
4. Marjorie Connelly, "Who Voted: A Portrait of American Politics 1976–2000," *New York Times*, November 12, 2000, sec. 4, p. 5.
5. Richard Seltzer, Judy Newman, and Melissa Leighton, *Sex As a Political Variable*, p. 11.
6. Connelly, "Who Voted," sec. 4, p. 4.
7. See Seltzer, Newman, and Leighton, *Sex As a Political Variable*, p. 129.
8. Seltzer, Newman, and Leighton, *Sex As a Political Variable*, p. 129; Cal Clark and Janet Clark, "Whither the Gender Gap? Converging and Conflicting Attitudes Among Women," in *Women in Politics: Outsiders or Insiders*, ed. Lois Duke, 2nd ed. (Englewood Cliffs, NJ: Prentice Hall, 1996).
9. Seltzer, Newman and Layton, *Sex As a Political Variable*, p. 33.
10. Barbara Norrander, "Is the Gap Narrowing" in *Reelection 1996;* Karen Kaufmann and John Petrocik, "Revenge of the Soccer Moms: Gender As a Party Cleavage in American Politics." 1997; Monica Johnson and Margaret Marini, "Bridging the Racial Divide in the United States: The Effect of Gender," *Social Psychological Quarterly* 61 (1998): 247–258.
11. Seltzer, Newman and Leighton, *Sex As a Political Variable*, p. 52; see also Daniel Wirls, "Reinterpreting the Gender Gap," *Public Opinion Quarterly* 50, no. 3 (1986): 316–330, and Karen Kaufmann and John Petrocik, "The Changing Politics of American Men: Understanding the Sources of the Gender Gap," *American Journal of Political Science* 43, no. 3 (1999): 864–887.
12. Susan Carroll, "Women's Autonomy and the Gender Gap: 1980 and 1982" in *The Politics of the Gender Gap*, ed. Carol M. Mueller. (Newbury Park, CA: Sage, 1998).
13. Mary E. Bendyna and Celinda C. Lake, "Gender and Voting in the 1992 Presidential Election," in *The Year of the Woman: Myths and Realities*, eds. Elizabeth Adell Cook, Susan Thomas, and Clyde Wilcox (Boulder, CO: Westview Press, 1994).
14. Bendyna and Lake, "Gender and Voting," p. 240.
15. Ibid., p. 249.
16. Seltzer, Newman and Leighton, *Sex As a Political Variable*, pp. 46, 53; Bendyna and Lake, "Gender and Voting," p. 245.
17. Kaufmann and Petrocik, p. 869.
18. Ibid., See n. 10.
19. It should also be noted, however, that in 1980, men began moving away from either party toward an independent preference. In the 1992 election, Perot enjoyed

much greater support among male voters than among female voters by about 12 percent (Norrander, "Is the Gender Gap Narrowing?", p. 152).

20. See, for example, Carole Chaney, R. Michael Alvarez, and Jonathan Nagler, "Explaining the Gender Gap in U.S. Presidential Elections, 1980–1992," *Political Research Quarterly* 51 (1998): 311–340; Norrander, "Is the Gender Gap Narrowing?", p. 146; Elizabeth Adell Cook and Clyde Wilcox, "Feminism and the Gender Gap—A Second Look," *Journal of Politics* 53 (1991): 1111–1122.

21. Martin Gilens, "Gender and Support for Reagan," *American Journal of Political Science* 32 (1988): 19–49.

22. Seltzer, Newman, and Leighton, *Sex As a Political Variable*, p. 114.

23. Chaney, Alvarez, and Nagler, "Explaining the Gender Gap," p. 316; Mueller, "Empowerment of Women," p. 17;

24. Kristi Anderson, "Gender and Pubic Opinion," in *Understanding Public Opinion*, ed. Barbara Norrander and Clyde Wilcox (Washington, DC: Congressional Quarterly, 1997); Robert Shapiro and Harpreet Mahajan, "Gender Differences in Policy Preferences: A Summary of Trends from the 1960s to the 1980s," *Public Opinion Quarterly* 50 (1986): 42–61; Gilens, "Gender and Support for Reagan," p. 34.

25. Chaney, Alvarez, and Nagler, "Explaining the Gender Gap," p. 333.

26. Norrander, "Is the Gender Gap Narrowing?", p. 150.

27. Kathleen Dolan, "Voting for Women in the 'Year of the Woman'," *American Journal of Political Science* 42 (1998): 272–293.

28. Michael X. Delli Carpini and Ester R. Fuchs, "The Year of the Woman? Candidates, Voters and the 1992 Elections," *Political Science Quarterly* 108, no. 1 (1993): 29–36.

29. James Gerstenzang, "Bush, Seeking to Narrow Gender Gap, Switches Focus to 'Family Issues'," *Los Angeles Times*, September 19, 1992, A14.

30. These numbers differ slightly from those reported by Bendyna and Lake, but show the same overall pattern.

31. Bendyna and Lake, "Gender and Voting," p. 249.

32. Ibid., p. 244.

33. Kaufmann and Petrocik, "Changing Politics of American Men," pp. 874–875.

34. Clark and Clark, "Whither the Gender Gap,"; Susan Carroll, "The Disempowerment of the Gender Gap: Soccer Moms and the 1996 Elections," *PS: Political Science and Politics* 32, no. 1 (1999): 7–12.

35. Kathleen A. Frankovic, "Why the Gender Gap Became News in 1996," *PS: Political Science and Politics* 32, no. 1 (1999): 20–23.

36. Norrander, "Is the Gender Gap Narrowing?" p. 160.

37. Seltzer, Newman, and Leighton, *Sex As a Political Variable*, p. 123.

38. Susan Carroll, "Disempowerment of the Gender Gap," p. 10.

39. Katharine Q. Seelye, "Dole Says He Has a Plan to Win Votes of Women," *New York Times*, May 8, 1996, A1.

40. Katharine Q. Seelye, "Politics: the Spouse: On the Trail, Dole's Wife Seeks Votes of Women," *New York Times*, October 5, 1996, A10.

41. Ronald Brownstein, "Clinton's Target Audience: Married, With Children," *Los Angeles Times*, June 13, 1996, A10.

42. Thomas B. Edsall and Richard Morin, "Clinton Benefited from Huge Gender Gap," *Washington Post*, November 6, 1996, A7.

43. Dan Balz, "Stands on Education Cost GOP Among Women," *Washington Post*, November 27, 1996, A6.

44. Ibid.

45. Robin Toner, "Presidential Race Could Turn on Bush's Appeal to Women," *New*

York Times, March 26, 2000 (available at <http://nytimes.com/library/politics/camp/032600wh-gop-bush-women.html>.

46. Available at the *Los Angeles Times* Web site at <www.latimes.com>.

47. Mary Leonard, "Campaign 2000/The Republican Convention/The Constituents: Convention Rhetoric Targets Women," *Boston Globe*, August 3, 2000, A28.

48. The figures were 55 percent for Gore and 43 percent for Bush among female respondents to the exit poll.

49. Mary Leonard, "Campaign 2000: Gore Falls Into 'Marriage Gap,' Losing Out to Bush in Polls," *Boston Globe*, May 28, 2000, A1.

50. Todd S. Purdum, "The 2000 Campaign: Gender Politics; Among Men, It's Bush the Maserati by a Mile," *New York Times*, October 8, 2000, sec. 1, p. 1.

51. Mary Leonard and Cindy Rodriguez, "Campaign 2000: Gore Speakers Try to Sell Candidate as a Man's Man," *Boston Globe*, August 18, 2000, A18.

52. Leonard, "Campaign 2000: Gore Falls Into 'Marriage Gap,' " A1.

53. Thomas B. Edsall, "Wooing Working Men: Gore Makes Inroads in Key Constituency," *Washington Post*, September 11, 2000, A1.

54. Balz, "Stands on Education," A6.

55. Ben White, "Presidential Race Evens Out; Gore Polls Well on Experience; Bush Is Closing Gender Gap," *Washington Post*, March 18, 2000, A7.

56. Robin Toner, "Presidential Race Could Turn on Bush's Appeal to Women," available at <http://nytimes.com/library/politics/camp/0326002h-gop-bush-women.html>.

57. Cathleen Decker, "Campaign 2000; Gore's Come a Long Way With Help of Women," *Los Angeles Times*, September 18, 2000, A1.

58. Leonard and Rodriguez, "Campaign 2000: Gore Speakers Try to Sell Candidate," A18.

59. Cathleen Decker, "Campaign 2000: Gore's Come a Long Way," A1.

60. Quoted in Ibid.

61. Ibid.

62. Ibid.

63. Frank Bruni, "The 2000 Campaign: The Families: Barbara Bush Joins G.O.P. Women on Stump to Bridge Gender Gap," *Washington Post*, October 19, 2000, A30.

64. Michael Cooper, "The 2000 Campaign/The Running Mate; Cheney, an Alpha Candidate, Casts His Line in a Sea of Men," *New York Times*, October 22, 2000, A22.

65. Leonard, "Campaign 2000: Gore Falls into 'Marriage Gap,' " A1.

66. Balz, "Stands on Education," A6.

67. Ronald Brownstein, "Campaign 2000: Education Surfacing as Key Issue for Bush," *Los Angeles Times*, March 24, 2000, A34.

68. Katherine Q. Seelye, "The 2000 Campaign: Women Voters, Marital Status is Shaping Women's Leanings, Surveys Find," *New York Times*, 20 September 2000, A1.

69. Leonard, "Campaign 2000: Gore Falls Into 'Marriage Gap,' " A1.

70. Katherine Q. Seelye, "The 2000 Campaign: The Rallying Cry," *New York Times*, August 22, 2000, A18.

71. *Los Angeles Times*, available at <www.latimes.com>.

72. Fay Fiore, "Campaign 2000: Married Women, Not Wedded to Either Camp, Could Be Deciding Bloc," *Los Angeles Times*, October 30, 2000, A16.

73. Connolly, "Who Voted.

Bibliography

Alvarez, R. Michael, and Jonathan Nagler. "Economics, Entitlements and Social Issues: Voter Choice in the 1996 Presidential Election." *American Journal of Political Science* 42, no. 4 (1998): 1349–1363.

Anderson, Kristi. "Gender and Public Opinion." In *Understanding Public Opinion,* ed. Barbara Norrander and Clyde Wilcox. Washington, DC: Congressional Quarterly, 1997.

Andersen, Kristi. "Working Women and Political Participation, 1952–1972." *American Journal of Political Science* 29 (1975): 439–453.

Balz, Dan. "Stands on Education Cost GOP Among Women." *Washington Post,* November 27, 1996, A6.

Bendyna, Mary E., and Celinda C. Lake. "Gender and Voting in the 1992 Presidential Election." In *The Year of the Woman: Myths and Realities,* ed. Elizabeth Adell Cook, Susan Thomas, and Clyde Wilcox. Boulder, CO: Westview Press, 1994.

Bennett, Linda L., and Stephen E. Bennett. "Enduring Gender Differences in Political Behavior: The Impact of Socialization and Political Dispositions." *American Politics Quarterly* 17 (1989): 105–122.

Bolce, Louis. "The Role of Gender in Recent Presidential Elections: Reagan and the Reverse Gender Gap." *Presidential Studies Quarterly* 15 (1985): 372–386.

Bonk, Kathy. "The Selling of the Gender Gap: The Role of Organized Feminism." In T*he Politics of the Gender Gap: The Social Construction of Political Influence,* ed. Carol M. Mueller. Newbury Park, CA: Sage, 1998.

Brownstein, Ronald. "Clinton's Target Audience: Married, With Children." *Los Angeles Times,* June 13, 1996, A10.

———. "Campaign 2000: Education Surfacing as Key Issue for Bush." *Los Angeles Times,* March 24, 2000, A34.

Bruni, Frank. "The 2000 Campaign: The Families: Barbara Bush Joins G.O.P. Women on Stump to Bridge Gender Gap." *Washington Post,* October 19, 2000, A30.

Carroll, Susan. "The Disempowerment of the Gender Gap: Soccer Moms and the 1996 Elections," *PS: Political Science and Politics* 32, no. 1 (1999): 7–12.

———. "Women's Autonomy and the Gender Gap: 1980 and 1982." In *The Politics of the Gender Gap,* ed. Carol M. Mueller. Newbury Park, CA: Sage, 1998.

CBS and CBS/*New York Times* polls, Roper Center for Public Opinion Research, available at Lexis Nexis Academic Universe <http://web.lexis-nexis.com/universe>.

Chaney, Carole, R. Michael Alvarez, and Jonathan Nagler. "Explaining the Gender Gap in U.S. Presidential Elections, 1980–1992." *Political Research Quarterly* 51 (1998): 311–340.

Clark, Cal, and Janet Clark. "Whither the Gender Gap? Converging and Conflicting Attitudes Among Women." In *Women in Politics: Outsiders or Insiders,* ed. Lois Duke, 2nd ed. Englewood Cliffs, NJ: Prentice Hall, 1996.

Connelly, Marjorie. "Who Voted: A Portrait of American Politics 1976–2000." *New York Times,* November 12, 2000, sec. 4.

Conover, Pamela Johnson. "Feminists and the Gender Gap." *Journal of Politics* 50: 985–1010.

Cook, Elizabeth Adell, and Clyde Wilcox. "Feminism and the Gender Gap—A Second Look." *Journal of Politics* 53 (1991): 1111–1122.

Cooper, Michael. "The 2000 Campaign/The Running Mate; Cheney, an Alpha Candidate, Casts His Line in a Sea of Men." *New York Times,* October 22, 2000, A22.

Dalto, Guy C., Robert Slagter, and Holly Tankersley. "Gendered Job Characteristics,

Gender Identity and Differences in the Political Ideology of Men and Women." Paper presented at the annual meeting of the Midwestern Political Science Association, Chicago, IL, April 27–30, 2000.

Decker, Cathleen. "Campaign 2000: Gore's Come a Long Way With Help of Women." *Los Angeles Times*. September 18, 2000, A1.

Delli Carpini, Michael X., and Ester R. Fuchs. "The Year of the Woman? Candidates, Voters and the 1992 Elections." *Political Science Quarterly* 108, no. 1 (1993): 29–36.

Dolan, Kathleen. "Voting for Women in the 'Year of the Woman'." *American Journal of Political Science* 42 (1998): 272–293.

Edsall, Thomas B. "Wooing Working Men: Gore Makes Inroads in Key Constituency." *Washington Post*, September 11, 2000, A1.

Edsall, Thomas B., and Richard Morin. "Clinton Benefited from Huge Gender Gap." *Washington Post*, November 6, 1996, A7.

Elder, Laurel, and Steven Greene. *Political Information, Gender and the Vote: The Differential Impact of Media, Organizations and Personal Discussion on the Electoral Decisions of Men and Women.* Paper presented at the annual meeting of the Midwest Political Science Association, Chicago, IL, April 27–30, 2000.

Fiore, Fay. "Campaign 2000: Married Women, Not Wedded to Either Camp, Could Be Deciding Bloc." *Los Angeles Times*, October 30, 2000, A16.

Fite, David, Marc Genest, and Clyde Wilcox. "Gender Differences in Foreign Policy Attitudes: A Longitudinal Analysis." *American Politics Quarterly* 18 (1990): 492–512.

Frankovic, Kathleen A. "Sex and Politics: New Alignments, Old Issues." *PS: Political Science and Politics* 15 (1982): 439–448.

Friedan, Betty, and Midge Dector. "Are Women Different Today?" *Public Opinion* April/May 1982: 20, 41.

Gerstenzang, James. "Bush Seeking to Narrow Gender Gap. Switches Focus to 'Family Issues.' " *Los Angeles Times*, September 19, 1992, A14.

Gilens, Martin. "Gender and Support for Reagan." *American Journal of Political Science* 32 (1998): 19–49.

Goertzel, Ted George. "The Gender Gap: Sex, Family Income, and Political Opinions in the Early 1980s" *Journal of Political and Military Sociology* 11 (1983): 209–222.

Hansen, Susan B. "Talking About Politics: Gender and Contextual Effects on Political Proselytizing." *Journal of Politics* 59 (1997): 73–103.

Johnson, Monica, and Margaret Marini. "Bridging the Racial Divide in the United States: The Effect of Gender." *Social Psychological Quarterly* 61 (1998): 247–258.

Kaufmann, Karen, and John Petrocik. "The Changing Politics of American Men: Understanding the Sources of the Gender Gap." *American Journal of Political Science* 43, no. 3 (1999): 864–887.

———. "The Revenge of the Soccer Moms? Gender as a Party Cleavage in American Politics." Paper presented at the annual meeting of the American Political Science Association, Washington, DC, August 27–31, 1997.

Klein, Ethel. "The Gender Gap: Different Issues, Different Answers." *Brookings Review* 3: (1985) 33–37.

Leonard, Mary. "Campaign 2000: Gore Falls Into 'Marriage Gap,' Losing Out to Bush in Polls." *Boston Globe*, May 28, 2000, A1.

———. "Campaign 2000: The Republican Convention/The Constituents: Convention Rhetoric Targets Women." *Boston Globe*, August 3, 2000, A28.

Leonard, Mary, and Cindy Rodriguez. "Campaign 2000: Gore Speakers Try to Sell Candidate as a Man's Man." *New York Times,* August 17, 2000, A18.
Mansbridge, Jane E. "Myth and Reality: The ERA and the Gender Gap in the 1980 Elections." *Public Opinion Quarterly* 49 (1985): 164–78.
Mueller, Carol M. "The Empowerment of Women: Polling and the Women's Voting Bloc." In *The Politics of the Gender Gap: The Social Construction of Political Influence,* ed. Carol M. Mueller, Newbury Park, CA: Sage, 1988.
Norrander, Barbara. "The Independence Gap and the Gender Gap." *Public Opinion Quarterly* 61 (1997): 464–76.
———. "Is the Gender Gap Narrowing?" In *Reelection 1996: How Americans Voted,* ed. Herbert F. Weisberg and Janet M. Box-Steffensmeier. Chappaqua, NY: Seven Bridges Press, 1999.
Paget, Karen M. "The Gender Gap Mystique." *American Prospect* 15 (Fall 1993): 93–101.
Purdum, Todd S. "The 2000 Campaign: Gender Politics; Among Men, It's Bush the Maserati by a Mile." *New York Times,* October 8, 2000, sec. 1, p. 1.
Radcliffe, Donna. "A Ford for Reagan?" *Washington Post,* July 13, 1982, C2.
Saad, Lydia. "Big Gender Gap Distinguishes Election 2000: Men Vote Overwhelmingly for Bush." *Gallup Poll Monthly,* 2000
Scholzman, Kay Lehman, Henry Brady, and Sidney Verba. "Gender and Citizen Participation: Is There a Different Voice?" *American Journal of Political Science* 39 (1995): 267–293.
Seelye, Katharine Q. "Dole Says He Has a Plan to Win Votes of Women." *New York Times,* May 8, 1996, A1.
———. "Politics: the Spouse: On the Trail, Dole's Wife Seeks Votes of Women." *New York Times,* October 5, 1996, A10.
———. "The 2000 Campaign: The Rallying Cry." *New York Times,* August 22, 2000, A18.
———. "The 2000 Campaign: Women Voters, Marital Status Is Shaping Women's Leanings, Surveys Find." *New York Times,* September 20, 2000, A1.
Seltzer, Richard, Judy Newman, and Melissa V. Leighton. *Sex As a Political Variable.* Boulder, CO: Lynne Rienner Publishers, 1997.
Shapiro, Robert, and Harpreet Majahan. "Gender Differences in Policy Preferences: A Summary of Trends from the 1960s to the 1980s." *Public Opinion Quarterly* 50 (1986): 42–61.
Tobar, Hector. "For White Males, Bush Is Their Guy." *Los Angeles Times,* September 11, 2000, A12.
Toner, Robin. "Presidential Race Could Turn on Bush's Appeal to Women." *New York Times,* March 26, 2000, <http://nytimes.com/library.politics/camp/032600wh-gop-bush-women.html>.
Welch, Susan, and Lee Sigelman. "A Black Gender Gap?" *Social Science Quarterly* 79 (1989): 120–133.
White, Ben. "Presidential Race Evens Out; Gore Polls Well on Experience; Bush Is Closing Gender Gap." *Washington Post,* March 18, 2000, A7.
Wirls, Daniel. "Reinterpreting the Gender Gap." *Public Opinion Quarterly* 50, no. 3 (1986): 316–330.
Zaller, John R. *The Nature and Origins of Mass Opinion.* New York: Cambridge University Press, 1992.

5

Back to the Future

Generation X and the 2000 Election

Molly W. Andolina

Every four years, as the presidential election nears, news media outlets return to a traditional storyline—the apathetic, uninterested cohort of Americans commonly called "Generation X." Typically, such coverage begins with an interview with a 20-something, who claims to be "too lazy" to vote, and then recounts the decline in turnout among young people nationwide, lamenting their inattention and comparing them, always unfavorably, to the image of 1960s youth as active, engaged, and heavily politicized.

At first, the 2000 election did not disappoint. From wire services to network news to cable outlets, news stories of the youth vote stuck to this traditional script.[1] Later, however, as Ralph Nader's college tour escalated, reporters suggested strong and growing support on university campuses for the Green Party candidate—and warned of his potential strength on election day.[2]

What was the story of Generation X in the first election of the new millennium? Was there a Gen X vote? Did it favor George W. Bush's compassionate conservatism or did it embrace the mountain-climbing Al Gore? Were reports of Nader's popularity among this age group accurate? Indeed, did Generation X even bother to go to the polls?

This chapter will discuss the role of Xers in the 2000 election—describing attempts to reinvigorate their participation, recounting efforts to lure them into different camps, and comparing the youth cohort to earlier generations in terms of participation and vote choice. First, however, we turn to the question of what it means to be a generation.

Political Science and Political Generations

Studies of political generations focus on the persistence of political orientations from childhood to old age.[3] Different scholars use competing models of persistence to represent their interpretation of the overall stability in an individual's attitudes and behavior over time. The first of these models, *lifelong persistence,* refers to the notion that political orientations of early childhood continue throughout the course of life, strengthening as one ages.[4] Research has provided support for this model, with evidence that while individuals' specific attitudes may change, their general attachments to the political system (such as partisan identification) or broad values (such as questions of racial equality) remain relatively stable over time.[5]

The polar opposite of lifelong persistence is *lifelong openness,* in which change, rather than stability, is the rule. Unlike the first model, this model suggests little or no connection between adult attitudes and behavior and childhood political orientations. Although researchers have demonstrated that individuals do indeed change over the course of their lives,[6] the change is not uniform at all ages, a finding that leads to a third conceptualization of persistence, the *life cycle model.* Adherents of the life cycle model, a hybrid of the first two, argue that "while persistence is the rule, certain orientations are very amenable to alteration at given life stages."[7] A classic example of the application of the life cycle model to mass politics is the work of Campbell et al. on party identification. In national surveys, older respondents expressed stronger partisan attachments than their younger counterparts, leading the researchers to conclude that strength of partisanship was influenced by the life cycle—that is, it increased over time.[8]

In some interpretations, the relative impact of change and stability can be understood as an outgrowth of particularly significant steps in life such as owning a home, becoming a parent, or retiring, all of which are loosely but not directly connected to chronological age. As these experiences teach individuals the effect that political issues have on their lives, they find it easier to understand the process, to follow the discussion, and to become involved.[9]

Finally, in the *generational* model of persistence, scholars argue that although all members of society can experience the same events (e.g., the Depression, World War II, Watergate), each age group may react differently. When the events are especially significant to a particular cohort, they can create cleavages between the generations. In this model, first articulated by the German sociologist Karl Mannheim, the confluence of political and social circumstances that occurs as individuals enter in political adulthood creates an atmosphere or *zeitgeist* that shapes the political orientations they will carry throughout the course of their lives.[10]

According to this theory, as societies change, the circumstances that inevitably shape the worldview of new members in the society change, creating distinct differences between generations. The Vietnam War, for example, affected the age group eligible to be drafted differently than older (or younger) Americans because the possibility of actually being called to fight had greater personal implications.[11] Another example of generational effects is the partisanship of the Depression generation. The political and social circumstances of the 1930s spawned a generation of Americans that, compared to their parents and their children, has been particularly loyal to the Democratic Party throughout the course of their lives.[12]

Importantly, generational effects and life cycle effects are not mutually exclusive. That is, any individual may have political attitudes and behavior that change as she travels through life (bringing her closer to her parents' generation) and at the same time have political orientations that, like those of others in her age cohort, both distinguish her from her elders and remain relatively stable as she ages. Moreover, all members of society may be subject to period effects—uniform change across all age cohorts—such as the decline in institutional trust that affected Americans of all age groups in the late 1960s and early 1970s. Indeed, most studies of political generations find evidence of both stability and change.[13]

Drawing Generational Lines

One of the most difficult tasks in generational research is determining where one generation ends and the next begins. As David Knoke writes, "[s]eldom do abrupt discontinuities in social behavior occur between aggregates of people characterized by birth date, so the cutting-points between generations must be somewhat arbitrary."[14] Traditionally, political scientists have defined generational boundaries by first identifying the critical events that are the source of intense societal upheaval and then designating the age cohort that is hypothesized to be most affected by the event. Studies of the baby boomer generation usually revolve around several events that were occurring simultaneously in society—e.g., Kennedy's assassination, the civil rights marches, the Vietnam War, and Watergate.[15] Similarly, studies of the Depression generation focus on the impact of this national catastrophe on the youth of the period.[16] This technique does not apply to Generation X, a cohort lacking in deep-seated or lasting events.[17]

Yet the very fact that they lack a defining event may distinguish Xers as much as the Vietnam War serves to identify baby boomers. The absence of a unifying force may leave an imprint on this generation, even if only in placing them in opposition to the generations that preceded them. As their moniker suggests, Xers are often defined as much by what they are not—boomers—as what they are. Moreover, Xers are distinct in that they have come of age during a period in which we have witnessed the deterioration of social institutions, a revolution in technological innovations, and a weakening of traditional political practices, creating the societal transformations that Mannheim wrote about almost seventy-five years ago. Many observers of this cohort argue that the social, political, and economic conditions of their youth and early adulthood are unique enough to have created a true generation, although there is not consensus in the discipline about this conclusion.[18]

Even among scholars who agree that changing conditions have created a distinct postboomer age group, there is considerable variation about what age groups actually make up the generation. Strauss and Howe have the broadest definition, designating Xers as including everyone born between 1961 and 1981. Their rationale is based in part on social phenomena (such as the introduction of the birth control pill on one end) and in part on the argument that "[h]istory shows that, on average, modern generations stretch across a little over 20 birth years."[19] Academic studies of Generation X conducted in the early 1990s concentrated in large part on the older members of the generation, born before 1972.[20] Attention to this older cohort was partly theoretical (as older Xers were seen as the "core" of the generation) and partly practical (since younger Xers had not yet reached voting age). Most mainstream accounts of Generation X since the mid-1980s have designated Xers as all adults under 30 (which suggests that membership in a generation can be fluid, in contradiction to traditional conceptions of social science).

By the 2000 election, all of the Strauss and Howe Xers—approximately 86 million adults ages 18 to 39—were old enough to vote. The analysis in this chapter takes advantage of this expanded pool but narrows the focus to the youngest Xers (those between the ages of 18 and 24). At times, the analysis will expand to ages 18 to 29, depending on the available data, the sample size, and the comparison groups. When possible, these age cohorts will be compared to their elder counterparts inside and outside the Gen X boundaries.

There are several reasons for this emphasis on the youngest adults. First, as Delli Carpini has illustrated, generations are not monoliths. In his study of the boomer genereration, he found differences among boomers who directly experienced the events of the sixties, those who had been socialized during this era, and older boomers who served almost as a transition between the values and practices of their parents' generation and their own.[21] Prior studies of Generation X have focused on the oldest subgroup; this election allows us to concentrate on the youngest element; future studies may test the intragenerational differences. In addition, focusing on 18- to 24-year-olds allows us a unique opportunity to highlight a distinct stage in the socialization process—the "impressionable years." This period— ranging from late adolescence to early adulthood—is significant because it is during this time that generational distinctiveness can take hold.[22]

Finally, a focus on this age cohort reflects the political reality of the 2000 election, in which organizations and groups concerned about the "youth vote" made concerted efforts to draw young voters into the political process. A systematic study of the age group should allow us to test any possible effects of these endeavors. Let us turn now to the politics of today's young adults.

Coming of Age in Y2K

Although popular accounts characterized youth outreach programs as attempts to inform the ignorant, register the uninterested, and get the apathetic to the polls, both nonprofit organizations and the candidates themselves made concerted efforts to reach this age cohort.

A New News

Bolstered by the belief that young people are not avoiding the news, but that the news is avoiding them, a handful of organizations developed innovative programs to inform young adults about the campaign. They argued that if the media discussed issues that are important to the X generation, if they framed stories in ways that connected with an Xer sensibility, and if they used technologies that appealed to an Internet savvy age cohort, they would find a following among young adults.

An example of one attempt to do so was "Y Vote 2000: Politics of a New Generation," launched by the Medill News Service, a program affiliated with Northwestern University and funded by the Pew Charitable Trusts. In an attempt to reestablish the links between young adults and American politics, Y Vote 2000 focused news coverage on issues of concern to youth and presented this coverage in a young, hip fashion. Its Web-based stories featured interviews with Americans in their late teens and early twenties, on and off the college campus, with a constant stream of links to other sites for political and policy information.[23]

Another voice in the fray was GenerationVote.com, a political news outlet created by Xers for Xers. Drawing on a nationwide network of contributors (all volunteers), the site targeted its political coverage toward this youngest generation. As with Y Vote 2000, when GenerationVote.com covered the presidential candidates, it highlighted statements relating to youth or youth issues. In launching the site, founder Alexis Rice repeated a common Xer lament that "many candidates do not speak to our generation or fail to relate to us. Traditional media outlets rarely report on issues specifically affecting us."[24] So she and her colleagues did so themselves.

Meanwhile, as these news organizations concentrated their efforts on informing youth, many other groups spent time and energy putting Xers on the registration lists and then pushing them toward the polls.

Raising X-pectations

Targeting and registering young adults has become a cottage industry in political circles, with players as diverse as well-funded foundations, media giants, and small community organizations all taking part. In the most recent election, one of the largest and most comprehensive programs fell under the helm of Youth Vote 2000, a conglomeration of over seventy-five nationwide organizations, including MTV's popular Choose or Lose campaign. Youth Vote 2000 workers, including almost two dozen full-time staff members, created a network of state and local groups aimed at registering young people and, on Election Day, getting them to the polls.[25]

After registering over 1 million young first-time voters, many of them online, Youth Vote 2000 then faced the difficult task of encouraging the newly enfranchised to actually cast a ballot. Employing traditional grass-roots efforts of door-to-door solicitations, calls from telephone banks, and actual rides to the polls, the organization also tapped into some newer methods, such as celebrity phone calls. Popular musicians such as Jewel, the Beastie Boys, and Third Eye Blind taped phone messages that were sent out to over 1 million young, registered voters, reminding them to vote.[26]

Rock the Vote, a ten-year veteran of youth vote drives, continued its tradition of nationwide bus tours, stopping for performances in twenty-five cities from coast to coast. The often daylong concerts featured speakers and workers prepared to register new voters, along with nationally and locally known musicians.[27]

Rock the Vote also sponsored commercials aimed at young people, encouraged online voter registration on the ChooseorLose.com Web site, and launched a Rap the Vote campaign, aimed at urban youth. In this effort, Sean "Puffy" Combs, Mary J. Blige, LL Cool J, and Rosie Perez taped public-service announcements that were aired in major metropolitan media markets.[28] Finally, Rock the Vote enlisted a handful of corporate media partners, including ABC, Alta Vista, Time, and Sony, to send out 10 million e-mail messages aimed at 18- to 24-year-olds. The messages focused on liberal issues, such as the opposition to the death penalty, support for same-sex marriages, and passage of hate crime legislation, in an attempt to spur this supposedly liberal cohort to the polls.[29]

Courting Generation X—The Candidates Come Calling

The major party candidates did not leave all the action to nonprofits and community groups. Indeed, despite Xers' reputations for ignoring news in general and politics in particular, both Gore and Bush courted their vote. Each sent out age-appropriate emissaries to rally a group that was often portrayed as largely unaware of both the intricacies and the principals of the two campaigns.

The Gore team's point person for youth issues was the vice president's daughter, Karenna Gore Schiff, a lawyer, a new mother, and a familiar face to most Xers. (*Saturday Night Live*'s playful homage to her good looks had become a stalwart of the 1992 season.) Schiff spoke to crowds of young people as one of them, declaring "we are the biggest potential voting bloc." At rallies on campuses throughout the key battleground states in the Midwest, Schiff attempted to personalize the Democratic candidate, describing him as a regular "dad." On the more progressive campuses of the University of Michigan at Ann Arbor and the University of Wisconsin at Madison, she touted her father's stand on traditional liberal issues—abortion rights, environmental protection, and education.[30] Lastly, Schiff, often accompanied by her father, hosted roundtable discussions with young people around the nation to discuss issues of concern to them.[31]

Bush turned to his nephew and namesake, George P. Bush, named by *People* magazine as one of the nation's most eligible bachelors[32] and dubbed a "bilingual Gen X heartthrob" by the New York *Daily News*.[33] The younger Bush spoke to crowds of young people in both English and Spanish, a particularly appropriate technique to use with the most ethnically diverse generation. Like his Democratic counterpart, he attempted to paint a picture of the Republican candidate as a real person, genuinely interested in the issues of importance to youth.

Neither candidate turned all the outreach efforts over to his relatives. Both candidates joined the late-night circuit, appearing on the David Letterman show with their "Top Ten Lists" in tow. A smart move, perhaps, as one poll found that almost half (49 percent) of 18- to 24-year-olds get political news from late-night talk shows at least occasionally.[34] Gore, following Clinton's 1992 example, held a town hall meeting broadcast exclusively on MTV, a mainstay of the Generation X television repertoire.[35] Finally, both candidates taped skits for *Saturday Night Live* that were aired on the Sunday before Election Day.[36]

Such efforts to connect with Xers were not limited to appearances on popular television shows; Bush and Gore also addressed issues traditionally associated with this age group. The Bush campaign produced a pamphlet entitled "Agenda for America's Rising Generation," in which the Texas governor laid out his positions on education, community service, and energy conservation. Bush's proposal to allow for a partial privatization of social security was said to resonate with a generation that has expressed doubts about the viability of the retirement program. For his part, Gore spoke to young people about providing tax cuts and grants for higher education and repeatedly hyped his record as an avid outdoorsman and a dedicated environmentalist.[37] The Gore Web site included a link to Gorenet, a site dedicated to young voters and the issues of concern to them.[38]

Finally, Ralph Nader, more popular among college students than he was nationwide, rewarded this particular cohort with special attention. He held rallies on college campuses, responding to their dissatisfaction with the political system, their concern for environmentalism, and their receptivity to his anticorporate message. Nader also exploited the popular culture leanings of Xers, appearing on Comedy Central's *The Daily Show* and including celebrities such as Pearl Jam's Eddie Vedder in his rallies.[39]

The Early Results

The first postelection reports now available indicate that attempts to focus Xers on the news, inform them about the politics and policies of the candidates, encourage them to vote, and even build an Xer agenda may have fallen short of their goals. By most measures, Generation X failed to reverse a youthful trend toward electoral apathy, ignorance, and inaction.

Campaign? Election? Whatever!

Despite the earnest efforts of Y Vote 2000 and others, initial studies of the 2000 campaign suggest little erosion in Xers' traditional inattention to the

Figure 5.1 **Inattentiveness Among Young Adults in 2000 Campaign**

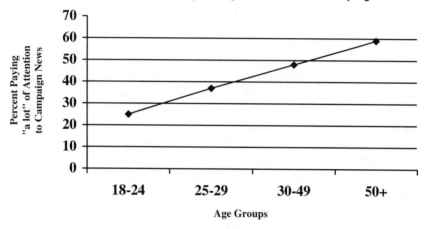

Source: Data provided to the author by The Pew Research Center for the People & the Press, Washington, D.C.

news. Over the past decade, Pew Research Center polls have documented a decline in news attentiveness among all Americans under age 30. Young adults are less likely to read a newspaper (29 percent vs. 46 percent overall) and less likely to watch television news (44 percent vs. 55 percent overall). They are, however, more likely to go online (74 percent vs. 54 percent overall) and to turn to the Internet at least once a week for news (46 percent vs. 33 percent overall).[40]

The first presidential election of the new millennium failed to change this trend. In a Pew poll conducted in the fall of 2000, about half of all older Americans (ages 30 and up) said that they had given "quite a lot" of thought to the presidential election. As Figure 5.1 shows, adults under age 30 were significantly less focused. Less than one-third of all 18- to 29-year-olds and only one-quarter of 18- to 24-year-olds were this involved.[41]

Surveys conducted by the Shorenstein Center at Harvard's Kennedy School of Government throughout the 2000 election also identified the under-30 cohort as especially inattentive to news of the campaign. Xers were not just watching news less than their elders; they were consistently less likely to talk about the campaign with others. They paid only passing attention to the primaries and largely ignored the televised debates.[42]

Yet such inattention and disinterest is nothing new for young adults. As Figure 5.2 illustrates, the 18 to 24 age cohort has always lagged behind

Figure 5.2   **Young Show Traditional Disinterest in Election**

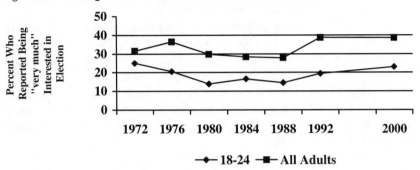

Source: Analysis based on data from the American National Election Studies, conducted by the University of Michigan, Center for Political Studies, Ann Arbor, Michigan.

the national average in attention to presidential campaigns. Even during the 1972 election, historic for its focus on youth issues, only 23 percent of those ages 18 to 24 told researchers that they were "very much interested" in the campaign, compared to about one-third of all adults.[43] Although the magnitude of this gap has varied over time, to condemn the youngest Xers for their negligence ignores the historical record.

Information Anyone?

This lack of attention to political news may explain why Xers in general were relatively uninformed about the details of the political race. A MTV poll conducted in October 2000 found one-fourth of 18- to 24-year-olds unable to name both presidential candidates without prompting and fully 70 percent unable to name their running mates.[44] In a Shorenstein Center survey conducted the week after the New Hampshire primary, adults ages 18 to 29 were three times more likely to know who won the Super Bowl than who had claimed victory in the first presidential primary.[45]

Young adults were even largely ignorant of proposals that were aimed at their age group. In a Pew Research Center poll of registered voters conducted in the beginning of September, almost half (48 percent) of 18- to 24-year-olds and almost as many (40 percent) of those ages 25 to 29 had not heard anything about George W. Bush's proposal to "allow younger workers to invest a portion of their payroll taxes in private retirement accounts" instead of social security. In comparison, at least two-thirds of those over age 30 were aware of this proposal.

Such reports of Xer ignorance, while disturbing, are not surprising. In a comprehensive study of political knowledge over four decades, Delli Carpini and Keeter demonstrate that postboomer generations know less about politics than do their elder counterparts. And, while boomers also entered the electorate less informed than their predecessors, they quickly closed the gap, a feat not yet accomplished by Generation X.[46] Unfortunately, the first election of the millennium does not appear to have led to any progress on this front.

Xer Issues

Reaching Xers may have been a tough prospect, but when the campaigns got their message through, it often met receptive ears. For example, while Xers were relatively uninformed about Bush's Social Security proposal, support was quite strong among young voters who had heard about it. In Pew's September poll, fully 83 percent of registered voters under 30 favored it, compared to about half of senior citizens.

This proprivatization stance is not the only issue area in which Xers stand out. They are unique both in the emphasis they place on particular agendas and the support they lend to some proposals. For example, when Pew asked voters prior to the election to pick the most important thing for the next president to do, no single issue captured the heart of the public: 24 percent of respondents placed Social Security and Medicare at the top of the list; 21 percent named education and almost as many (19 percent) preferred heath care. However, among 18- to 24-year-old voters, education swamps everything else: 42 percent placed it first, compared to 12 percent who chose Social Security and Medicare and an equal number picking health care.

And, when it comes to specific policies, Xers are also more unified than their elders. About half (53 percent) of all voters in the Pew preelection poll supported federal funding for school vouchers, compared to two-thirds of those under 30. Similarly, while older voters divided evenly (46 percent to 49 percent) over whether to allow government funding for religious groups to provide social services, two-thirds of voters under 30 endorsed this proposal.

Xers also stand out in their attitudes toward the budget surplus. Among registered voters in the Pew poll, 42 percent of 18- to 29-year-olds wanted to spend the surplus on domestic programs such as health, education, and the environment. Just 30 percent of 30- to 49-year-olds and even fewer (15 percent) of older voters agreed. Overall, most voters opted to use the surplus to shore up Social Security and Medicare, a goal that ranks a distant second with Generation X.

Finally, Xers indicated a very status-quo stance toward defense spending: 57 percent wanted to keep it about the same, about 19 percent wanted to increase it, and a similar number (22 percent) chose to cut it back. Voters ages 50 and older were divided between keeping defense spending at the current level (42 percent) and increasing it (43 percent). Only 10 percent supported reduction.

For many of these issues, the differences across age groups is not surprising. For example, opting to invest Social Security funds in the stock market does not pose the same risk for Xers, who have a longer time period to allow such investments to grow, as it does for those nearing retirement, who may fear for the solvency of a program with diminished funds. Similarly, concern for educational issues might be expected from an age group that has just recently graduated from high school. At this point, it is too early to tell if these issue preferences represent true generational effects that will continue to differentiate Xers over the course of their lives or merely life cycle effects that will diminish as they age. For now, it is a distinguishing characteristic of the age group.

On other areas in the Pew poll, Xers were less distinct. Like all voters, they overwhelmingly (91 percent) supported making prescription benefits a part of the Medicare program. They preferred targeted tax cuts for lower- and middle-income families over across-the-board tax cuts by a 58 percent to 40 percent margin, similar to voters in all age groups. And solid majorities (60 percent) supported eliminating the inheritance tax, as did over 70 percent of voters ages 30 and up.

These indications of an Xer agenda, however limited, would matter only if Xers actually turned out to vote and if one candidate was able to build on this agenda to create a solid bloc of youth voters. Each of these prerequisites will be addressed within the historical context.

A Tradition of Low Turnout

In 1972 Americans ratified the Twenty-sixth Amendment to the Constitution, extending the legal voting age from 21 to 18 years of age. Young adults' successful drive to gain the right to vote was seen as a harbinger of their active participation in the presidential election of that same year. However, in the first year of eligibility, less than half of the newly enfranchised even made it to the polls. Only 48 percent of 18- to 20-year-olds voted, compared to an only slightly higher 51 percent of 21- to 24-year-

Figure 5.3   **Reported Voting Rates**

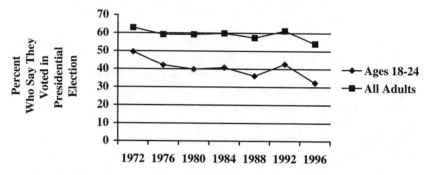

Source: Current Population Reports, Series P20–504, available on the census Web site <www.census.gov>.

Note: Because these data are *self-reported* measures of voting, they are larger than the percentage who actually voted. For example, while the 1996 numbers indicate that 54.2 percent of all Americans voted for president, better estimates suggest that the real number was closer to 48.9 percent.

olds and a full 12 percentage points less than the national average of 63 percent.[47]

So, contrary to popular myth, the youth of 1970s America began their entrée into politics with a less than stellar reputation for electoral participation, a phenomenon that has grown as each successive cohort achieved adulthood. That is, while turnout for all Americans, regardless of age or generation, has generally declined over the decades, the falloff has been greatest among youth. Indeed, as Figure 5.3 indicates, the poor poll showing by young people in the 1970s pales in comparison to the absence of Xers on voting day in the mid-1990s. By 1996, when 54 percent of all Americans reported casting a ballot for president, just 32 percent of 18- to 24-year-olds did so—fully 22 percentage points below the national average.[48] Xers may deserve a reputation for apathy after all.

Preliminary reports of voter turnout among 18- to 24-year-olds in the 2000 election are mixed. Using data from the Associated Press, Curtis Gans, a veteran of turnout studies and vice president and director of the Committee for the Study of the American Electorate, estimates that official turnout levels rose to 51 percent from the record low level of 49 percent in 1996.[49] Gans's early projections of turnout among the crucial 18- to 24-year-old age group suggest little or no increase, however. Slightly more college students may have made it to the polls, but this advantage appears to be counterbalanced by a slight decline in voting among non-college students.[50]

Figure 5.4 **Youth Cohort Targeted for Voter Mobilization**

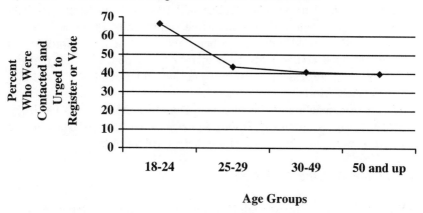

Source: Analysis based on data from 2000 American National Election Studies, conducted by the University of Michigan, Center for Political Studies, Ann Arbor, Michigan.

Other studies are more optimistic. Although official turnout data for 18- to 24-year-olds is not yet available, the Voter News Service estimates that almost 39 percent of 18- to 29-year olds showed up at the polls, a rise over their 1996 participation rates, an indicator of a possible uptick for the 18- to 24-age group as well.[51] Moreover, in the American National Election Studies (ANES), which provide a self-reported (and thus inflated) measure of turnout, 52 percent of 18- to 24-year-olds say they voted—almost as many as the 53 percent who reported doing so during the high watermark of 1992. If Xers have managed to narrow the turnout gap, they may lose their generational distinctiveness—but gain some long denied respect.

Reaping What Was Sown

If turnout did increase, was it a result of the well-organized and sincere attempts to contact young voters described earlier? Perhaps. Young Xers are more likely than any other age group to report being the object of get-out-the-vote and registration drives. According to the ANES, two-thirds of 18- to 24-year-olds said that someone contacted them during the campaign about registering to vote or voting, as shown in Figure 5.4. No other age group reports such a high contact rate. Older Xers were not the subject of such levels of attention in their youth. In 1984, just under half of 18- to 24-year-olds were contacted; in 1988, only 39 percent were. The 2000 rates are especially impressive, because young adults are notoriously difficult to contact. They tend to be more mobile and less likely to have a routine-oriented lifestyle than older people. More significantly, in the ANES survey, 18- to 24-year-olds who report being the target of such efforts bested their uncontacted counterparts by a margin of 59 percent to 38 percent. (Although they are less likely to be contacted, older adults are also influenced by such efforts.)

Did these contacting efforts also lead Xers to unite behind a particular candidate? To answer this question, we once again turn to history to see if young people have ever formed a coherent voting bloc.

A Tradition of Being Traditional

When the Twenty-sixth Amendment was ratified, amid the fervor of Vietnam War protests and the rise of the counterculture, it was believed that the newest bloc of voters would greatly influence the outcome of the general election. The number of young people protesting American involvement in Southeast Asia convinced many (especially Democrats) that an antiwar candidate could carry the votes of the newly enfranchised, thus propelling himself into the White House. However, despite repeated attempts by both parties to court the youth vote, young people have never joined together to form a single political force. Indeed, with the exception of George McGovern's slight victory among the youngest cohort in 1972, young people in general have served as a microcosm of the larger nation.[52]

When the first Xers entered the voting mix, rumors of a new conservative movement took hold, bolstered by Ronald Reagan's reelection to the White House in 1984. Indeed, young people did throw their support behind Reagan, voting for him by a margin of 3 to 2. However, this overwhelming endorsement of Reagan was simply a reflection of Reagan's trouncing of Walter Mondale among all age groups, young and old.[53]

When Clinton first ran for president in 1992, with explicit appeals to Xers on MTV and the Arsenio Hall television show, pundits argued that the youngest generation would fall in line behind the first baby boomer candidate. And again, they were wrong—at least partially. Clinton captured 43 percent of the popular vote nationwide, and 43 percent of those ages 18 to 29.[54] Among the youngest age cohort, however, Clinton did do well, pulling in 52 percent of those under age 25.[55]

With history as our guide, in a tight race we would expect under-30 voters to split their votes evenly. This is just what happened. According to Voter News Service exit polls, 48 percent of 18- to 29-year-olds voted for Gore, 46 percent pulled the handle for Bush, and 5 percent cast a ballot for Nader. Older age groups were similarly divided: 49 percent of 30- to 44-year-olds voted for Bush; 48 percent for Gore. The same is true for 45- to 59-year-olds. Among those 60 and older, 51 percent cast Gore ballots, 47 percent opted for Bush.[56]

The 2000 ANES indicates similar results nationally, with 50 percent of voters opting for Gore, 47 percent saying they voted for Bush, and the remaining 3 percent choosing Nader. Among younger adults in this survey, however, there was a decided pro-Gore sentiment. He topped Bush by a 56 to 37 percent margin among 18- to 29-year-olds and received a whopping 59 percent from those ages 18 to 24. We will have to wait another election cycle to see if these young voters remain loyal to the Democratic nominee in 2004. In the meantime, President Bush may take heart in knowing that the advantage Clinton received among 18- to 24-year-olds in 1992 did not translate into an edge for Gore in 2000. These young adults (now ages 26 to 32) split their votes evenly between the two major party candidates, with 48 percent voting for Gore and 47 percent voting for Bush.[57]

While Nader was more popular among younger voters than he was nationwide, this is hardly surprising since youth cohorts are traditionally less allegiant to the candidates of the major political parties. In 1980, independent candidate John Anderson garnered 11 percent of the under-30 vote, compared to 7 percent overall. Similarly, Ross Perot drew 22 percent of this cohort in 1992 (compared to 19 percent among all voters) and 10 percent in 1996 (compared to 8.5 percent overall).[58]

Conclusion

Does the 2000 election help us to determine if Xers have a true generational identity? Maybe. On some fronts, it is too early to tell if their distinctiveness (in issue positions and candidate preferences) are age effects or the results of generational influences. We need to wait a few more election cycles to chart these developments. On other fronts (such as political knowledge), there is some confirmation that certain characteristics are not simply a reflection of their youth, but a feature of their generational identity. In other areas (such as low levels of turnout and disinterest in politics in general), Xers merely illustrate changes in the larger society.

Yet, even though generational scholars would label these "period" effects (influencing all members of society), they pose unique ramifications for Xers in particular and for our political system in general. In relative terms, Xers may be no less interested in politics than were the youth of the early 1970s. In absolute terms, however, they are entering the political realm at historically low levels. Put differently, although Americans of all ages are shunning politics, the effect is greatest among young adults, who, in starting at a lower point, may never reach the participatory levels of older generations—even as they increase their involvement over the life course.

However, elsewhere there are signs of hope. For one, although Xers may not have made strides in their poor record of turnout, early indications suggest that they may have stemmed the tide. The 18- to 24-year-old age cohort did not rush to the polls in droves, but they at least matched the 1996 standard.

Second, as postelection polls indicated, Xers may be shunning traditional news outlets, but more and more of them are logging onto the Internet. And, among all age groups, they are the most likely to actually get political news online.[59] By the year 2004, news organizations may be able to exploit this habit to reach and inform a greater proportion of Generation X.

Third, while Xer electoral participation may be in a slump, studies have repeatedly found Xers to be active in other areas of civic life—volunteering in soup kitchens, tutoring elementary school students, and taking part in environmental cleanup days. Such "record high levels of volunteerism"[60] are not surprising, given that 24 percent of 18- to 24-year-olds say that they make "more of a difference by getting involved" in their communities than by voting.[61]

Thus, candidates and organizations hoping to build on the Xer identity need to first understand that Generation X is more nuanced—and more promising—than traditional characterizations of it allow. Only then can they confront the challenge of convincing it that politics and elections, like volunteerism, are worthwhile ventures.

Notes

1. Associated Press, "Low Turnout Expected among Young Voters," November 6, 2000; Dori Meinert, "Young Adults Tune Out Campaign," Copley News Service, October 20, 2000.

2. Kate N. Grossman, "Nader Draws Sellout Crowd," *Chicago Sun Times*, October 11, 2000, p. 32.

3. David O. Sears, "Political Socialization," in *Handbook of Political Science*, vol. 2, ed. Fred I. Greenstein and Nelson W. Polsby (Reading, MA: Addison-Wesley Publishing 1975); Norval D. Glenn, "Values, Attitudes and Beliefs," in *Constancy and Change in Human Development*, ed. Orville G. Brim Jr. and Jerome Kagan (Cambridge: Harvard University Press, 1980); M. Kent Jennings and Richard B. Niemi, *The Political Character of Adolescence* (Princeton: Princeton University Press, 1974); Donald R. Kinder and David O. Sears, "Public Opinion and Political Action," in *Handbook of Social Psychology*, vol. 2, ed. Gardner Lindzey and Elliot Aronson (New York: Random

House, 1985); T. Allen Lambert, "Generations and Change: Toward a Theory of Generations as a Force in Historical Process," *Youth and Society* 4 (1972): 21–45; Howard Schuman and Jacqueline Scott, "Generations and Collective Memories," *American Sociological Review* 54 (1989): 359–381; and Abigail J. Stewart and Joseph M. Healy Jr. "Linking Individual Development and Social Changes," *American Psychologist* 44 (1989): 30–42.

4. Glenn, "Values, Attitudes and Beliefs," terms this the "aging-stability" thesis to capture the notion that as one ages, one is less likely to change.

5. Sears, "Political Socialization"; Kinder and Sears, "Public Opinion and Political Action."

6. M. Kent Jennings and Richard B. Niemi, *Generations and Politics* (Princeton: Princeton University Press, 1981); Glenn, "Values, Attitudes and Beliefs."

7. Jennings and Niemi, *Generations and Politics*, p. 20.

8. Angus Campbell, Philip E. Converse, Warren E. Miller, and Donald E. Stokes, *The American Voter* (Chicago: University of Chicago Press, 1960).

9. Sidney Verba and Norman H. Nie, *Participation in America* (Chicago: University of Chicago Press, 1972); Raymond E. Wolfinger and Steven J. Rosenstone, *Who Votes* (New Haven: Yale University Press, 1980); and John M. Strate, Charles J. Parrish, Charles D. Elder, and Coit Ford III, "Life Span Development and Voter Participation," *American Political Science Review* 83 (1989): 443–464.

10. Karl Mannheim, "The Problem of Generations," in *Essays on the Sociology of Knowledge*, ed. Paul Kecskemeti (1928; London: Routledge & Kegan Paul, 1952).

11. Michael X. Delli Carpini, "Generations and Sociopolitical Change," in *Political Learning in Adulthood*, ed. Roberta A. Sigel (Chicago: University of Chicago Press, 1989).

12. Campbell et al., *The American Voter;* Philip E. Converse, *The Dynamics of Party Support: Cohort-Analyzing Party Identification* (Beverly Hills: Sage, 1976).

13. Michael X. Delli Carpini, *Stability and Change in American Politics* (New York: New York University Press, 1986).

14. David Knoke, "Conceptual and Measurement Aspects in the Study of Political Generations," *Journal of Political and Military Sociology* 12 (1984): 192.

15. Delli Carpini, *Stability and Change.*

16. Glen H. Elder, *Children of the Depression* (Chicago: University of Chicago Press, 1974).

17. Saul Wisnia, "Moments to Remember? A Tough Question for Generation X," *Washington Post*, July 26, 1994, E5.

18. Bill Strauss and Neil Howe, *13th Gen: Abort, Ignore, Retry, Fail?* (New York: Random House, 1993); Blayne Cutler, "Up the Down Staircase," *American Demographics* 11 (1989); Stanley W. Moore, James Lare, and Kenneth A. Wagner, *The Child's Political World: A Longitudinal Perspective* (New York: Praeger, 1985); Richard A. Easterlin and Eileen M. Crimmins, "Private Materialism, Personal Self-Fulfillment, Family Life, and Public Interest: The Nature, Effects and Causes of Recent Changes in the Values of American Youth," *Public Opinion Quarterly* 55 (1991): 499–533. For dissenting opinions on the generational distinctiveness of Xers, see Everett Carl Ladd, "The Twentysomethings: Generational Myths Revisited," *Public Perspective* 5 (1993): 14–18.

19. Strauss and Howe, *13th Gen*, p. 13.

20. Stephen Earl Bennett and Eric Rademacher, "The Politics of 'Generation X': America's Post Boomer Birth Cohort Comes of Age," paper presented at the annual meeting of the American Association for Public Opinion Research, Danvers, Massachusetts, 1994; Stephen C. Craig and Angela C. Halfacre, "Political Issues and Political

Choice: Belief Systems, Generations, and the Potential for Realignment in American Politics," paper presented at the annual meeting of the Southern Political Science Association, Tampa, Florida, 1995; Michael A. Maggiotto, "Partisanship, Federalism and Generation X," paper presented at the annual meeting of the Southern Political Science Association, Tampa, Florida, 1995; Stephen K. Medvic, "The Political Attitudes of Generation X: A Preliminary Inquiry," paper presented at the annual meeting of the Midwest Political Science Association, Chicago, Illinois, 1994; Diana Owen and Jack Dennis, "The Political Orientations of the *Grunge Generation*: The Development of Partisan Orientations," paper presented at the annual meeting of the American Association for Public Opinion Research, Danvers, Massachusetts, 1994; and Diana Owen and Molly W. Sonner, "Think Globally, Act Locally: Why Political Science Underestimates the NEXT Generation," paper presented at the Midwest Political Science Association Annual Meeting, Chicago, Illinois, 1995.

21. Delli Carpini, *Stability and Change*.

22. Mannheim, "The Problem of Generations"; Lambert, "Generations and Change"; Schuman and Scott, "Generations and Collective Memories"; Stewart and Healy, "Linking Individual Development and Social Changes"; Glenn, "Values, Attitudes and Beliefs"; and Jennings and Niemi, *Generations and Politics*.

23. See Web site: yvote2000.com.

24. See the press release, June 29, 2000, on the Web site: <www.generationvote. com>.

25. Ethan Zindler, "Over One Million Served," yvote2000.com, November 2, 2000.

26. Ibid.

27. Karen MacPherson, "Big Drop in Under-30 Voters a Concern," *Pittsburgh Post-Gazette,* October 22, 2000, p. A14.

28. See Web site: <rockthevote.org/press.html>.

29. Stuart Elliott, "The Media Business: Advertising—Addenda: Campaign to Use E-Mail to Promote Youth Vote," *New York Times*, September 25, 2000, p. C19.

30. Associated Press, "Gore's Daughter Courts Youth Vote," September 20, 2000.

31. Russ Freyman and Brent McGoldnick, "They Pretend to Talk to Us and We Pretend to Vote: Candidates and Young Adults in Campaign 2000 and Beyond," Neglection 2000 Report, pp. 38–39, available online: <www.neglection2000.com>.

32. "Candidates Struggle to Attract Young Voters," *Dubuque Telegraph Herald,* October 25, 2000, p. B5.

33. Timothy Burger, "Bush Nephew a Big Hit," *New York Daily News,* August 4, 2000, p. 5.

34. Krista Larson, "Bush Hits the Late-Night TV Circuit," yvote2000.com, October 20, 2000.

35. Associated Press, "Gore's Daughter Courts Youth Vote."

36. Larson, "Bush Hits the Late-Night TV Circuit."

37. Associated Press, "Low Turnout Expected among Young Voters"; Freyman and McGoldnick, "They Pretend to Talk to Us," p. 37; Otto Kreisher, "Gore Turns Education Speech Into Pitch for Black, Youth Vote," Copley News Service, September 15, 2000.

38. Associated Press, "Candidates Struggle to Attract Young Voters."

39. Freyman and McGoldnick, "They Pretend to Talk to Us," p. 40; Grossman, "Nader Draws Sellout Crowd."

40. Pew Research Center for The People and The Press, "Internet Sapping Broadcast News Audience," June 11, 2000, available online: <www.people-press.org>.

41. Pew Research Center for The People and The Press survey of 2,799 adults 18 years of age or older, conducted during the period August 24–September 10, 2000. Data supplied directly to the author from Pew. Unless otherwise noted, all analyses of Pew surveys were conducted using this data set.

42. Vanishing Voter Project, "Young Adults Largely Ignoring Presidential Campaign," December 28, 1999; "Election Apathy Pervasive Among Young Adults," May 12, 2000; "Nearly Half of Young Adults Say They Will Not Watch the First Presidential Debate," September 30, 2000, available online: <www.vanishingvoter.org>.

43. American National Election Studies, conducted by the University of Michigan, Center for Political Studies, Ann Arbor, Michigan.

44. MacPherson, "Big Drop in Under-30 Voters a Concern." (There are no older cohorts included for comparison.)

45. Vanishing Voter Project, "Nearly Half of Young Adults." The project did not provide the percentage of older Americans who could answer each of these correctly, although its news release indicates that older Americans were better informed than their younger counterparts about political issues.

46. Michael X. Delli Carpini and Scott Keeter, *What Americans Know about Politics and Why It Matters* (New Haven: Yale University Press, 1989), p. 163.

47. U.S. Census Bureau.

48. The 1992 election stands out as an exception to the overall downward trend in participation, both for the nation at large and for young people specifically. More Americans cast ballots in 1992 than in 1998. And more 18- to 24-year-olds joined in the action than had bothered to do so four years earlier. By 1996, however, overall turnout reached an all-time low, with official estimates of actual turnout falling below 50 percent.

49. The Committee for the Study of the American Electorate analysis of turnout in the 2000 election was provided to the author by Tobi Walker of the Pew Charitable Trusts.

50. Telephone conversation with Curtis Gans, January 3, 2001. Gans's official analysis does not include breakdowns by age.

51. Wendy Sandoz, "GenY Voter Turnout Increased, Experts Say," yvote2000.com, November 8, 2000.

52. Rhodes Cook, "Whatever Happened to the Youth Vote?" *Congressional Quarterly Weekly*, July 15, 1987, pp. 1782–1795.

53. Rhodes Cook and Tom Watson, "New Generation Poised to Tip Voting Scales," *Congressional Quarterly Weekly*, November 23, 1985, pp. 2421–2427.

54. Marjorie Connelly, "Portrait of the Electorate," *New York Times*, November 10, 1996, A28. (Clinton did do somewhat better among 18- to 29-year-olds in 1996, besting Dole by 19 percentage points among this age cohort and only 8 percentage points overall. This may be due in part to young Americans feeling especially distant from the older Dole. One bumper sticker declared, "Dole *is* 96.")

55. American National Election Studies cumulative data set.

56. Voter News Service exit polls are available online at most major new media outlets, such as msnbc.com or cnn.com.

57. Importantly, in a multivariate logistic regression analysis designed to determine what factors best predict that an individual will cast a vote for Gore, age is not a significant predictor. Other traditional political, social, and demographic characteristics (party identification, religiosity, race) are both more significant and more powerful. This may be due in part to the preference of 18- to 24-year-olds to align themselves with the Democratic Party by a margin of almost two to one over the Republican Party.

58. Connelly, "Portrait of the Electorate."

59. Pew Research Center for The People and The Press, "Internet Election News Audience Seeks Convenience, Familiar Names," December 3, 2000, available online at <www. people-press.org>.

60. "New Millenium Project–Phase I," a report issued by the National Association of Secretaries of State, January 1999, available online at <www.stateofthevote.org>.

61. Princeton Survey Research Associates, "Youth, Voting and the 2000 Election," a survey commissioned by the Kaiser Family Foundation and MTV, September 2000, available online at <www.kff.org>.

6

Wither the Christian Right? The Elections and Beyond

Clyde Wilcox

Before the 2000 elections, political scientists who studied the Christian Right generally agreed on three things. First, one of the major strengths of the movement was its strong organization, which was evident at the state, local, and sometimes even precinct level. Second, the movement was populated with political "purists" who would rather back a candidate whose views fully matched their own than support a candidate who could win an election but whose stands on key issues were "soft." Finally, the movement had its greatest successes in mobilizing voters in general elections, when it could contrast the positions of liberal Democrats with conservative Republicans, but was generally less successful in GOP primary elections in which the choice was between conservatives of various ideological flavors.

The 2000 campaign turned each of these truths on its head. The organizational structure of the Christian Coalition crumbled before the election, and yet the movement managed to mobilize voters in the GOP primaries. Most activists in the movement got behind George W. Bush early in the primary elections, instead of backing ideological favorites such as Gary Bauer, Alan Keyes, or Patrick Buchanan. Finally, the greatest impact of the Christian Right in the 2000 elections was during the GOP primaries, when the movement delivered the nomination to George W. Bush. During

---

An earlier version of this paper was presented at a special conference on religion and the 2000 elections at Rice University in March 2000.

the general election, the movement was less active and influential than it had been in 1996.

Conventional Wisdom: The Movement's Strength Is in Its Organization

During the 1980s, the Christian Coalition and other contemporary Christian Right built grassroots organizations that were the envy of liberal groups. The Christian Coalition claimed organizations in all 50 states and in many countries. It was widely believed that this organizational structure gave the movement its strength, for it helped movement activists influence local party organizations and distribute voter guides in churches across the country.

But by the fall of 1999, the Christian Right appeared to be a movement in deep trouble. The Christian Coalition had suffered major defections: a wave of resignations by national, state, and local leaders had left it with at best a handful of functioning state chapters and few county organizations. In the national offices, morale was low and many of the most able leaders were gone. The organization's membership had clearly declined, and the coalition required a substantial infusion of funds from founder Pat Robertson to manage its growing debt.

The Christian Coalition had been the most pragmatic of Christian Right organizations. As it struggled, Focus on the Family grew steadily, and its founder, James Dobson, became more influential in the movement. Dobson's uncompromising rhetoric and frequent threats to bolt from the Republican Party made it seem even more likely that the movement in 2000 would back a strong social conservative during the GOP primaries, making it difficult for the GOP to find unity. The debate between purists and pragmatists, typical of most social movements, appeared to be won by those who abhorred compromise.

Moreover, elites in the movement were engaged in a growing debate over the efficacy of electoral politics. Influential movement activists such as Paul Weyrich, Cal Thomas, and Ed Dobson argued that electoral politics had failed and that it was time for conservative Christians to focus more on building alternative institutions, especially churches. This internal debate appeared to rob the movement of much of its grassroots vitality.

With its organizational structure in disarray, many observers expected the Christian Right to be much less important in the 2000 elections than in previous campaigns. Yet within a few months, the movement had virtually united behind the candidacy of a "compassionate conservative" governor whom they had previously criticized as being too moderate, and delivered to him the nomination. In doing so, they ignored the candidacy of one of their own, Gary Bauer from the Family Research Council, and became involved in a heated attack on Senator John McCain, who arguably was more of a social conservative than George W. Bush. The movement proved effective in mobilizing its activists in the GOP primaries, as we shall see below, despite the weakness of its organizational base.

Conventional Wisdom: The Movement Is Composed of Purists Who Will Not Compromise

The early and unified support of the Christian Right behind George W. Bush in the primaries came as a surprise to many. Gary Bauer's candidacy would normally have been expected to attract considerable support, for he was a longtime movement activist. Presidential candidates Alan Keyes and Patrick Buchanan, perennial Christian Right favorites, were in the early field, along with other social conservatives. Yet by the start of the primary season, most of the movement's leadership had either endorsed George W. Bush or were conspicuous in the absence of their support for Bauer and the rest.

The decision of Pat Robertson, former Christian Coalition director Ralph Reed, and other Christian Right leaders to back Bush was a pragmatic one, but borne of the intense dismay of the movement at the presidency of Bill Clinton. Most Christian Right leaders saw Clinton as a moral cripple, a man who could not tell right from wrong and who provided a terrible example for the nation. Moreover, many Christian Right leaders believe that God visits his judgment on nations based on the actions of their leaders. They believed that it was vitally important to elect a "true Christian" to the White House.

Many Christian Right leaders blamed Clinton for the failure of their policy agenda. GOP congressional leaders fed this belief, arguing that there was little reason to take up controversial social issues because there were not enough votes to override a presidential veto. Any Republican president, they argued, would sign the bills and thus free the Congress to create moral policy. "Work to elect a Republican to the White House," they promised, "and we will engage your agenda."

The urgency of replacing Clinton with a "true Christian" made many Christian Right activists amenable to the pragmatic arguments of the Bush campaign. Yet the movement would never have backed Bush with such unity had not Bush himself actively courted movement support. In 1999, Bush, traveled the country and met with many Christian Right leaders singly and in groups, and provided his personal testimony—the story of his acceptance of Christ and redemption, a conversion that changed him from an alcoholic party boy into a family man who read the Bible and prayed regularly. Indicating that Christ was important in his life, Bush promised to "hold Christ up" as president. During the campaign, Bush identified Jesus as his personal hero and the Bible as his favorite book, leading many activists to believe that he would use the presidency as a bully pulpit to testify publicly of his faith.

Among evangelicals, the testimony is a central element in establishing the validity of a person's faith, and Bush by all accounts presents a powerful, riveting testimony. Many generally purist Christian Right leaders were persuaded by Bush's testimony to support his candidacy, in part because they believe that any truly "saved" Christian would follow God's will and thereby implement their policy preferences.

Bush was apparently quite careful in his policy promises, but his pledge to appoint "strict constructionists" to the Supreme Court, along with his statement that Antonin Scalia was his model justice, convinced many that it would be possible to overturn *Roe v. Wade* with a Court influenced by Bush. His support for vouchers for private schools and for faith-based welfare initiatives was also attractive to some but not all Christian Right activists.

The seeming inevitability of Bush's nomination—his scores of endorsements and record fund-raising—made it seem to many movement leaders that Bush was a train ready to leave the station, whether or not they were on board. Although they may have preferred other candidates, they knew that it would be difficult to defeat a sitting vice president in boom times. Movement leaders cast their lot with Bush early in an unprecedented display of pragmatism because they believed that he could defeat Al Gore but that more ideologically "pure" candidates, such as Bauer, would lose to Clinton's heir.

Once they had thrown their support behind Bush, movement leaders rallied to promote his candidacy when he lost the New Hampshire primary to McCain. To a primary electorate focusing for a brief time on the two candidates, McCain's was the better biography. Bush was the son of a president who called himself a self-made man, and had served in the Texas National Guard. McCain was a decorated war hero who bucked party leaders to clean up campaign finance and fight big tobacco. Bush's defeat in the primary tarnished his aura of invulnerability and made McCain the center of media attention.

McCain's military record, his strongly conservative voting record, and his consistent prolife record made him a candidate who would initially seem appealing to evangelical voters, especially in the South. However, Christian Right leaders opposed McCain's candidacy for several reasons. First, Bush had lined up pledges of support early in the campaign, before McCain's viability had become evident. Most activists felt bound by those pledges. Second, many believed that only Bush could beat Gore, and thus were intensely motivated to support his cause. Third, many opposed McCain's campaign finance reform proposals, which they believed would harm the movement. Finally, McCain was less deferential to movement leaders, and less eager to talk about his personal faith.

Many Christian Right leaders, especially Pat Robertson of the Christian Coalition, launched strong attacks on McCain in South Carolina and in later primaries. Movement leaders in the Bush camp had to wage a spirited war to bring evangelical primary voters to Bush, especially in South Carolina. Campaign observers generally agreed that if McCain beat Bush in South Carolina, McCain would be the favorite to win the nomination. Robertson was a ubiquitous presence on television and radio, announcing that Christian conservatives might well sit out an election if McCain were the standard bearer. Robertson and others attacked McCain's conservative credentials, including his prolife record. McCain had temporarily appeared to waffle on abortion early in the campaign, and this was trumpeted in phone calls, mailings, and other communications.

The National Right-to-Life Committee, which had previously rated McCain at close to 100 percent, mailed a package to registered GOP voters in South Carolina with a picture of a baby on the front with the words "This little guy wants you to vote for George Bush."[1] The committee also ran radio and television spots. A number of groups mounted a phone campaign, including recorded messages from Pat Robertson attacking McCain's record on abortion and his commitment to profamily issues. The magnitude of the South Carolina effort was remarkable.

As the campaign moved into Michigan, religion remained at the core of the debate. Robertson's taped message in the state attacked McCain's New Hampshire campaign manager, former senator Warren Rudman, as a "vicious bigot." McCain responded with a phone call campaign to Catholic voters, alerting them to Bush's appearance at Bob Jones University, a fundamentalist school with explicit attacks on Catholicism on its Web page. After McCain won in Michigan, he flew to Virginia Beach and made a highly publicized speech that endorsed evangelical politics but denounced Robertson and former moral Majority Leader Reverend Jerry Falwell, and linked Bush to these two movement leaders. McCain professed his personal faith, claiming the mantle of a prolife, profamily Republican. Yet the Bush campaign easily spun the speech into an attack on religious conservatives, and from that time on the Christian Right was united in its opposition to McCain.

In the final analysis, Bush won the GOP nomination because of the Christian Right. The exit polls show a consistent pattern: Bush won overwhelmingly among Republicans who identified as members of the Religious Right and generally lost among voters who did not.

In South Carolina, for example, McCain beat Bush 52 to 46 among non–Christian Right voters, but Bush carried the Christian Right 68 to 24 in a state where more than a third of primary election voters identified with the movement. In Michigan, only 27 percent of voters called themselves members of the Religious Right, but they split 66 to 25 for Bush, with McCain winning the others 60 to 36. This pattern was repeated in most other states—Bush carried the Christian Right overwhelmingly, and McCain had a majority among other voters. The magnitude of McCain's margin with non-Christian Right voters declined over the course of the campaign and was generally higher in states that allowed independents and/or Democrats to vote in the GOP primary.

Before McCain blasted the Christian Right, Gary Bauer had endorsed his candidacy. Although Bauer was critical of McCain's remarks, he remained in the McCain camp and earned the enmity of many movement activists. After the campaign he was not welcomed back to the Family Research Council and was thus left trying to build a political action committee from the detritus of his campaign.

The Lessons of the GOP Presidential Primary

The mobilization of the Christian Right in the GOP primaries, despite a crumbling infrastructure, suggests a need to revise the conventional wisdom. The movement was able to contact and mobilize evangelicals without its grassroots organizations, and it backed a pragmatic and ideologically agile candidate instead of movement favorites. Yet there were some special circumstances in the 2000 campaign that made such activity more likely than in past elections, and those circumstances might not be repeated in future elections.

First, the Bush campaign dominated the free media, outspent its opponents by huge margins, and locked up early endorsements from key party officials. Thus the Christian Right leadership was swimming with the tide, which certainly made its work easier. Second, the task of the Christian Right was made much easier by McCain's attack on movement leaders, which brought some leaders off the sidelines and enabled the movement to paint McCain as a religious bigot in their communications to their supporters. Bush's strong personal testimony made it easier for evangelicals to support his campaign. Finally, the heritage of the Clinton presidency made it possible to convince many activists that, in 2000, it was important to back a candidate who could win.

Yet there are also reasons to believe that the success of the movement in the primaries may reflect more long-term changes in the way the movement is active in politics. First, many activists are firmly ensconced in the party apparatus, and thus in many states the movement is now part of the party in a real sense. Second, for many evangelicals, voting has become a habit, so voter mobilization efforts may be less important than in past elections. Third and perhaps most importantly, changes in campaign laws that allow unlimited and unreported issue-advocacy spending make the presence of formal organizations less important. Whereas once the Christian Coalition argued for a grassroots strategy, in 2000 the movement was influential through mass mailings, computerized phone calls, and other efforts. The funding for these efforts need not come from thousands of volunteers—it can come from a few rich individuals or even from other interest groups. The success of such efforts may be contingent on the previous existence of grassroots organizations, but the 2000 election showed that the movement can at times be successful even without that organization.

The 2000 campaign demonstrates that the movement can be a kingmaker when it is united. As Table 6.1 demonstrates, the McCain mobilization and the collapse of the Christian Coalition actually diluted the Christian Right share of the primary election vote in most states. Even in South Carolina, Religious Right members constituted 34 percent of the primary electorate in 2000, a decline of 2 percent from 1996. Turnout surged in South Carolina in 2000, so the absolute numbers of Religious Right voters did not decline. But among those states where the exit poll measured Religious Right support in both years, the vote share of the movement declined in 19 states, increased in 2, and remained the same in 2.

But the data in the Table 6.1 also show the significance of the movement throughout the South, through the heartland, and in the Pacific Northwest. Throughout the South, the Christian Right constituted roughly a third of the primary electorate, and even in New England support was not negligible. Clearly the movement retains the support to make it a critical player in close primary races.

Table 6.1

Strength of the Christian Right in GOP Primaries, 2000 and 1996

State	Percent of voters belonging to Religious Right—2000	Percent of voters belonging to Religious Right—1996
Arizona		29
California	17	26
Colorado	26	31
Connecticut	13	16
Delaware	24	22
Florida	30	32
Georgia	30	36
Illinois		25
Iowa	37	35
Louisiana	38	53
Maine	21	27
Maryland	22	28
Massachusetts	8	15
Michigan	27	29
Mississippi	27	54
Missouri	24	
New Hampshire	16	17
New York	15	19
North Dakota		24
Ohio	23	26
Oklahoma	40	40
Oregon		36
Rhode Island	11	18
South Carolina	34	36
South Dakota		30
Tennessee	34	46
Texas	37	37
Vermont	14	16
Virginia	19	
Washington		32
Wisconsin		27

Source: Presidential Primary Exit Polls by Voter News Service.

Conventional Wisdom: The Movement Is Strongest in the General Election

In past elections, the Christian Right has been most effective in general elections, when the movement can build upon growing Republican partisanship and use more clearly contrasting candidate positions on issues to mobilize its members and other conservative Christians who attend churches where voter guides are distributed. The real difference between George W. Bush and Al Gore on abortion, for example, was far greater than the difference between Bush and McCain, and thus under normal circumstances we might have expected the Christian Right to be even more mobilized in the general election than in the primaries.

Bush made a number of important symbolic gestures to the Christian Right after he clinched the nomination. He declared June 10 to be "Jesus Day" in Texas. The declaration read:

> Throughout the world, people of all religions recognize Jesus Christ as an example of love, compassion, sacrifice and service. Reaching out to the poor, the suffering and the marginalized, he provided moral leadership that continues to inspire countless men, women and children today. To honor his life and teachings, Christians of all races and denominations have joined together to designate June 10 as Jesus Day. Jesus Day challenges people to follow Christ's example by performing good works in their communities and neighborhoods.[2]

Bush's convention focused on tax cuts, social security reform, and especially education, and featured many prochoice and moderate Republicans. Bush announced his support for the prolife plank of the platform, but abortion was seldom mentioned at the convention, which emphasized instead inclusion. Unlike his father's convention eight years before, Bush did not allow social conservatives to make highly publicized speeches that might frighten moderate suburban voters. Yet Bush also maintained firm control over the speakers, and Colin Powell did not mention his prochoice views in 2000 as he had in 1996.

During the campaign, Bush steered away from the social issues of the Christian Right. Yet he made a number of symbolic gestures and sounded some themes that resonated in the community. First, Bush campaigned hard on restoring morality to the White House, doing his best to draw the distinction between his behavior and that of the current occupant. He declined to make abortion a litmus test for judges, but did promise to appoint strict constructionists to the Supreme Court. His education platform had as a central element the possibility that parents of children in failing schools could get government money to help pay for private schools, including religious ones. He called openly for the involvement of faith-based communities in welfare services.

Near the end of the campaign it was revealed that Bush had been convicted for drunken driving as a young man and had earlier answered a reporter's question about the incident in a way that seemed to many to be dishonest. One pollster told me that he believed that this incident depressed the turnout of older evangelical women, but for most evangelicals, sinful

behavior before a born-again experience is merely testimony to the power
of God to change an individual's life.

Exit polls showed that the percentage of the electorate who identified
as members of the Religious Right in 2000 was only 14 percent, a decline
of slightly over 3 percent since 1996. The National Election Study data for
2000 showed a decline in support for the Christian Coalition as well, from
more than 15 percent in 1996 to barely 13 percent in 2000. The data are
presented in Table 6.2.

The evangelical core constituency of the movement also voted less frequently in 2000 than it had in 1996. Between 1996 and 2000 the National
Election Studies showed a decline in turnout among white Catholics of 1
percent, a decline for white mainline Protestants of 2 percent, and a decline
among white evangelicals of 6 percent.[3] Clearly the Christian Right was
less mobilized in 2000 than it had been in 1996.

But the voting loyalty of Religious Right identifiers was very strong:
exit polls revealed that fully 80 percent of those who identified as members
of the Religious Right voted for Bush, compared with only 65 percent for
Dole four years earlier. Clearly Bush could not have won the election
without the concentrated support of the Christian Right, although any group
of 500 voters in Florida could make the same claim.

Christian Right Activity in the General Election: Evidence of a Decline

It is always difficult to obtain accurate estimates of the activity of Christian
Right organizations. Groups have several incentives for exaggeration: it
helps in intraparty bargaining over policy and personnel, it helps keep
members satisfied and willing to give again to the organization, and it helps
in media relations. Republican activists complained in 2000 that the Christian Coalition was not as active or effective as in the past and that fewer
voter guides were distributed. The Christian Coalition claimed to have
distributed 70 million voter guides in churches on the Sunday before the
election, but that figure is doubtlessly exaggerated. It is fair to say that the
coalition did better than many had expected in producing and distributing
these "nonpartisan" guides, which were as carefully skewed to GOP candidates as ever, but that it was significantly less active in the 2000 general
election than it had been in 1996.

Concerned Women for America (CWA) distributed voter materials to its
members to share with neighbors, and this might have had some impact.
Political science research shows that old-fashioned personal contact is the

Table 6.2

Evidence of Activity of the Christian Right in General Elections

	2000	1996
	(in percent)	
Vote share in general election	14	17
Percent who support Christian Coalition	13.7	15.5
Self-reported turnout rate for white evangelicals	67	73
Contacted by religious or moral group: white evangelicals	22	24
Information about candidates available in churches: white evangelicals	18	21

Source: Analysis based on data from the American National Election Studies 1996 and 2000 conducted by the University of Michigan, Center for Political Studies, Ann Arbor, and the Voter News Service Exit Polls.

best way to stimulate voter turnout.[4] If CWA members shared these voter guides with their neighbors, it may have made a difference in some votes.

Yet the National Election Study once again shows a decline in overall Christian Right activity. Compared with 1996, the percentage of white evangelicals who had been contacted by a religious or moral group prior to the election declined by more than 2 percent, and the percentage who reported that there was information available about candidates in their church declined by 3 percent. These data are presented in Table 6.2.

On television advertising, the Christian Right was invisible but its opponents spent sizable amounts. A study by the Annenberg Public Policy Center found significant spending by prochoice groups but relatively little by Christian conservative organizations.[5] A number of organizations used their weekly radio programs to communicate with supporters and members, to stress issues, and even to mention candidates by name. Radio is a more targeted medium; television campaigns are likely to prompt countermobilization, but radio programs reach mostly group supporters.

Compared to previous election cycles, Christian Right Political Action Committees (PACs) were more active. The largest was Gary Bauer's Campaign for Working Families, which primarily helped fund Bauer's early presidential campaign, flying him across the country to deliver contributions to candidates and make speeches. The PAC had almost $2.7 million in total receipts and directed about $45,000 of that to candidates. Some of this money was listed as independent expenditures or in-kind contributions that appear to be costs of the Bauer presidential campaign, but the PAC did make sizable contributions to several candidates. After the campaign Bauer took up work on the PAC full-time.

The two most interesting Christian Right PACs are the Madison Project and the Susan B. Anthony List. The Madison Project began as a state PAC in Virginia, where homeschool advocate and former Moral Majority head Michael Farris encouraged the PAC's donors to bundle additional contributions to candidates supported by the PAC. The Madison Project asks only that $10 be pledged to five candidates, but the PAC claims to have generated more than $1 million over the past six years to fifty candidates. In 2000, the PAC focused on defending the House impeachment managers and gave mostly to incumbents.

The Susan B. Anthony List is fashioned after EMILY's List and its smaller GOP counterpart, WISH List, which raise early money for pro-choice women candidates. The Susan B. Anthony List does support male candidates, but also encourages women to run and seeks to channel early money to their cause. Members agree to contribute to at least two candidates backed by the organization, making the checks payable to the campaign itself. These earmarked contributions are less effective than bundled ones, but they do serve to inflate the revenues of the PAC itself. The PAC received contributions from quasi-party PACs and from candidate campaign committees as well, raising more than $300,000 in the campaign. It claimed to direct some $160,000 to candidates and did indeed make significant cash contributions, along with independent expenditures and in-kind contributions that may or may not have been an allocation of overhead costs.

Yet overall, the conventional wisdom that the movement was most effective in general elections proved inaccurate in 2000, and the movement appears to have done less voter contacting and distributed fewer voter guides than in past years. Given the urgency that Christian conservatives felt about the 2000 election, the inability of the movement to fully mobilize in the general election may be a sign that the movement entered a period of decline.

Wither the Christian Right?

Thus in 2000 the Christian Right made a pragmatic choice, and was able to mobilize its supporters in the presidential primaries despite a crumbling infrastructure. But in the general election the movement was less effective than in past elections. What is the likely future of the movement?

The events of the 2000 campaign are consistent with different accounts of the Christian Right, each of which paints a somewhat different picture of the movement's future. It is possible to read the 2000 election as the last gasp of the current incarnation of the movement. As the infrastructure crumbled, the movement managed a very focused push in the South Carolina GOP primary, certainly one of the very best states in which to wage such a last battle because of the earlier strength of the Christian Coalition there and the continuing infrastructure of Baptist churches. This effort was aided by the overwhelming organizational and financial advantages of George W. Bush. By the general election, the movement was less able to distribute its voter guides and less able to mobilize its supporters, even in an election in which Bill Clinton's heir was the Democratic candidate.

The notion that the movement is in decline is bolstered by events that have occurred since the election. In April 2001, Pat Robertson argered many by telling a television interviewer that he understood why China used forced abortions, although he did not approve of the policy, and that population control was vital for the country's future. He then worried about the effects of abortion, not on the "unborn babies," but on the racial purity of the Han Chinese, who might need to dilute their genetic heritage by importing Indonesian women to make up for all of the aborted female fetuses. Robertson's remarks were greeted with anger and dismay by many movement leaders, and thus by spring 2001 both Robertson and Gary Bauer had lost much of their ability to motivate and mobilize the movement.

Yet scholars and others have written the obituary for the Christian Right many times, and like Lazarus it has generally risen from the dead. It is also possible to imagine a far rosier scenario. Despite the declining efforts of the movement, the Christian Right constituted 14 percent of the 2000 general electorate, a figure equal to that of union members and significantly higher than that of African Americans. By the numbers, the Christian Right remains an important electoral force even when it is not fully mobilized. And in some states the impact is far greater: in Tennessee, for example, the Religious Right constituted 27 percent of the electorate and gave Bush 78 percent of its votes—far more than his narrow margin in Gore's home state. In normally Democratic West Virginia, the Christian Right constituted 31 percent of the electorate and gave Bush 69 percent of its votes—easily more than his narrow margin.

Having invested so much in the Bush campaign, however, the movement will find its future dependent in part on the policies and payoffs of the Bush administration. Bush's victory seems to have settled, at least temporarily, two internal movement debates. The pragmatists who counseled the movement to support the most conservative candidate who could win a general election seem to have been vindicated, as were those who advised the movement not to abandon electoral politics. But the ultimate outcome of these debates will hinge on the policies of the Bush administration. In many ways Bush is the Republican version of Clinton—ideologically agile and able to provide rhetorical and symbolic reassurances to a wide range of his party's ranks. If Bush backs the movement on key issues so activists see "progress," they will likely remain active in the GOP coalition in future elections. If Bush accomplishes little or focuses on economic and other issues, the purists and those who argue that electoral politics are futile may again join the debate.

It is too early to tell which will occur, but to date it appears that Bush will provide the Christian Right with key positions in the administration, key rhetorical assurances, and key policies. The nomination of John Ashcroft as attorney general was an obvious coup for the movement. Although the Bush team told reporters that Ashcroft was a late and reluctant choice for the position, movement leaders privately announced the pick the day after the election. Ashcroft has received most of the attention, but secretary of health and human services, Tommy Thompson, and secretary of interior Gale Norton are also movement favorites, as was Linda Chavez. Yet Bush reportedly declined to nominate former senator Dan Coates as secretary of defense because of Coates's strong stand against gays in the military, and Bush has delayed significantly the appointment of a head for the Food and Drug Administration (FDA), which may revisit the decision to permit the sale of RU-486, the French abortion pill, a move that may signal ambivalence on this topic.

Not surprisingly, one of Bush's first actions was to reinstate earlier executive orders banning U.S. funds to overseas population agencies that perform abortions, and he ordered an investigation of the FDA's approval of RU-487. Yet he resisted demands for more sweeping executive orders on abortion. Bush's early policy initiatives on spending and tax cuts are generally popular among all Republicans. By May he was quietly cutting a deal on education policy that would apparently remove vouchers from his plan. Such a retreat may well anger Christian conservatives who remember all too well Ronald Reagan's promises but lack of performance.[6] Bush appeared to be surprised by the strongly negative reaction to his initiatives in faith-based support of welfare policy by Christian Right leaders, who feared government regulation of religious activity.

Despite the electoral activities of the Christian Right, it has yet to win public policy victories or to effect a social transformation. It is often argued that the Christian Right provides the shock troops for a culture war between Christian conservatives and social liberals. Yet this culture war has thus far been waged primarily in the electoral battlefield, and there have been precious few victories for the movement in the larger policy arena. Most Americans are noncombatants in any culture war, preferring moderate policies on most social and moral issues.

After some twenty-two years of activity in its most recent incarnation, the movement's core policy agenda remains unfulfilled. Since 1980 abortions have become only slightly more difficult to obtain, women have entered the labor force in larger numbers, school curricula continue to teach sex education and evolution, and gays and lesbians have won political battles in a number of cities and private battles within companies that now pay benefits to domestic partners.

The Christian Right has enjoyed some policy success: in most states teenage girls must notify parents or even get their consent for an abortion, abstinence is a critical element of the sex education curricula in many more states and local districts, and homemakers can now contribute to an Independent Retirement Account (IRA). Evolution is not included in the high school biology curriculum in many local jurisdictions and is deemphasized in a number of states. Yet when activists are asked their greatest victories, they usually tell stories of liberal policies prevented, rather than conservative policies enacted.

All of this could change, of course, with two or three carefully selected Supreme Court justices. The Court is only a vote or two away from overturning its decision legalizing abortion, from relaxing its criteria for church-state separation, and from returning major power to the states—which might allow the movement to enact conservative social policy in many states. If Bush appoints the kind of judges that the Christian Right wants, it is possible that all of the efforts and prayers of the movement will be answered. And that might begin a true culture war in the United States.

Notes

1. For a detailed account of the involvement of the movement in the primary election campaign, see Mark J. Rozell, "The Christian Right in the GOP Primaries," paper presented at the annual meeting of the International Association of Americanists, Warsaw, Poland, July 19, 2000.

2. Bush was not the only southern governor to sign this proclamation, and his aides insisted that his action was routine. Nonetheless, the proclamation sent a strong signal to Christian conservatives that was amplified by the media attention and liberal attacks on Bush's action.

3. In 2000 the National Election Studies used a far better turnout question, which may have resulted in fewer respondents who did not vote claiming that they had. There is no reason to believe that this would have disproportionately affected evangelicals, however.

4. See Alan Gerber and Donald P. Green, "The Effects of Personal Canvassing, Telephone Calls, and Direct Mail on Voter Turnout: A Field Experiment," *American Political Science Review* 94 (2000): 653–664.

5. See Lorie Slass, "Spending on Issue Advocacy in the 2000 Cycle," Annenberg Public Policy Center at the University of Pennsylvania, February 2001.

6. Although Reagan took strong prolife stands, his first appointment to the Supreme Court, Sandra Day O'Connor, upheld the *Roe v. Wade* decision. Reagan also refused to push for a constitutional amendment to permit prayer in schools.

Bibliography

Persinos, John. "Has the Christian Right Taken Over the Republican Party?" Campaigns and Elections, September 1994, 21–24.

Wilcox, Clyde. "Political Action Committees of the New Christian Right: A Longitudinal Analysis." *Journal for the Scientific Study of Religion* 27 (1988): 60–71.

III

The Partisan Perspective

7

It's Party Time

Stephen J. Wayne

Since the beginning of the 1970s, political scientists have pointed to a weakening of partisan identities, the attachments people feel toward political parties. Not only do people feel less strongly about their own partisan affiliation, but an increasing number of people identify themselves as independents. Some scholars see a trend toward dealignment, with partisanship in general exercising less influence on voting behavior while issues and personalities become more important. One evidence of the decline in partisanship has been the rise of split ticket voting.[1] Another has been the atrophying of party organizations at the grass roots level.

A variety of factors has been advanced to explain the loosening of partisan ties. The reforms in the nomination process, which were initiated in the 1970s, have factionalized the parties, weakened their leadership, and turned them increasingly into candidate-driven organizations. The influence that party activists have exercised during the nomination process has resulted in the selection of candidates and delegates who are more ideologically extreme than are most rank-and-file partisans. As a consequence, those partisans who hold more moderate political beliefs have greater difficulty in identifying with the rhetoric and policy positions of their elected party leaders.

Changes in the way in which candidates communicate to the electorate have also worked to weaken the parties. Campaign resources have been disproportionately devoted to television and radio advertising, to polling and focus groups, not to developing broad-based party organizations. Moreover, the growth and involvement of interest groups in the electoral and governing processes have also diluted the party's influence and reduced its representational functions.

If partisanship is declining, then parties would be expected to exercise less influence on who votes and how they vote. If partisanship is declining, then support for the party's nominees should relate less to partisan identities and more to other factors. If partisanship is declining, then group partisan preferences should be less distinct and more variable. The empirical evidence, however, points in the other direction.

This chapter will explore that evidence. It will examine partisan voting patterns since 1988 in presidential elections and in Congress to see whether some of the implications of the conventional wisdom are valid: that partisan affiliation is more tenuous today and thus has less influence on voting in elections and in government. The chapter is divided into five parts. The first examines partisan voting during the contested phase of the 2000 presidential primaries; the second looks at partisan attitudes during the non-contested stage between Super Tuesday and the national nominating conventions; the third analyzes partisan preferences during the general election campaign and voting patterns on Election Day; the fourth part of the chapter discusses partisanship and public opinion during the Florida vote controversy; the final section presents trends in party unity in Congress over the last three decades.

Partisan Voting in the 2000 Primaries

Since primary elections are contests within a party, partisan voting in a primary sounds like a contradiction, but it is not. Some states permit *crossover* voting, by which independents and those whose allegiances are with another party may vote in a different party's primary by simply requesting a ballot. Others hold *open* primaries, in which voters are given two primary ballots and choose one of them on which to vote. In 2000, California instituted a *blanket primary,* in which voters could cast ballots for any candidate for any position regardless of party, although the Supreme Court later declared such a ballot unconstitutional on the grounds that it violated the rights of parties in selecting their nominees.[2]

In 2000, exit polls were conducted by the Voter News Service in many of the states that held primaries and also in Iowa, which held the first caucus. These polls evidence voting patterns at the presidential level in each party's primary elections. Over all, they permit analysts to discern the composition of the candidates' principal support. What follows is an analysis of the four principal candidates' electoral base in the Iowa caucus and the presidential primaries that were held during the competitive stage of

the nomination process, from the caucus on January 21 through the first
Tuesday in March.[3]

Democrats for Gore

Two-thirds of the self-declared Democrats voted for Vice President Al
Gore. He won the Democratic vote in every competitive state and led
substantially among the four groups that comprise the party's core electoral
coalition: labor, African Americans, Latinos, and women. Gore's proportion of the vote among self-declared Democrats ranged from a low of 59
percent in New Hampshire to a high of 82 percent in California. The vice
president received almost two-thirds of the vote of those with a union
member in their household, 81 percent of the African American vote, 87
percent of the Latino vote,[4] and 63 percent of women who voted in these
Democratic contests.

The preferences of self-declared independents in the Democratic primaries were much closer, with former senator Bill Bradley winning among
this group in nine of twelve competitive races. Overall, Bradley won 48
percent of the independents who voted in the Democratic primaries compared to Gore's 45 percent. Bradley's problem was that independents constituted only one-fourth of the Democratic primary electorate. Had that
independent proportion been larger, and it would have been had Republican
senator John McCain not attracted so many independent voters to his
party's primaries, Bradley would have done better. In addition to independents, Bradley did best among younger voters and those in the highest
income bracket in the survey, $75,000 and over, but again, both of these
groups represented relatively small percentages of Democratic voters in
their states.

Republicans for Bush

Although McCain posed a serious challenge to Governor George W. Bush,
he did not do so among most self-declared Republican voters. With the
exception of his home state of Arizona, McCain lost the Republican vote
to Bush in every other contest. Nor was it close among Republican identifiers. Bush won 59 percent of this group compared to 34 percent for
McCain, with the remainder going to other Republican candidates.

Much like Gore, Bush benefited from the support of his party's electoral
core: conservatives and, especially, the Religious Right. Bush won 58 percent
of the conservative vote compared to 33 percent for McCain, a considerable
advantage since self-declared conservatives constituted over half of the vote

in the GOP's primaries. Although the religious right was a smaller proportion of the Republican primary vote than were people who considered
themselves conservative, this group was even more pro-Bush. Sixty-three
percent favored the Texas governor compared to only 22 percent for
McCain. In states in which the Religious Right was a substantial proportion
of the Republican electorate, such as South Carolina (34 percent), Bush's
almost 3 to 1 advantage counterbalanced the independent and Democratic
support that McCain received in that state. Even though only 19 percent
of the Republican voters claimed an affiliation with the religious right,
Bush's 80 to 14 margin among this group more than offset McCain's much
smaller 7 percent lead among those who were not affiliated with this group.

McCain did best among independents and, in those states that permitted
crossover voting, among Democrats. He received the votes of two out of
three independents. In every state except California, he received more votes
from independents than did Bush. McCain's support from Democrats was
even greater although Democrats represented less than 10 percent of the
total Republican vote in all states but Michigan, where it was 17 percent.

In short, in both major parties, partisans stuck with their front-runner.
The organizational support that these front-runners were able to muster
from party officials and group leaders in these states undoubtedly contributed to the size and cohesion of this vote. Democratic and Republican
partisans obviously liked their anointed nominees and supported them. This
high level of partisan support continued throughout the general election
campaign.

Partisan Preferences During the Noncompetitive Phases of the Nomination

The intraparty divisions generated by the nomination process quickly faded
once a presumptive nominee had emerged. With each of the defeated candidates endorsing his primary opponent, each party's electoral coalition
coalesced behind its new leader. Moreover, both Bush and Gore were
viewed favorably by their rank and file as were their respective choices for
vice president, Richard Cheney and Joseph Lieberman. The national conventions marked the nadir of partisan support at this final stage of the
nomination process.

Table 7.1 shows the level of support each of the winning nominees received from his respective partisans from the end of the competitive phase of
the nomination to the beginning of the general election campaign. Table 7.2
indicates how independents were inclined over the course of this period. As
the figures indicate, there was little variation among partisans in support of

Table 7.1

Partisan Support for the Parties' Nominees: After the Contested Primaries to the Beginning of the 2000 General Election

Dates of poll	Percent Republican support for Bush	Percent Democratic support for Gore
March/10–12	92	89
March/30–April/02	91	88
April/07–09	92	86
April/28–30	91	88
May/23–24	95	82
June/06–07	89	86
June/23–25	90	80
July/06–09	91	86
July/14–16	92	89
July/25–26	97	86
August/04–05	95	83
August/11–12	93	85
August/18–19	91	89
August/24–27	90	87
September/04–06	88	89

Source: Gallup Poll <http://www.gallup.com/Election2000/bushgoretrialheat.asp>.

Table 7.2

Independent Support for the Presidential Candidates After the Contested Primaries to the Beginning of the 2000 General Election

Dates of poll	Bush/Percent	Gore/Percent
March/10–12	50	32
March/30–April/02	45	36
April/07–09	42	36
April/28–30	47	40
May/23–24	37	38
June/06–07	39	43
June/23–25	57	31
July/06–09	48	32
July/14–16	41	44
July/25–26	53	34
August/04–05	59	32
August/11–12	59	43
August/18–19	41	25
August/24–27	47	22
September/04–06	47	42

Source: Gallup Poll <http://www.gallup.com/Election2000/bushgoretrialheat.asp>.

Table 7.3

Partisan and Independent Support During the Nine Weeks of the 2000 Presidential Election

Dates of poll	Percent Republicans for Bush	Percent Democrats for Gore	Percent Independents for	
			Bush	Gore
September/04–10	85	86	22	31
September/11–17	88	86	18	26
September/18–24	87	86	28	29
September/25–October/1	88	85	24	31
October/02–08	89	85	28	23
October/09–15	87	86	24	24
October/16–22	89	83	17	25
October/23–29	90	84	28	25
October/30–November/4	90	83	31	25

Source: Gallup Poll <http://www.gallup.com/Election2000/aggregate.asp>.

their standard-bearers but more variation among independents. In short, during the period after the nominations were effectively decided but before the nominating conventions, partisans rallied behind the acknowledged winners while the winners reached out to those who were disaffected and had supported their primary opponents. Unity was the order of the day.

Partisan Preferences and Voting Behavior During the General Election

The Campaign

The steadiness of partisan support for the party's respective standard-bearers continued throughout the general election campaign. Daily tracking polls by the Gallup organization show practically no change in the preferences of self-declared Republicans, only slight variation among Democrats, but more among independents. Although Republican support for Bush was slightly higher than Democratic support for Gore, both major party candidates had strong partisan backing throughout the campaign. Independents' evaluations of both candidates fluctuated slightly with about 40 to 50 percent of this group expressing no preference. (See Table 7.3.) Thus, with the parties unified and near parity, attention turned to independent and third-party voters.

Table 7.4

Ideology and the Vote, 1988–2000 (in percent)

Year	1988		1992			1996			2000	
Candidate	Bush	Dukakis	Clinton	Bush	Perot	Clinton	Dole	Perot	Bush	Gore
Liberal	18	81	68	14	18	78	11	07	13	80
Moderate	49	50	48	31	21	57	33	09	52	44
Conservative	80	19	18	65	17	20	71	08	81	17

Source: Calculated by author from Voter News Service Exit Polls, 1992–2000.

The Election

Since 1988, partisanship has been strongly related to voting behavior. According to exit polls, there has been a discernible relationship between partisanship and political ideology, with liberals overwhelmingly Democratic and conservatives Republican. (See Table 7.4.) Political scientists who have analyzed data from the national election studies have also reached similar conclusions. They have found partisanship to be related to turnout and to voting itself.[5] Today's electorate is closely divided between the two major parties and has been since the 1980s. The Democrats enjoy a slight advantage in the proportion of the population which identifies with them, but Republicans generally turn out at a slightly higher rate than do Democrats. According to the 2000 election exit poll, 39 percent of the electorate indicated they were Democrats, 35 percent Republicans, and 27 percent independents.

One of the reasons for the continuing partisan divide has been the consistency with which core groups in each party's electoral coalition have maintained their loyalty to that party in recent elections. Table 7.5 documents this loyalty. It indicates the extent to which the key Democratic groups of women, African Americans, Latinos, and labor voted for their party's candidates and the extent to which white men, the religious right, and those with the highest incomes voted Republican. Moreover, the proportion of these groups within the electorate has not shifted dramatically in the last twelve years, thereby reinforcing the stability of partisan voting patterns.

Table 7.6 indicates the vote according to partisan allegiance. Democrats overwhelmingly voted for Gore, Republican for Bush, and independents were nearly evenly divided. Hence the outcome—a very close popular vote.

Table 7.5

Groups in the Democratic and Republican Electoral Coalitions, 1988–2000 (in percent)

Year	1988		1992			1996			2000	
Candidate	Bush	Dukakis	Clinton	Bush	Perot	Clinton	Dole	Perot	Bush	Gore
Democratic										
Women	50	49	46	37	17	54	38	07	43	54
African Americans	12	86	82	11	07	84	12	04	09	90
Latinos	30	69	62	25	14	72	21	06	35	62
Labor*	42	57	55	24	21	59	30	09	37	59
Lowest income bracket (under $15,000)	37	62	59	23	18	59	28	11	37	57
Liberals	18	81	68	14	18	78	11	07	13	80
Republican										
Men	57	41	41	38	21	43	44	10	53	42
Whites	59	40	39	41	20	43	46	09	54	42
White† born-again Christians	81	18	23	61	15	26	65	08	80	18
Upper income bracket (over $100,000)	65	32	—	—	—	38	54	06	54	43
Conservatives	80	19	18	65	17	20	71	08	81	17

* Union member in household.

† In 2000, the reference was to the Religious Right.

Source: Calculated by author from Voter News Service Exit Polls, 1992–2000.

Partisanship in the Florida Vote Controversy

The election ended on November 7 but it was not resolved until December 11, when the Supreme Court issued its judgment on the Florida vote controversy.[6] In most respects the partisan preferences of the electorate continued to affect public perceptions of the candidates, the controversy, and the fairness of the Supreme Court's judgment.

In examining public opinion during this period, the Gallup organization

Table 7.6

Partisanship and the Vote, 1988–2000 (in percent)

Year	1988		1992			1996			2000	
Candidate	Bush	Dukakis	Clinton	Bush	Perot	Clinton	Dole	Perot	Bush	Gore
Republican	91	8	10	73	17	13	80	06	91	08
Independent	55	43	38	32	30	43	35	17	47	45
Democrat	17	82	77	10	13	84	10	05	11	86

Source: Calculated by author from Voter News Service Exit Polls, 1992–2000.

took six national polls. It found Bush and Gore's supporters as divided over the Florida vote count as they had been in the election. Gore voters approved of his challenge of the Florida vote; Bush voters did not. Gore's partisans favored a hand count of the disputed ballots; Bush's did not. Gore's supporters believed that an accurate tally of the Florida vote was possible; Bush's did not. Gore's backers wanted the Florida courts to intervene; Bush's did not.

Over the course of the controversy, Bush's supporters said that they were less willing "to wait a little longer" for a resolution, were more anxious for Gore to concede, and less likely to view Gore as the legitimate president were he to be declared the winner of the Florida vote. Table 7.7 indicates the opinion of partisans and the nation as a whole on these issues.

Partisan differences were also evident in the reaction to the Supreme Court's decision. At first, a majority of the population, including the electoral supporters of both major party candidates, said that they trusted the United States Supreme Court more than the Congress, the Florida legislature, or the Florida Supreme Court to resolve the controversy and make the final decision. When the Court did so, however, Gore's backers saw the decision as unfair and partisan; they expressed less confidence in the Supreme Court as a result. The reaction of Gore's partisans differed from that of the nation as a whole and obviously from that of Bush's supporters. Table 7.8 summarizes Gallup's polling data on the public's response to the Court's decision.

Throughout the electoral controversy, more than 70 percent of the population indicated that they would accept whichever candidate was ultimately declared the winner by the electoral college. And they did. Two out of three Gore supporters said that they regarded George W. Bush as the legitimate president after he received Florida's vote and, thereby, an

Table 7.7

Partisan Opinions on the Florida Vote Controversy (in percent)

	Supporters of		
	Bush	Gore	National adults
Accurate tally possible?			
Yes (11/19)	13	24	19
Florida court intervention:			
Bothers me (11/19)			
A great deal	47	17	30
A fair amount	31	27	29
Not much	14	34	23
Not at all	07	21	17
Hand count of ballots:			
Favor (11/19)	23	92	60
Election timetable:			
Wait a little longer			
(11/19)	16	82	51
(11/26–27)	9	67	37
(12/2–4)	9	69	36
Should Gore concede:			
Yes			
(11/19)	70	28	46
(11/26–27)	81	36	56
(12/2–4)	84	27	58
Regard Gore as legitimate president if he was declared Florida winner:			
Yes			
(11/11–12)	66	97	82
(11/19)	58	98	80
(11/26–27)	46	97	74
(12/2–4)	46	97	71

Source: Gallup Polls <http://www.gallup.com/poll/releases/pr001120.asp>; <http://www.gallup.com/poll/releases/pr001206.asp>.

electoral college majority. Of the core groups within the Democrat Party's electoral coalition, African Americans expressed greatest reluctance to do so. More embittered than other groups, two-thirds of African Americans polled indicated that they felt cheated, while 42 percent indicated that they did not feel that George W. Bush was the rightful president. African Americans' skepticism of Bush's "legitimate" victory continued through the first six months of the new administration.[7] A comparison of the opinions of white and African Americans on the controversy and the outcome appears in Table 7.9.

Table 7.8

Public Reaction to the Supreme Court's Decision (in percent)

| | Supporters of | | |
	Bush	Gore	National adults
Decision fair?			
Yes	94	17	54
Basis of decision:			
Legal merits of the case	87	22	54
Supreme Court Justices wanted Bush to win	06	65	35
Both/Neither/No opposition	07	13	11
Public view of court:			
Lose confidence	05	54	30
No effect	93	39	66
Accept Bush as legitimate president:			
Yes (11/12)	97	61	79
(11/19)	98	72	86
(11/26–27)	100	65	84
(12/2–4)	100	68	85
(12/13)	99	61	80
Reaction to Bush as president:			
Thrilled	33	0	15
Pleased	63	09	33
Disappointed	01	66	34
Angry	0	22	11

Source: Gallup Poll, "Eight in Ten Americans to Accept Bush as 'Legitimate' President," December 14, 2000, <http://www.gallup.com/poll/releases/pr001214.asp>.

Partisanship and Governing

With political emotions still raw from the election outcome and the new Congress very evenly divided, partisanship threatened to undercut attempts by the new president to pursue his campaign agenda, build a cohesive majority, and govern with public support. The good news for Bush was that his party initially controlled both houses of Congress, the first time Republicans did so under a GOP White House since the first two years of the Eisenhower presidency, 1953–1954. Moreover, there was a public consensus on the most important issues: education, health care, tax relief, and Social Security. The bad news was that this consensus did not extend to policy solutions. Moreover, Congress had been plagued by partisan division since 1985. More than half of the roll call votes in Congress during this period pitted a majority of Republicans against a majority of Democrats.[8]

Although party voting declined in 2000, during the last session of the

Table 7.9

Reaction of African Americans and Whites to the Election (in percent)

	Respondents	
	African Americans	Whites
The way Bush won:		
Fair and square	07	54
On a technicality	39	31
Stole the election	50	14
Accept Bush as legitimate president:		
Yes	58	86
Think Bush will work hard to represent interests of black Americans:		
Yes	22	67
Florida vote:		
Fraud involved	64	26
Errors, but no fraud	33	68
Confidence in the system by which votes are cast and counted:		
A great deal	09	16
Quite a lot	06	16
Some	28	33
Very little	51	33
None/No opposition	06	02

Source: Gallup Poll, "Black Americans Feel 'Cheated' by Election 2000," December 20, 2000.

106th Congress, partisan animosities remained high.[9] They had been re-inforced by the Republican takeover of Congress in the 1994 elections, the pursuit by the Republicans of their "Contract with America," the Clinton impeachment, and finally, the 2000 election campaign and controversy.

It was these angry politics, strident rhetoric, and lack of civility among members of Congress and with the White House that candidate George W. Bush had promised to reduce, if elected. By making overtures to Democrats, by compromising on the issues, and by pursuing a bipartisan approach, Bush hoped to overcome the self-righteous attitudes and noncompromising behavior that had characterized legislative-executive relations throughout most of his father's presidency and the Clinton years.

Bush's goal was based on an assumption, which many political pundits shared, that the electorate was as evenly but not deeply divided as Washington. Hence, the problem was not partisan parity but partisan politics—Washington style. Members of Congress had become too ideological, too personal, and too suspicious of their political opponents. They had lost touch with the average American.

The president's campaign promise to reduce the partisan rhetoric, to end the name calling and finger pointing, and to build a consensus through compromise rather than impose it by partisan politics also hinged on the perception that people were tired of the bickering and personal attacks that characterized contemporary national politics. Much of the cynicism toward government, mistrust of public officials, and apathy in the electoral process was attributable to this style of vitriolic partisan politics.

Thus the president's objective was to reduce dysfunctional partisanship in Washington, a goal that he claimed much of the public shared. As he began his presidency, Bush had two strategic choices: to redefine his policy agenda and personnel appointments in terms of the election result or to stick with his campaign agenda and make those appointments that would please his electoral constituency. He chose the latter strategy but his rhetoric and style were more informal and inclusive. Bush's personal manner tempered his political nominations and policy decisions and resulted in a "wait and see" attitude on the part of Washington Democrats. Overall, the initial public reaction, taken in the first two weeks of the administration was favorable, but partisan divisions continued to be evident in the evaluation. Eighty-eight percent of Republicans approved of the way the new president was doing his job compared to 52 percent of independents and only 32 percent of Democrats. Racial and gender gaps remained large: 61 percent of whites approved of his performance compared to only 35 percent of nonwhites; 64 percent of men approved compared to only 50 percent of women.[10] The people remained divided; the wounds of the election had not healed. The new president had his work cut out for him in this divisive political environment.

Conclusion

If partisan allegiances have weaken since the end of the 1960s, if candidate orientation is stronger in this age of electronic campaigning, and if issue preferences are more pronounced as a consequence of special interest politics, then why does partisanship continue to be such a strong influence on who turns out in elections and how they vote? If parties are weaker, if the nomination process factionalizes and personalizes them, if television now intercedes between the party and the electorate, then how come partisan perceptions, evaluations, and voting behavior continue to be evident in American elections? If interest groups are stronger, if they are more directly involved in elections and governing, if the public perceives them to be more influential on public policy decisions, then why do parties still oversee campaigns, organize government, and dominate congressional voting behavior? If third-party candidates are able to wage a national campaign and gain attention from the media and the major party candidates, if the people are tired of partisan bickering, if the public continues to express cynicism toward politics, politicians, and parties, then why haven't the major parties lost their attraction for the American electorate?

The answer may have to do with the utility of partisanship as an organizing framework for the people, the press, and politicians to understand, evaluate, and influence the personnel and policy decisions of government. The news media present the story of elections and government within the context of a partisan prism. Elected officials and party organizations, monitoring the views of their constituents, appeal to their interests, and claim positions and make decisions with their constituents in mind. And they do this to maintain their own popularity and electability in the performance of their representative functions. Partisanship is an easy-to-use mind-set, which frames and influences electoral decisions because values, beliefs, and opinions contribute to partisan attitudes and behavior rather than detract from them much of the time. We have already noted the reinforcing effect that ideology has on contemporary partisan perspectives.

The parties as institutions may be weaker than they were several decades ago; the allegiances people have to the parties may also lack the intensity of the past; the parties may no longer mediate as effectively between their candidates and the electorate; nor may they exercise as much influence on who those candidates will be. But parties remain important, if not as organizations then as states of mind, as filters through which the electorate weighs the issues, evaluates the candidates, and then decides whether to vote and, if so, for whom. In this way partisanship frames and influences electoral decisions. It is still party time in America.

Notes

1. Samuel J. Eldersveld and Hanes Walton Jr. *Political Parties in American Society*, 2nd ed. (Boston: Bedford/St. Martin's, 2000), pp. 94–95.

2. In the case of *California Democratic Party v. Jones* (2000), the Supreme Court held that California's primary, which permitted voters, regardless of their party affiliation, to vote for any candidate in any party for any position, violated the political party's right to organize and run candidates for office as protected by the First Amendment to the Constitution.

3. Eleven Democratic and sixteen Republican primaries are included in the analysis. The exit poll in Iowa is used for the Democrats but not for the Republicans since John McCain was not a candidate in Iowa and did not campaign in that state. Bill Bradley was a candidate and did campaign. Delaware is included in the Republican list. McCain did not campaign in that state but he did receive 25 percent of the vote, 5 percent more than did Steve Forbes, who did campaign.

4. Since most of the early Democratic contests were in the Northeast, the Latino vote was too small to measure in most states' exit polls. In two states, California and

New York, however, it was large enough to do so. In California, Gore received 89 percent and in New York, 84 percent of the Latino vote.

5. Paul R. Abramson, John H. Aldrich, and David W. Rohde, *Change and Continuity in the 1996 and 1998 Elections* (Washington, DC: Congressional Quarterly, 1999), pp. 164–190.

6. In the case of *George W. Bush, et al. v. Al Gore Jr., et al.*, (2000), a 5 to 4 majority of the Supreme Court ruled that the recount of Florida's undercounted and voided ballots as ordered by the Florida Supreme Court violated the equal protection clause of the Constitution because of the absence of a uniform system of determining valid votes throughout the state. Moreover, a bare majority of the Court held that there was not sufficient time to create such a system in order to meet the legislature's deadline of December 12 for the selection of the state's presidential electors.

7. Gallup Poll, "Seven out of 10 Americans Accept Bush as Legitimate President," July 17, 2001. <http//www.gallup.com/Poll/releases/pr010717.asp>.

8. "2000 Party Unity Votes," *Congressional Quarterly*, January 6, 2001, p. 68.

9. There were fewer roll call votes in 2000 in large part because Congress was so divided and the Republicans were fearful of losing their congressional majority. For a discussion of why the decrease in party unity was not a consequence of weakening partisan loyalties and behavior, see Adriel Bettleman, "Votes Belie Partisan Intensity," *Congressional Quarterly*, January 6, 2001, pp. 56–57.

10. Gallup Poll, "Initial Job Approval for Bush at 57%," February 6, 2001.

8

Standoff in the House

Democrats Come Up Short in the Trenches

Michael A. Bailey and Keiko Ono

In the summer of 2000, it looked like House Minority Leader Richard Gephardt (D-MO-3) could start measuring for curtains in the Speaker's office. The Democrats needed to pick up only a handful of seats to take over the House, and they had to do so in a year in which almost three times as many Republicans as Democrats had announced they would not seek reelection. Democrats also had good issues on which to run. Survey after survey showed that voters favored Democrats on key issues such as education, health care, Social Security, and gun control. On top of that, Democrats expected a boost from the presidential ticket, led by an experienced politician who had presided over a booming economy.

The Democrats devised a straightforward and aggressive strategy to turn these advantages into victory. They raised more money than ever—their campaign committee even outraised the Republican campaign committee and used the funds to run ads praising Democratic approaches and attacking vulnerable Republicans.

The election did not depend only on the Democrats, however. The Republicans recognized their own weaknesses and worked hard to minimize them. They closeted away their unpopular congressional leaders such as Richard Armey (R-TX-26) and Tom DeLay (R-TX-22) and pushed legislation that was designed to take the edge off Democratic issues.[1] The Republicans also benefited from George W. Bush's well-run presidential campaign that distracted many Democratic voters and activists from House races.

In the end, a handful of extremely competitive districts determined the fate of the House. Campaigning in these districts was hot and heavy, in stark contrast to the minimal efforts put into most House races. Candidates and their campaigns poured millions of dollars into television ads, logged millions of phone calls, and posted hundreds of thousands of lawn signs. The Democrats did well in some of these battleground districts, but not in enough districts to achieve their goals. After all the dust settled, Democrats had picked up only two seats. They lost several others by remarkably slim margins. Many races were decided by less than 10,000 votes. A swing to the Democratic candidates of a mere 2,400 votes across five districts (CA-38, FL-22, MN-2, MI-8, NM-1) would have been enough to give the House to the Democrats.

This chapter discusses the 2000 House elections from the Democratic perspective, covering important trends, issues, and strategies that influenced the outcome. We proceed more or less sequentially, beginning with factors that were determined well before the election and moving on to factors that played out in the last days and hours of the campaign. We finish with a retrospective analysis of results and a comparison to previous years.

Speaker Gephardt?

In the summer of 2000, things looked good for the Democrats. They were presented with mostly good news in terms of which seats would be competitive. Out of the thirty-five seats in which the incumbent was either retiring, running for another office, or defeated in a primary, twenty-six belonged to the Republicans.[2] On top of that, Democrats had good issues to run on, and it looked like they would have a solid team at the top of the Democratic ticket. We consider each of these factors in turn.

Open Seats and Competitive Districts

On paper, congressional elections occur every two years in 435 different districts. In reality, the typical congressional election is little more than an afterthought that ratifies a foregone conclusion. The campaign for such an election may feature a few desultory trips through the district by a well-known incumbent. The challenger—if there is one—is a retired school-teacher or a religious zealot. All but the hardest-core partisans spend their falls raking leaves and watching football, giving scant attention to their local House campaign.

The election is not this way in all districts. In every election cycle there are anywhere from 50 to 150 districts in which the election is in doubt. This is where the action is. These competitive races attract the money, press, and energy. They determine who will control Congress. In 2000, *Congressional Quarterly* identified ninety-one House races in which there was any possibility of a partisan takeover as of late September. Of those ninety-one seats, however, one party or the other was clearly favored to keep the seat in its column in a little over half of them, leaving around forty-five truly competitive seats.[3]

The most competitive seats tend to be open seats. This is a direct consequence of the first law of congressional elections: Bet on the incumbent. In 1998 and 2000, 98 percent of incumbents who ran won. Even in 1994, when Republicans made breathtaking gains in the House, incumbents won 92 percent of their races. Incumbents have many advantages. The most important is simply that incumbents have won before, not only demonstrating a familiarity and aptitude for the task at hand, but also discouraging quality challengers. Incumbents have more concrete advantages as well. Some are literally concrete in the form of roads and bridges brought to the district by the incumbent's hard work in Washington. Others are no less tangible, arising from the concerted efforts of a large congressional staff dedicated to building goodwill with constituents. Incumbents keep in touch with voters via free ("franked") mailings, e-mailings, and congressional television and radio facilities. Incumbents also are able to build connections to political interest groups that can, if needed, infuse the incumbents' campaign with cash or other useful resources.

Sometimes the advantages of the incumbency have absurd consequences. In Utah, vulnerable Republican incumbent Merrill Cook (R-UT-2) sent a full color, heavy-stock flyer to several hundred thousand constituents just before the Republican state convention. The flier boldly stated: "It's time to stop the IRS from making off with your money" and described Cook's efforts to prevent wasteful spending. The kicker, though, was in small print at the top of the flier: "This mailing was prepared, published, and mailed at taxpayer expense."[4]

It is open seats, then, in which the ground is level and campaigns are crucial. In these races, neither candidate has the broad name recognition of an incumbent and neither can mobilize the resources of office on his or her behalf. If the district is not overwhelmingly disposed toward one party or the other, the races are decided by the quality of the candidates and their campaigns. Hence, high-quality candidates on both sides will be attracted to the race, as will big-time money from interest groups and the parties.

Strategic behavior also adds to the allure of open seats for high-quality challengers. Politicians like nothing less than running and losing. The toll of a modern campaign for Congress is extraordinary, and the result of a losing campaign is to end up with nothing. Hence the most likely incumbents to retire or run for another seat are the ones who face a tough re-election battle. In other words, the seat not only may be competitive because it is open, it may be open because it is competitive.

Open seats bring unexpected opportunities. Republican William McCollum's (R-FL-8) decision to run for Senate opened a seat in Orlando, Florida. The district was not an obvious target for Democrats, as Robert Dole had beaten Bill Clinton in the district in 1996 and McCollum had cruised to victory throughout the nineties. However, the Republican primary turned into a bloodbath and only late in the season did a right-wing candidate with no political experience emerge. The Democrats, in contrast, united early around Linda Chapin, a former Orange County Commission chairwoman with extensive experience and broad support. Chapin came up short with 49 percent of the vote, but made a much better run at the seat than any Democrat in recent memory.

In 2000, the residual effects of the term limit included more Republican open seats than expected. Many Republicans elected in 1994 made campaign pledges to limit their service in Washington. Five such Republican House members kept their word and retired after serving three terms. This hurt the Republicans, as it opened up seats they had controlled comfortably since 1994. In fact, Democrats seized two of the five seats in 2000 (OK-2, WA-2).

Candidates who broke their pledge, on the other hand, came away victorious, if bruised. Republican George Nethercutt (WA-5) is the most famous. He had come to Congress in 1994 in a historical upset of then Speaker Thomas Foley. A large part of Nethercutt's campaign was based on the term limit pledge. Not only did the pledge distinguish Nethercutt from the long-serving Foley, but it also highlighted the fact that Foley had fought term limits politically and in the courts. In 2000, Nethercutt decided not to honor his term limit pledge and ran again. Supporters of term limits were horrified to see the poster child of their movement "go native" and turned on Nethercutt with a fury. U.S. Term Limits, an interest group advocating term limits, circulated posters depicting Nethercutt as Pinocchio and shadowed him with a character called "George the Weasel King."[5] But, despite the attacks, Nethercutt won easily with 59 percent of the two-party vote. Martin Meehan (D-MA-5) and Scott McInnis (R-CO-3) also broke their term limit pledges and both won easily (69 percent and 78 percent of two-party vote respectively).

Not all news on the open seat front was good for Democrats. In particular, Democrats worried about seats vacated by Democrats in western Pennsylvania and southeastern Virginia. Both districts had been trending Republican and were only Democratic due to the strength of popular Democratic incumbents. In Virginia, Owen Pickett's (D-VA-2) district had been carried by George H. W. Bush in 1992 and Dole in 1996. Pickett had thrived by building a moderate voting record and by working tirelessly on behalf of the district's military bases from his senior position on the Armed Services Committee. Another Democrat would not be able to offer such services and would be easy prey to a Republican candidate who presumably would be closer to the ideological sympathies of the district. Once Pickett announced his retirement, few Democrats expected the seat to remain in their hands. Democrat Jody Wagner tried to emulate Pickett's hawkish talk on defense, but was decisively beaten by Republican state senator Edward Schrock, a 24-year Navy veteran.

Ronald Klink's district in western Pennsylvania was another open seat that the Democrats did not expect to hold. Although Clinton had carried the district in 1992 and 1996, it is a culturally conservative stronghold. Klink (D-PA-4) did very well in the district by being liberal economically and conservative on abortion and gun control. However, it was clear that were the seat to open, Republicans would be much better positioned to win, due to the hot-button cultural issues. In the end, conservative Republican state senator Melissa Hart won easily with 59 percent of the votes.

Other districts were competitive because the incumbent was not, for one reason or another, a good fit. Some incumbents were simply ideologically out of step with the district. For example, Republican Jay Dickey (R-AR-4) was living on borrowed time as a solid conservative in a district in which Clinton had received twice as many votes as Dole in 1996. Other incumbents were vulnerable because of a scandal. Two-term Republican congressman Merrill Cook (R-UT-2) became a prime target after being accused of everything from "road rage" to profane, angry outbursts against colleagues. His frequent and sometimes bizarre staff shake-ups prompted the *Salt Lake Tribune* to label Cook's tenure "the Alice in Wonderland saga."[6] Cook could not even survive the primary, as a 35-year-old entrepreneur handily beat Cook in the race for the Republican nomination. The Democrats eventually took the seat in the general election.

In summary, open seats define the battle lines of every election, and in 2000 Democrats looked to benefit from a generally advantageous crop of open seats.

Issues

Democrats also had a lot going for them on issues. The Republicans had few accomplishments in the 106th Congress (1999–2000). The biggest story was the impeachment trial of President Clinton, hardly a political winner for the Republicans. The majority of voters were consistently opposed to impeaching Clinton and removing him from office.[7] Little else emerged from the 106th Congress. Congress passed legislation to create permanent normal trade relations with China, but this was not exactly a political barn-burner on the campaign trail. Most important legislation sank in a quagmire of partisan acrimony or, if passed, was vetoed by the president. Congress was unable to deliver a final product on many of the hotly debated issues: comprehensive reform of health maintenance organizations (HMOs) that would include expanding a patient's right to sue HMOs in case of injury or denial of care, prescription drug benefits for Medicare, repeal of estate taxes, easing of the tax marriage penalty, and background checks on all gun buyers.

Voters' response to the work of the 106th Congress was lukewarm at best. Fifty-six percent of Americans disapproved of the way the congressional Republicans were doing their job according to a March 1999 survey, and 47 percent said the Democrats better represent their own personal values, compared with 39 percent who said Republicans do so. On the generic question, "Which party do you trust to do a better job in coping with the main problems the nation faces over the next few years?" the Democrats had a ten-point lead over the Republicans in March 1999 (47 to 37 percent).[8]

These advantages extended to specific issues. More voters trusted the Democrats to do a better job on most of the top national issues of the 2000 cycle: health care, prescription drug coverage, the economy, Social Security, and education. The issues on which voters trusted Republicans— crime, moral values, foreign affairs—were less important to most voters.[9]

President Clinton summed up the Democrats' optimism about issues by stating that the Democrats would sweep the two chambers of Congress and the White House "when the American people understood what the issues were and what the choices were."[10]

The Presidential Election

Traditionally, winning presidential candidates were believed to "pull some of their party's candidates into office along with them, riding, as it were, on their coattails."[11] The coattail effect, however, has become increasingly attenuated in recent years. In 1992, the Democrats lost ten seats in the House despite winning the race for the White House. Clinton's reelection in 1996 brought a modest three-seat gain for the Democrats. Nonetheless, the Democrats were hopeful in 2000 that the energetic presidential ticket headed by an experienced, solid candidate would at least set a positive tone for their candidates.

Democrats also thought that the extra attention the presidential election would bring would help them by bringing more people out to vote. In particular, the plans of both parties to spend unprecedented sums on get-out-the-vote (GOTV) drives in key states and districts in the final weeks were expected to help Democrats. High levels of turnout among African Americans and union households indicate that these expectations were borne out, at least in part.

There was another wrinkle to the connection between presidential and congressional voting in the 2000 campaign. The Democrats were concerned that the Green Party presidential candidate, Ralph Nader, was going to siphon precious votes away from Al Gore, which they feared could ultimately give the election to George W. Bush. Survey results, however, presented a dilemma for the Democrats. The surveys showed that a significant portion of would-be Nader voters would not be voting at all if it were not for Nader.[12] Assuming that in these areas (CA, OR, WA, MN, WI) anyone who turned out for Nader would certainly vote for the Democratic candidate for the House, the Democrats reasoned that the more Nader voters turned out, the better for the House Democrats.[13]

Translating Optimism into Seats

The above factors gave the Democrats reasons to be hopeful. But in order to be the majority party, Democrats needed to produce a slate of quality candidates who had enough money and a coherent set of issues on which to run.

Candidate Recruitment

The most important step in turning opportunities into Democratic pickups was to field strong candidates. As House Minority Leader Richard Gephardt said, "if you don't have the players, you're not going to win."[14]

A strong candidate is usually a local politician who is established, famous or rich—preferably all three. Jane Harman (D-CA-36) was the archetypal strong challenger. A millionaire and a former member of Congress, she was widely known not only as a House member, but for a run for governor in 1998. She clearly had the experience, name recognition and money to make Republican incumbent Steven Kuykendall's life miserable. Former Democratic representative Scott Baesler also typified what it means to be a strong candidate. He not only had held the seat in Kentucky's sixth district before he ran for Senate in 1998, but held a place in many voters' hearts as a former basketball star at the University of Kentucky.

Democrats also had many strong new faces in their lineup. Many currently served in state legislatures. For example, state Representative Elaine Bloom brought experience from eighteen years in the Florida state legislature to her race against Republican incumbent E. Clay Shaw in the state's twenty-second district. Others brought a different kind of political asset to their race: a prominent family name. In Utah's second district, James Matheson was aided by the popularity of his father, the late former governor Scott Matheson. In Pennsylvania's sixth district, voters' memories of the late former governor Robert Casey helped his son Patrick Casey. Steve Danner, the son of outgoing incumbent Patsy Danner, was also expected to do well in Missouri's tenth district.

Not all the Democratic candidates were strong, however, and several otherwise promising races were done in by candidates' weaknesses. For example, in the traditionally Democratic second district of West Virginia, trial lawyer James Humphreys carried the banner for the Democrats. While he had a lot of money to spend on the race, he also came into the race with a fair bit of baggage, including liens placed on his house for being $38,000 behind in paying his state income taxes. How did he become the candidate? It is here that money probably played its biggest role, as his bottomless pockets scared out opposition in the Democratic primary and meant that he was not seriously scrutinized until the general election.

Strong candidates do not simply emerge out of thin air. The Democratic Congressional Campaign Committee (DCCC) made a concerted effort to recruit qualified candidates, particularly in top target districts such as California's fifteenth district, an open seat where Republican incumbent Thomas Campbell was running for Senate. National Democrats had identified Michael Honda, a state assemblyman representing the Silicon Valley area as the best challenger, but he was reluctant and, after extensive lobbying, informed the DCCC that he would not run out of consideration for his wife and family. Upon hearing this, Gephardt stated that "No is not the right answer" and redoubled his efforts to convince Honda to run. After another round of extensive lobbying that included efforts by many members of the California delegation to the House and President Clinton, Honda relented and decided to run.[15]

A similar story was playing out in southern California. State senator Adam Schiff was an experienced Democrat with a record of running strong campaigns. However, he had run against and been defeated by Republican incumbent James Rogan (R-CA-27) twice and was not sure he wanted to try again. Gephardt and DCCC chairman Patrick Kennedy (D-RI-1) viewed Schiff as their best bet and badgered him throughout the spring of 1999. Sciff finally admitted, "Talking with them helped me put the race in a national context, that I could be part of a very few races that would decide if the country would make progress on key issues."[16]

In summary, recruiting a strong cast of candidates is a key step in taking advantage of open seat opportunities. By and large, in 2000 the extraordinary recruiting efforts of the Democratic leadership paid off with candidacies by many experienced politicians and locally prominent individuals.

Money

The DCCC also worked extremely hard raising money. Strong candidates do not win by filing for the office and waiting for results. They have to work their districts very hard. And while legwork is important, money is indispensable. It is very difficult to win a competitive House race without raising at least $1 million. That is almost $1,500 per day every day for two years.

House Democrats dived into the fund-raising game with all their effort. "The only way to raise this kind of money is to be on the road all the time," said DCCC National Finance Director Noah Mamet. This meant that Minority Leader Gephardt and DCCC Chair Kennedy were traveling almost every minute the House was not in session. They paid particular attention to Silicon Valley, where newfound wealth coupled with ideological liberalism proved a fertile ground for Democratic fund-raising.

Their efforts paid off in a big way. In 1998, the DCCC had raised $37 million, a modest sum compared to the National Republican Congressional Committee's $130 million. In 2000, the Democrats set a goal of raising $50 million. They almost doubled it, raising $97 million. Not only did they exceed their own goals, but they outraised the Republicans.

However, money raised and spent by candidates accounts for a smaller and smaller share of total political spending today as parties and interest groups start to pour large amounts of money into congressional races. In fact, express advocacy and issue advocacy independent expenditures have become a major part of modern campaigns.[17] In the 1999–2000 cycle, issue advocacy advertising included $80 million spent on the 2000 House races by Citizens for Better Medicare, a front group for pharmaceutical companies. This group spent almost $1.5 million defending Republican incumbent Brian Bilbray (R-CA-49) in San Diego.[18] Interestingly, Bilbray was one of the few incumbents to lose, even with such largesse.

According to an Annenberg Public Policy Center study, issue advocacy advertising (for both congressional and presidential races) dramatically increased from the two previous cycles. The estimated dollar amount spent in the 1999–2000 cycle ($509 million) was more than three times as much as that for the 1995–1996 cycle ($135 million–$150 million.)[19] The sheer size of the issue advocacy expenditures was staggering given that the total spending by congressional candidates was a little over $850 million. The number of interest groups sponsoring issue ads also jumped, from 77 (1997–1998) to 130.

Where did the money come from? The Annenberg study shows about two-thirds of the issue ad spending came from non-party organizations, many of which represented business interests. In fact, three pro-business groups (Citizens for Better Medicare, the Coalition to Protect America's Healthcare which represents hospitals, and the U.S. Chamber of Commerce) accounted for 24 percent of the total issue ad spending. The rest of the issue advertising dollars came from the Republican and Democratic parties. The Democrats were able to spend almost as much on issue ads ($78.4 million) as did the Republicans ($83.5 million).

The Democrats' success in raising money did not mean that they could buy their way to victory. It simply meant they could compete in the tough districts. In fact, in some districts, it is not clear that more money would have helped much. The airwaves were already saturated with campaign ads, making it hard to get messages into the voters' heads. In some places, ad time was literally sold out.

"No race was lost because of a lack of money," said election analyst Amy Walter of *The Cook Political Report*. The flush parties were even able to spend money rather extravagantly. Democratic challenger Patrick Casey spent $200,000 on ads for the Pittsburgh and Harrisburg markets even though the combined range of these markets reaches less than 5 percent of his district.[20] Democrats also ran ads for the New Jersey race against Republican Richard Zimmer in the extraordinarily expensive New York media market, while West Virginia's James Humphreys spent $250,000 for 155 airings of a health care ad in the extremely expensive Washington, D.C. market, a market that covered only a slice of the district.[21]

Message

Having strong candidates and a pocketful of cash means little if you have little to spend it on. There are many examples of candidates who poured money into their campaigns and lost. Democrats Roger Kahn (GA-7) and James Humphreys (WV-2) spent nearly $11 million between them in 2000, including millions of their own money, but neither was successful. In fact, sixteen of the top fifty spenders running for House seats lost.[22]

Hence it was crucial that Democrats find messages that would resonate with voters. Campaign issues come in two types: national and local. The Republican sweep in 1994 was based mostly on national issues, as the Republicans turned race after race into a referendum on Bill Clinton and Democratic efforts to expand government. In 1996, Democrats in turn ran a nationalized campaign demonizing then House Speaker Newt Gingrich and other Republican leaders as heartless and hostile to working families and the elderly.

The Democrats thought that the issue advantages discussed above gave them a strong platform to build a national campaign with three themes. First, Democratic leaders and candidates attacked the Republican 106th Congress as a do-nothing congress. Hours after Congress adjourned for the summer in late July 2000, Democratic leaders in the House and the Senate and President Clinton presented a united Democratic front at the White House and accused the Republican leadership of "leaving town with a trunk full of unfinished business vital to the health of our economy and the well-being of our people."[23] The Democrats charged that the Republicans squandered a great opportunity to lift up those "who may not be riding so high on the wave of prosperity in our country."[24]

Second, the Democrats painted the Republicans as agents of special interests and the wealthy. The plans to repeal estate taxes and cut other taxes were easily portrayed by Democrats as favoring the rich. Democrats also argued that special interests such as the insurance industry, pharmaceutical companies, and the National Rifle Association benefited from the failure of Congress to act. According to House Minority Leader Gephardt, the minimum wage hike failed because "the Chamber of Commerce didn't want it, and so the Republican leaders won't go forward with it."[25] Gephardt also argued that patients were left waiting for necessary health care because HMOs had the Republican majority in their pocket.

Third, the Democrats accentuated the differences on issue positions between the two parties. The Democratic leadership managed to unite the party caucus behind a clear-cut, partisan agenda called "Families First" and used it to educate the voters. The Democratic agenda included reforming Social Security and Medicare, providing prescription drug coverage for seniors, increasing funding for public education, passing a patients' bill of rights, implementing targeted tax cuts, tightening restrictions on sales of weapons at gun shows, and raising the minimum wage by one dollar an hour over two years.

Co-optation

As attractive and, perhaps, as necessary as developing a national message was for the Democrats, the strategy could not guarantee success because it was vulnerable to co-opting by the Republicans. That is, the issues were seldom so stark that the Republicans could not create an agenda that at least partially addressed the underlying concerns in a politically attractive way. In fact, the Republicans' ability to blunt Democratic issue advantages with action on several major issues may be the major story of the election.

The Republicans were keenly aware of the Democratic issue advantage on health care and Medicare. Public opinion surveys showed that the voters thought the Democrats would do a better job dealing with health care by a 51 percent to 38 percent margin and that Democrats would do better on Medicare by a 52 percent to 39 percent margin.[26] The Republicans desperately needed political cover to avoid appearing to be on the wrong side of the issues. Accordingly, a Republican pollster told the House Republican conference regarding Medicare prescription drug coverage that "passing some plan—any plan—was a 'political imperative' for the party. It is more important to communicate that you have a plan as it is to communicate what is in the plan.' "[27]

In June, the House narrowly passed a bill that would provide prescription drug benefits to Medicare recipients by encouraging private insurers to set up such plans. Under a veto threat by the president, the Senate failed to pass comparable legislation.[28] Nonetheless, 211 House Republicans could now claim they voted for Medicare prescription drug benefits.

Many Republican House incumbents also trumpeted their votes for *a* patient's bill of rights in their campaigns, a bill that relied on tax deductions to help people pay medical insurance premiums. They tended not to mention the fact that they voted against the far more comprehensive patient's bill of rights that enjoyed broader public support.[29]

Education was another issue candidates simply could not afford to ignore. And here again, it was the Republicans who narrowed the gap between the two parties. Congress increased federal funding for education by more than $12 billion in the last four years. That is a far cry from 1995, when House Republicans called for eliminating the department of education.[30] The disagreement between the parties was in details about state autonomy and other technical issues. "The fact is, the Republicans have gotten smarter about education, not in terms of their policies, but in the way they talk about them. So it's harder than it used to be to create big differences on education," Democratic pollster Mark Mellman told *Congressional Quarterly* in September 2000.

The Republican strategy of co-optation drove the Democrats crazy. The

Republicans were, as one Democratic consultant put it, "trying to reinvent themselves after a pretty solid record against these things, including a comprehensive patient's bill of rights and prescription drug benefit for Medicare."[31]

Frustrated House Democratic leader Gephardt called the Republican leaders "master illusionists" creating the impression of doing something about the rising costs of medicine.[32] It prompted President Clinton to question, "Only the Democrats want you to know what those differences are. What does that tell you about who you ought to vote for?"[33]

Local Factors

A second reason the national Democratic message strategy alone could not win back the House was that politically popular issues varied dramatically across districts. In order to maximize their chances, candidates in most competitive districts sought to tailor their campaigns to local conditions.

The Republicans were particularly intent on "localizing" elections. National Republican Congressional Committee (NRCC) chairman Thomas Davis (VA-11) thought the Republican effort to nationalize the election in 1998 was a huge mistake." The NRCC sponsored ads in the 1999–2000 cycle reflected the change of tactic: many campaign commercials associated Democratic candidates with efforts to raise *local* taxes. "The days of nationalized Congressional campaigns are over," an NRCC spokesperson told *Roll Call*.[34]

The Democrats clearly recognized that they could not run a one-size-fits-all national issues campaign and retake the House. "If we're going to win the House back, we have to win seats in conservative areas," said Minority Leader Gephardt. "There's no way to do it otherwise."[35] In order for the Democrats to win, they had to win in places such as Indiana's eighth and Missouri's second district, where Democratic candidates had to be pro-gun, pro-life and anti-spending even to be considered for office. There were "half a dozen pro-gun, antiabortion Democrats running this year in competitive House races and an equal number of candidates who supported at least one of those positions."[36] Democrats justified supporting candidates who seemed at odds with most of their core beliefs by arguing that the only vote that matters is the first vote taken in the 107th Congress, the vote that elects the Speaker of the House.

James Matheson in Salt Lake City provided a good example of locally tailoring national issues. Instead of emphasizing the national Democratic platform, Matheson's ads stuck to themes that resonated with Utah voters, such as paying down the debt and cutting estate taxes. Not surprisingly for a Democrat running in a Republican district, Matheson emphasized that "it is time to get beyond party politics" and hardly mentioned his partisan affiliation.

However, there are limits to a candidate's ability to localize elections. Even when Democrats ran on conservative platforms, they were vulnerable to being linked to the national party. Brian Roy in Kentucky's first district was a pro-life and pro-gun Democrat. His Republican opponent, incumbent Ed Whitfield, used images of Democratic incumbents Patrick Kennedy (RI-1), Rosa DeLauro (CT-3), Charles Rangel (NY-15), and Steven Rothman (NJ-9) to run against Roy. "Let's take a look at who's bankrolling his campaign. It's a who's who of national liberals who support early release of violent felons, more gun control laws, partial birth abortions—they even supported trial lawyers over Kentucky tobacco farmers," said Whitfield's ad, which finished with "You can tell a lot about a man by the company he keeps."[37]

Interplay of National and Local Issues

Often, the dynamics of races were determined by an interplay of national and local issues. The relevance of national issues largely depends on characteristics of the districts and the individuals running. For example, Colorado's sixth district was the site of the Columbine High School massacre. Not surprisingly, gun control was a particularly important issue there, with Democrat Kenneth Toltz attacking Republican incumbent Thomas Tancredo for cosponsoring "The Gun Manufacturers Protection Act" one week after the tragedy at Columbine.[38] In Florida's twenty-second district, Democrat Elaine Bloom was hit hard by Republican incumbent E. Clay Shaw's ads for her association with Fort Lauderdale-based drug manufacturer Andrx. The ads alleged that she helped the company accept $89 million from a competitor in exchange for not marketing a less expensive generic drug.[39] The controversy involved a particular local company, but Shaw took advantage of the voters' widespread distrust of the health care industry and frustration with the rising costs of drug to successfully fend off the strong challenge by Bloom.

The race in Pennsylvania's tenth district is another good example of how local issues often supersede national ones. Democrat Patrick Casey started the race by attacking Republican incumbent Donald Sherwood on national issues such as Social Security and prescription drugs. But Sherwood parried with ads that defended his positions, leaving Casey with little traction. By the end of the campaign, Democrats were reduced to running on extremely local issues, at one point accusing Sherwood of promoting the outbreak of the West Nile virus because mosquitoes were breeding in water standing in tires in a tire dump owned by Sherwood.[40]

Another example was the widely watched race in San Diego between Rogan and Schiff. The race caught people's attention because the incumbent, Rogan, had served as a prominent manager of the impeachment case against President Clinton. Impeachment itself was not a big issue in the campaign. However, "impeachment created a context in which it was easy for Schiff to portray Rogan as too conservative for the district," said Amy Walter of the *Cook Political Report*.[41] Because of impeachment, voters had a framework for believing that Rogan was in fact too conservative, as Schiff charged when he attacked Rogan's anti-abortion rights and pro-gun record. Local issues also mattered, though. One was an issue that seemed distant physically and historically: whether the United States should label the 1915 massacre of Armenians by the Ottoman Empire as genocide. The issue was far from obscure for the district's large Armenian community and both candidates worked the issue very hard. Rogan had produced a pledge from Speaker J. Dennis Hastert to include provisions favored by the Armenians in legislation, only to see the provisions scuttled when they produced a diplomatic outcry by the Turkish government. Schiff, in turn, had secured public money for a documentary on the massacre, a fact he made sure to publicize in the Armenian community.[42]

Did Democratic Messages Work?

Were the Democrats able to translate national issue advantages into votes? On the aggregate level, exit poll data suggests that most of the voters did perceive the difference between the two parties and voted accordingly. The voters for whom education, Social Security, or prescription drug benefits were the single most important issue facing the country—approximately 60 percent of all voters—voted for Democratic House candidates in their districts by 56 to 42 percent.[43]

The Democrats did not win on all issues, however. Republican presidential candidate Bush's emphasis on his across-the-board tax cut package made that issue quite prominent. As of September, the overwhelming majority of Americans (74 percent) were in favor of a cut in federal income taxes, though they were split on the issue of broad, across-the-board tax cuts versus targeted tax cuts.[44] In the end, 27 percent of the voters for whom a tax cut was the top priority voted overwhelmingly Republican (66 to 32 percent) in their choice of a House member, according to the exit polls. The Republicans also may have benefited from Bush's emphasis on education. In a June poll, Bush and Gore were rated roughly even on their abilities to deal with the problem of education, a historic shift away from the typical advantage Democrats have had on the issue.[45]

In the end, the Republicans were able to bring up their numbers enough to make sure that the Democrats would not be able to sweep the election. While approval of the way Congress was handling its job had fallen as low as 37 percent in September 1999, it rose to 49 percent just before the election.[46]

Campaign Strategies and Tactics

With candidates, money, and message usually in place by midsummer, the last weeks of the campaign are usually dominated by campaign tactics. One tactic that Democrats relied heavily on was turning out their core supporters—African Americans and union members. African Americans turned out in record numbers and voted overwhelmingly Democratic. People from union households also turned out at higher rates than in earlier elections. In 1996, they comprised 23 percent of the electorate, while in 2000 they comprised 26 percent.[47]

One issue that many candidates had to ponder was whether to link themselves to presidential candidate Al Gore or not. While Gore was strong in many districts, these districts tended not to have competitive races. In fact, the competitive races were in districts where Gore was weakest and the Democratic candidates who ran in them made sure that they were never linked to Gore in any way.

In fact, candidates sometimes linked themselves to presidential candidates of the opposite party in order to distance themselves from the national party. In Democratic-friendly Connecticut, Republican Mark Nielsen ran a TV ad presenting Democratic vice presidential candidate Joseph Lieberman in a favorable light (and contrasting him to Nielsen's Democratic opponent). This led Republican vice presidential candidate Richard Cheney to snub Nielsen by not shaking his hand or acknowledging him at a public appearance where they both were on stage. Cheney's snub probably did not hurt Nielsen with liberal Connecticut voters. Nielsen received a respectable 44 percent against 54 percent for Democratic incumbent James Maloney (D-CT-5).[48]

Another tactical decision campaigns have to make is whether to go negative or not. Most campaigns have some form of attacks—or, to use more polite language, contrast messages. This is especially true for challengers who have to convince voters to make a change. For example, Democratic challenger Michael Ross in Arkansas attacked incumbent Jay Dickey (R-AR-4) for being hostile to teachers, the working poor, and seniors. Dickey responded with ads that portrayed Ross as a captive of drug and insurance companies.[49]

Democrats had negative ads backfire in several cases. After Democrat Patrick Casey attacked Republican incumbent Donald Sherwood of Pennsylvania in an ad, Sherwood responded with a split screen ad that showed Casey's ad and audiences' negative reactions to it. The people in Sherwood's ad stated that Casey lied about Sherwood.[50] In other races, such dynamics helped Democrats. In the open seat in San Jose, California Republican James Cunneen sent out a mailer with Democratic candidate Michael Honda's face superimposed on jailhouse bars with the tagline "Mike Honda's criminal record." Honda has no criminal record, but was imprisoned by the U.S. government in a Japanese internment camp during World War II, making Cunneen's attacks seem especially cheap.

Analysis of Results

The final tally for the Democrats was a net pickup of two seats. They beat four Republican incumbents and picked up six open seats that had been held by Republicans. However, two Democratic incumbents were defeated and six open seats that had been held by Democrats were won by the Republicans.

In order to get a sense of the results from a recent historical perspective, we conducted some basic statistical analysis of congressional results from 1992 to 2000. In these years, the congressional districts were the same, facilitating comparison. We estimated a simple regression model in which the percentage received by the Democratic candidate was the dependent variable and incumbency and district-based presidential results from the most recent presidential election were the independent variables. All variables were statistically significant at conventional levels.[51]

The first thing we wished to assess was whether the Democratic issue advantages translated into a larger swing to the Democrats relative to other years. As we can see in Figure 8.1, this did not occur. The figure plots the baseline level of support predicted for a district with the national average level of support for Clinton in the most recent election. In 2000, this amount was 51 percent, an amount comparable to—although lower than—1998, 1996, and 1992. This amount was substantially higher than the 47 percent baseline for Democrats that occurred in their 1994 drubbing.

We also wished to address the power of incumbency. Figure 8.2 displays the advantage to the incumbent by party and by year for all congressional races. In general, the advantage is quite large, averaging over 10 percentage points for each party. In several years, the Democrats had a larger incum-

Figure 8.1 **National Trends—Baseline Support Levels in All House Districts**

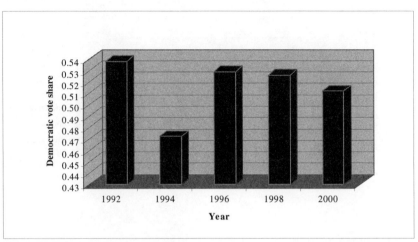

Source: Authors' analysis of CQ election data.

bency advantage, which was true in 2000 as well when Democratic incumbents had a 16 percentage point bump and Republican incumbents had only a 10-point bump. Interestingly, we could also isolate the results for House impeachment managers. While House managers of President Clinton's impeachment generally did quite well (with the prominent exception of Rogan in California), they did not run as far ahead of Republican non-incumbents as did other Republican incumbents. Specifically, the estimated incumbency advantage for them was half that of the rest of the Republicans.

Figure 8.2 includes all House races, which means that many noncompetitive races are in the mix and drive up the value of being an incumbent. Figure 8.3 displays the results for only competitive races, defined as races in which the Democratic candidate received between 40 and 60 percent of the two-party vote. In these races, the incumbency advantage is smaller in terms of percentage points, but still substantial. For example, in 2000, an incumbent Democrat could expect a 5.8 percentage point bump and an incumbent Republican could expect a 4.5 percentage point bump. Again, we see that House impeachment managers ran behind their Republican incumbent colleagues, with an incumbency advantage of around 2 percentage points. We also see that while the Democrats ran behind in incumbency advantage in 1992 and close in 1994, they have been clearly ahead since 1996, indicating reasonable success in protecting incumbents.

Figure 8.2   **Incumbency Advantage—All House Races**

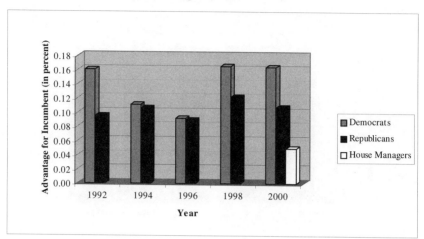

Source: Authors' analysis of CQ election data.

Figure 8.3   **Incumbency Advantage—Competitive House Races**

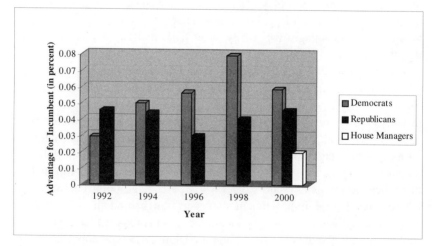

Source: Authors' analysis of CQ election data.

So what can we say about the Democrats' efforts in the 2000 elections? Several themes emerge. First, incumbency was a strong advantage in 2000. A total of nine incumbents lost in the general and primary elections, well below the postwar average of thirty-three. Not only did most incumbents win, but even most vulnerable incumbents won, as well. Democrats such as Rush Holt (NJ-12) and William Luther (MN-6) won, as did Republicans such as E. Clay Shaw (FL-22), Anne Northup (KY-3), and Donald Sherwood (PA-10). Few would have expected all of these individuals to win, yet they did, and their small margins of victory could easily be attributable to the resource advantages of incumbents.

Second, while congressional races have become famously individualistic in the postwar era, they became even more candidate-centered in this election. There is very little evidence that national trends decided the competitive seats. Instead, they were each fought based on the policies and personalities of the candidates in each race.

Third, money is not enough. Democratic fund-raisers repeatedly made their pitch to potential contributors that Democrats would be almost unstoppable if they could play on an even financial playing field. That was so because they had been able to pick up seats in 1996 and 1998 while being vastly outspent by the Republicans. In 2000, Democrats raised more than enough money and yet the results were pretty much the same as in the previous two elections. Many factors determine the outcome of an election and, clearly, money alone is not pivotal. The Democrats' discouragement led George Miller (D-CA-7) to label Michael Ross (D-AR-4), the party's lone pickup outside of California, as the "$90 million man" as that is almost all the Democrats had to show for their fund raising success.[52]

Fourth, the election did a remarkable job selecting the weak from the strong. Most incumbents who lost were either bad ideological fits—for example, Dickey in Arkansas and the three incumbent Republicans who lost in California—or were not considered hardworking representatives—for example, Cook in Utah and Matthew Martinez in California's thirty-first district. In short, in a time when the economy was doing well and crime was declining, voters made a change only when there was a clear reason.

Fifth, the election reflected a clearly divided electorate. The split is almost perfectly in half: Republicans received approximately 50.7 percent of the two-party vote for House candidates. The split also reflects clear cultural and geographic differences. Democrats run well in culturally liberal areas such as big cities and the West Coast. They have a much more difficult time in more rural, culturally conservative areas. The fact that a credible Democratic candidate such as former congressman Scott Baesler in Kentucky could only get 35 percent of the vote is a bad sign for Democrats. On the other hand, Democrats have shown their ability to win in California, even against relatively moderate Republicans.

Conclusion

In the end, the elections of 2000 were a disappointment for Democrats. Yes, they picked up two seats, building off gains in 1996 and 1998. But they expected more, possibly much more. Facing a good slate of open seats with almost unlimited cash and popular issues, the Democrats gained only two seats. "People were definitely terming it a failure," one Democratic aide told *Roll Call* to describe a postelection leadership meeting. The members demanded a "complete review" of what went wrong.[53] The lesson seems to be that there just was not enough political wind to sail the Democrats to victory. In the calm political environment of 2000, the Republicans' efforts to defend their seats stalled Democratic advantages in almost every area.

What does this all mean for the 107th Congress, the 2002 elections, and beyond? After the virtually tied presidential election and the seating of a very evenly divided Congress, players at both ends of Pennsylvania Avenue began to emphasize the need for bipartisanship.[54] The electoral implications of bipartisan cooperation were very much on the mind of Democrats. "The American people want this country and this president to succeed and as members of the loyal opposition, we have to make a good faith effort to work with Bush. If we don't, we won't be rewarded for it two years from now," said Senator Richard Durbin (D-IL).[55] One House Democratic leader observed, "the bottom line is that for the Democrats to win back the majority, we can't be perceived as an obstructionist party."[56]

The spirit of compromise and cooperation, however, may be short-lived. If recent years are any indication, the permanent nature of modern congressional campaigns will deeply color everything Congress does. As a midterm election, the 2002 elections will likely be a low-turnout affair whose results may depend on which party can do a better job of energizing its core partisans. The natural impulse of incumbents "may well be to position themselves closer to the ends of the spectrum, rather than the center, on the issues that most resonate with their core constituencies."[57]

The prospects for Democrats in 2002 are mixed. On the one hand, midterm elections tend to favor the party that does not hold the White House.[58] However, other structural factors do not favor Democrats. Right before the

2000 elections, the House Democrats were concerned that if they failed to capture the House, "the party will be beset by a rash of retirements that, coupled with the redrawing of congressional districts next year, will only increase the odds against their regaining the majority in 2002—and perhaps for some time to come."[59] In addition, the decennial reapportionment of House seats that will take effect in 2002 will shift seats away from the more Democratic Northeast and Midwest to the more Republican South and West. How exactly these factors will play out is not clear. What is certain is that the consequences will be with us for a very long time.

Notes

1. House Republican leaders did not play a prominent role at the Republican national convention, for example. Eric Pianin, "A Diminished Role for GOP's Hill Leaders," *Washington Post,* August 2, 2000: A23.

2. Gregory Giroux, "GOP Maintains Thin Edge," *Congressional Quarterly Weekly Report,* November 11, 2000: 2652–2654.

3. "CQ's House Race Ranking Update." *Congressional Quarterly Weekly Report,* September 23, 2000: 2186.

4. Paul Rolly and Joann Jacobsen-Wells, "Cook Battling IRS—With Taxpayer Cash," *Salt Lake Tribune,* April 3, 2000: B1.

5. Rachel Van Dongen, "Promises, Promises: Two Members Tested After Abandoning Term-Limit Pledges," *Roll Call,* September 18, 2000: 15, 22.

6. Paul Rolly and Joann Jacobsen-Wells, "Does Merrill Believe in Love Thine Enemies?" *Salt Lake Tribune,* January 11, 1999: B1.

7. Richard Morin and Claudia Deane, "Public Against Impeachment, but Clinton Support Has Limits," *Washington Post,* December 15, 1998: A1, A19.

8. Richard Morin and David S. Broder, "Poll: GOP Leads on Foreign Policy, Trails on Domestic Issues," *Washington Post,* March 17, 1999: A1, A15.

9. Ibid.

10. The White House, transcript. *Remarks by the President at Reception for Congressman Richard A. Gephardt.* July 27, 2000: p. 2.

11. Gary Jacobson, *The Politics of Congressional Elections,* 4th ed. (New York: Longman), 28, 1997.

12. Based on telephone interviews with 193 likely Nader voters who were asked, "Who would be your second choice for president or would you not vote at all?" Forty-three percent said they would be voting for Gore, 21 percent for Bush, and 21 percent said they would not be voting at all. The Gallup Organization, "Nader Voter Second Choices," November 2, 2000, <http://www.gallup.com/poll/releases/pr001102c.asp>.

13. Susan Crabtree, "Democrats Mull Whether Nader Will Help Take Back House," *Roll Call,* November 2, 2000: 8.

14. Matthew Vita, "Make-or-Break Quest Is Driving Gephardt," *Washington Post,* October 24, 2000: A1, A8, A9.

15. Interview, Noah Mamet, National Finance Director, Democratic Congressional Campaign Committee, December 15, 2000.

16. Peter Wallston, "Rogan's Run: The GOP Fights for a Crucial Swing District." *Congressional Quarterly Weekly Report,* June 10, 2000: 1366–1370.

17. Express advocacy ads use explicit language that advocates the election or defeat of specific candidates. Issue advocacy ads do not.

18. *Campaign Media Analysis Group,* November 2000, 1 (8): 42.

19. Annenberg Public Policy Center of the University of Pennsylvania, "Issue Advertising in the 1999–2000 Election Cycle," February 1, 2001, www.appcpen.org.

20. *Campaign Media Analysis Group,* Nov. 2000, vol. 1, issue 8, p. 43.

21. Ibid.

22. Federal Election Commission. "Congressional Financial Activity Soars for 2000." January 9, 2001: 49.

23. Remarks by President Clinton. The White House transcript. *Remarks by the President, Senator Tom Daschle and Congressman Dick Gephardt at Democratic Agenda Event.* July 27, 2000: 1.

24. Remarks by House Minority Leader Gephardt. The White House transcript. *Remarks by the President, Senator Tom Daschle and Congressman Dick Gephardt at Democratic Agenda Event.* July 27, 2000: p. 5.

25. Ibid., p. 6.

26. Richard Morin and David S. Broder. "The Big Issues: A Health Care Muddle: Voters Agree Only That It's Top Issue," *Washington Post,* July 28, 2000: A17.

27. Mary Agnes Carey. "Insurers' Queasiness About Costs Helped Sink GOP Prescription Drug Bill," *Congressional Quarterly Weekly Report,* October 28, 2000: 2520.

28. Adam Clymer and Lizette Alvarez. "With Minimal Fanfare, Congress Calls It Quits," *New York Times,* December 17, 2000: 36.

29. Howard Kurtz, "Some GOP Hopefuls Echo Democrats on Health Care," *Washington Post,* July 29, Adam: A7.

30. David Nather, "School of Hard Knocks," *Congressional Quarterly Weekly Report,* September 23, 2000: 2190–2192.

31. Kurtz, "Some GOP Hopefuls Echo Democrats."

32. Vita, "Make-or-Break Quest," A8.

33. *Remarks by the President at Reception,* 3.

34. Ethan Wallison and Rachel Van Dongen, "GOP Takes Ad Fight to DCCC," *Roll Call* September 18, 2000: 1, 26.

35. Juliet Eilperin, "Democrats Diversify in Bid for House," *Washington Post,* October 16, 2000: A1, A8.

36. Ibid., A1.

37. Ibid., A8.

38. Charles Cook, *Cook Political Report,* December 20, 1999: 18.

39. John Mercurio, "Shaw's Ads Leave Challenger Reeling," *Roll Call,* October 26, 2000: 1, 19.

40. Interview, Amy Walter, January 8, 2001.

41. Ibid.

42. Peter Wallston, "Rogan's Run: The GOP Fights For a Crucial Swing District," *Congressional Quarterly Weekly Report,* June 10, 2000: 1366–1370.

43. Calculated by authors from Voter News Service exit poll data. These data are available on most news network Web sites such as <http://www.cnn.com/ELECTION/2000/epolls/US/P000.html>.

44. Gallup Organization, "Americans Split on Issue of Targeted Versus Across-the-Board Income Tax Cuts," September 18, 2000, <http://www.gallup.com/poll/releases/pr000918.asp>.

45. Dan Balz and Richard Morin, "Education Voters Pose a Tough Test: Poll Shows Gore, Bush Face a Conflicted Group," *Washington Post,* June 30, 2000: A1.

46. Based on a survey of national adults. "Do you approve or disapprove of the way Congress is handling its job?" Gallup Organization, 2001. "Poll Trends: Congress Job Approval," January 14, 2001, <http://www.gallup.com/poll/trends/ptjobapp_cong.asp>.

47. Celinda Lake, "Issue Kleptomania," *Campaigns and Elections*, December–January 2001: 81–82.

48. David Herszenhorn, "Connecticut Congressman Gets Help of President in Close Race," *New York Times*, September 12, 2000: B6.

49. *Campaign Media Analysis Group*, Nov 2000 vol. 1, issue 8, p. 41.

50. Ibid.

51. Details are available from the authors upon request.

52. Ethan Wallison, "House Democrats Look for Answers," *Roll Call*, January 25, 2001: 21.

53. Ibid.

54. Following the postelection death of Rep. Julian Dixon (D-CA-32), the 107th Congress opened with 222 Republicans, 210 Democrats, 2 independents, and 1 vacancy. The last time there was such a close party ratio was 1953–1955, when there were 221 Republicans and 213 Democrats.

55. Lizette Alvarez, "On Capitol Hill, Feelings of Finality and Disappointment and Sighs of Relief," *New York Times*, December 14, 2001: A21.

56. Rep. Cal Dooley (D. CA-20) quoted in Wallison, "House Democrats Look for Answers," 21.

57. Susan Benkelman, "Victorious Candidates Face Hard Choices in Governing," *Congressional Quarterly Weekly Report*, January 13, 2001: 98–99.

58. The president's party lost House seats in every midterm election in the postwar era except 1998.

59. Vita, "Make-or-Break Quest," A1.

Bibliography

Annenberg Public Policy Center of the University of Pennsylvania. "Issue Advertising in the 1999–2000 Election Cycle." February 1, 2001, <www.appcpen.org>.

Alvarez, Lizette. "On Capitol Hill, Feelings of Finality and Disappointment and Sighs of Relief." *New York Times*, December 14, 2001: A21.

Balz, Dan, and Richard Morin. "Education Voters Pose a Tough Test: Poll Shows Gore, Bush Face a Conflicted Group." *Washington Post*, June 30, 2000: A1, A22, A23.

Benenson, Bob. "Proudly Worn Party Label Missing in Key Contests." *Congressional Quarterly Weekly Report*, September 23, 2000: 2182–2185.

Benkelman, Susan. "Victorious Candidates Face Hard Choices in Governing." *Congressional Quarterly Weekly Report*, January 13, 2001: 98–99.

Campaign Media Analysis Group, November 2000 1 (8): 36–45.

Carey, Mary Agnes. "Insurers' Queasiness About Costs Helped Sink GOP Prescription Drug Bill." *Congressional Quarterly Weekly Report*, October 28, 2000: 2520.

Clymer, Adam. "The Democrats: the Battle for Congress: White One Isn't Only House the Democrats Have Eye On." *New York Times*, August 16, 2000: A27.

Clymer, Adam, and Lizette Alvarez. "With Minimal Fanfare, Congress Calls It Quits." *New York Times*, December 17, 2000: 36.

Cook, Charles. *Cook Political Report*, December 20, 1999: 18.

"CQ's House Race Ranking Update." *Congressional Quarterly Weekly Report*. September 23, 2000: 2186.

Crabtree, Susan. "Democrats Mull Whether Nader Will Help Take Back House." *Roll Call,* November 2, 2000: 8.

Eilperin, Juliet. "Democrats Diversify in Bid for House." *Washington Post,* October 16, 2000: A1, A8.

Federal Election Commission. "Congressional Financial Activity Soars for 2000." January 9, 2001.

Gallup Organization. "Nader Voter Second Choices." November 2, 2000. <http://www.gallup.com/poll/releases/pr001102c.asp>.

———. "Americans Split on Issue of Targeted Versus Across-the-Board Income Tax Cuts." September 18, 2000. <http://www.gallup.com/poll/releases/pr000918.asp>.

———. "Poll Trends: Congress Job Approval," January 14, 2001. <http://www.gallup.com/poll/trends/ptjobapp_cong.asp>.

Giroux, Gregory. "GOP Maintains Thin Edge." *Congressional Quarterly Weekly Report,* November 11, 2000: 2652–2654.

Herszenhorn, David. "Connecticut Congressman Gets Help of President in Close Race." *New York Times,* September 12, 2000: B6.

Jacobson, Gary. *The Politics of Congressional Elections.* 4th ed. New York: Longman, 1997.

Kurtz, Howard. "Some GOP Hopefuls Echo Democrats On Health Care." *Washington Post,* July 29, 2000: A7.

Lake, Celinda. "Issue Kleptomania." *Campaigns and Elections,* December–January 2001: 81–82.

Mercurio, John. "Shaw's Ads Leave Challenger Reeling." *Roll Call,* October 26, 2000: 1,19.

Morin, Richard, and Claudia Deane. "Public Against Impeachment, but Clinton Support Has Limits." *Washington Post,* December 15, 1998: A1, A19.

Morin, Richard, and David S. Broder. "Poll: GOP Leads on Foreign Policy, Trails on Domestic Issues." *Washington Post,* March 17, 1999: A1, A5.

———. "The Big Issues: A Health Care Muddle: Voters Agree Only That It's Top Issue." *Washington Post,* July 28, 2000: A1, A17.

Nather, David. "School of Hard Knocks." *Congressional Quarterly Weekly Report,* September 23, 2000: 2190–2192.

Pianin, Eric. "A Diminished Role for GOP's Hill Leaders." *Washington Post,* August 3, 2000: A23.

"Remarks by the President, Senator Tom Daschle and Congressman Dick Gephardt at Democratic Agenda Event." The White House transcript issued by Office of the Press Secretary, July 27, 2000.

"Remarks by the President at Reception for Congressman Richard A. Gephardt." The White House transcript issued by Office of the Press Secretary, July 27, 2000.

Rolly, Paul, and Joann Jacobsen-Wells. "Does Merrill Believe in Love Thine Enemies?" *Salt Lake Tribune,* January 11, 1999: B1.

———. "Cook Battling IRS—With Taxpayer Cash." *Salt Lake Tribune,* April 3, 2000: B1.

Taylor, Andrew. "Symbolism and Stalemate Closing Out 106th Congress." *Congressional Quarterly Weekly Report,* October 28, 2000: 2518–2523.

Van Dongen, Rachel. "Promises, Promises: Two Members Tested After Abandoning Term-Limit Pledges." *Roll Call,* September 18, 2000: 15, 22.

Vita, Matthew. "Make-or-Break Quest Is Driving Gephardt." *Washington Post,* October 24, 2000: A1, A8, A9.

Voter News Service. National Presidential Exit Polls, 2000. <http://www.cnn.com/ELECTION/2000/epolls/US/P000.html>.

Wallison, Ethan. "House Democrats Look for Answers." *Roll Call,* January 25, 2001: 1, 21.

Wallison, Ethan, and Rachel Van Dongen. "GOP Takes Ad Fight to DCCC." *Roll Call,* September 18, 2000: 1, 26.

Wallston, Peter. "Rogan's Run: The GOP Fights For a Crucial Swing District." *Congressional Quarterly Weekly Report,* June 10, 2000: 1366–1370.

9

The Real "Survivors" of 2000
The House Republican Majority

G. Patrick Lynch and Hayden Milberg

Introduction

Washington is a town where political predictions and punditry are more popular than even the hometown Redskins. Most of the talk around town for the year leading up to election night was that the Democrats had a very good chance to take control of the House of Representatives and retain the White House. Most political observers believed that the Republican House leadership could not recover from the bruising it took in 1998 and that the nation's strong economy would send Al Gore to the White House. But the conventional wisdom also held that the Democrats had a very slim chance to gain parity in the Senate, much less a majority. Of course Al Gore lost, the Republicans retained the House, and the Democrats almost won control of the Senate. So much for the conventional wisdom.

In this chapter we will take a look at how the Republicans in the House pulled off perhaps the most overlooked upset of election night 2000, retaining their majority—albeit narrowly. We will do this by reviewing the events between the 1998 midterms and the 2000 election that helped to shape the electoral landscape for the House GOP. Next we'll discuss some of the structural constraints the GOP leadership faced during the campaign. Finally, we will draw on a series of interviews with prominent Republican staffers and strategists who helped to shape the image and signature issues for Republican House members running in 2000.

As we shall see, the Republicans in the House made a conscious effort to learn from their mistakes in the 1998 campaign. However, they also tried to change their public image from a party of firebrands to one that was "doing the people's work."[1] But before we can understand the wholesale changes the Republicans made to prepare for the 2000 election, we must first revisit the 1998 midterm elections.

The Disastrous 1998 House Elections and Their Political Aftermath

The 1998 House midterms were, in a word, awful for the GOP. Normally, the president's party loses seats in midterm House elections, and with a Democrat in the White House, the Republicans should have gained seats in that election. In addition, President Clinton was saddled with the Monica Lewinsky scandal leading up to the 1998 campaign. Theoretically, the Republicans were in a great position to strengthen their majority in both houses of Congress. The last time a scandal-ridden second-term president had faced a midterm election—President Nixon in 1974—the Republican party lost forty-eight seats. However, breaking almost seventy years of historical precedence in 1998, the Democrats picked up seats, narrowing the Republican majority. Why did this happen?

There is probably one overriding reason why the Republicans lost seats. The House's impeachment proceedings against President Clinton were widely unpopular among independent and Democratic voters. Moreover, most Americans viewed the House leadership, in particular then Speaker Newt Gingrich, as confrontational and largely ineffective in dealing with major legislative issues. A CNN/Gallup poll immediately following the midterm elections showed that 62 percent of Americans disapproved of the GOP's handling of the Clinton investigation, and 54 percent disapproved of the job that the Congress was doing.[2] In contrast, President Clinton's approval rating, even as he was being investigated for perjury, was 66 percent.[3]

Many analysts felt that the Republican House leadership, most notably Speaker Gingrich, had not effectively capitalized on its majority. The GOP had only a few major legislative victories, most notably the welfare reform legislation of 1996, and more than a few embarrassing losses, such as being blamed by the public for the government shutdown of 1995. The belief that Gingrich, who had helped to catapult the GOP into the majority in 1994 with a style that some analysts referred to as "bomb throwing," might not be suited to lead the House as Speaker was gaining strength in Republican circles.[4]

Gingrich had proven to be a polarizing figure. By and large, the public did not care for him, and his very conspicuous and confrontational leadership style had alienated members of both parties in the House. Faced with an embarrassing defeat in the 1998 midterms and growing discontent among House Republicans, Gingrich stepped down from the Speakership after the election. Initially, his resignation did little to stop the public relations bleeding.

The GOP first turned to a widely respected Republican leader, Robert Livingston (R-LA), as the new Speaker, but his candidacy was derailed when Livingston admitted to having had extramarital affairs. In the wake of the Clinton impeachment proceedings, this issue made it impossible for him to lead the House effectively. Livingston retracted his candidacy and resigned from the House six months later. Faced with yet another public relations nightmare, the Republicans decided to make a most unlikely and, in retrospect, very wise choice, Dennis Hastert (R-IL).

An "affable and respected Illinois Republican known for his relaxed style and low profile," Hastert quickly gained the support of Republican moderates who were looking for a less prominent and confrontational leadership style and conservatives who respected his voting record.[5] Although Hastert had a reputation as a competent and well-liked legislator, he was virtually unknown to the press and the public. Viewed as honest, a family man, and someone who would shun the spotlight that Gingrich had so clearly loved during his Speakership, Hastert represented a conscious break from the Gingrich era.

The new Speaker faced numerous challenges both within his own party and from across the aisle as his term began in 1999. House Democrats had narrowed the Republican majority to just five seats, a number that grew to six when Virgil Goode (I-VA) joined the Republican caucus in 1999. Governing with a six-seat majority is exceedingly difficult, particularly in the light of the Democrats' incentive to block Republican efforts to pass major pieces of legislation in order to make the case for change in 2000. Would Hastert be able to keep the Republicans together? How would he position the party for the approaching 2000 elections?[6]

When the Republicans took over Congress in 1994, they had laid out a brashly conservative political agenda, based in large part on the "Contract with America." Included in the contract was a proposal to eliminate the Department of Education. In 1999, chastened by their losses in the midterm elections, Speaker Hastert and Senate Majority Leader Trent Lott issued a statement at the beginning of the session that they agreed to work with Democrats to improve education.[7] The Speaker also softened the partisan rhetoric that characterized the Gingrich era. "I will meet you halfway, maybe more so on occasion. But cooperation is a two-way street," he said.[8] The problem was that Hastert's rhetoric didn't always match the actions of the House leadership. The GOP budget bill that reached the floor in March 1999 contained tax cuts and increases in defense spending. During debates over gun control, the Speaker held firm in his support of the right to bear arms. He also opposed a Democratic-sponsored patient's bill of rights that eventually passed the House.

Hastert's solid conservative voting record, and the fact that he was not as easy a target for Democrats as Gingrich, incurred Democratic complaints that the Speaker really had no interest in cooperating with them on legislation. This perception was reinforced by the persistence of hard feelings over the Clinton impeachment. Even Minority Leader Richard Gephardt (D-MO) maintained a frosty relationship with Hastert. In fact, they rarely communicated. The Democrats remained suspicious and hostile.

Although the Congress was still badly divided along partisan lines, the public perception of the Republican Congress improved. By August 2000, polls showed that more than half of the public approved of Congress, a dramatic increase over the previous year.[9] Moreover, Republican representatives were praising Hastert's low-key style as a refreshing change from Gingrich. Hastert's success and the rising popularity of the House unified the Republicans as they headed into the late summer and fall campaign season.

The Money Challenge for the 2000 Elections

Despite the improvements in the Republicans' public image, the political landscape still favored the Democrats' winning control of the House. The *Congressional Quarterly* gave the edge in vulnerable seats to the Democrats in 2000 as did Stuart Rothenberg, a noted Capitol Hill observer of congressional campaigns. Rothenberg projected a very close race for control of the House, but he gave the early edge to the Democrats.[10]

Why all the pessimism about the Republicans' chances? In his research on congressional elections, political scientist Paul Herrnson argues that successful candidates must win two campaigns if they want to win a seat in the House. The first campaign is for resources. Candidates must get money and help from their parties and contributors in order to run competitive races. The second campaign is for votes. In this campaign, candidates must have issues, or records, that will help them convince voters to choose them come Election Day.[11]

The parties must help their candidates win both of these campaigns. The parties must raise money, and they must provide the candidates with winning issues, although neither guarantees victory. The candidates themselves are also an important factor, as are local district issues. National conditions can also affect House races, as can incumbency and the presidential and vice presidential nominees.

Normally, the majority party in Congress has a sizable advantage in campaign fund-raising. Interest groups, which need to get access to politicians during the legislating process, give to those in power. Second, and just as importantly, incumbent House members rarely lose elections when they decide to run for reelection. That means that giving money to incumbents in the majority is likely to get an interest group more bang for the buck than giving to either candidates in the minority or to challengers. Together, these factors should have put the GOP in great position financially for the 2000 campaign, but they did not.

The perception that the Democrats might win control of the House prompted a number of business groups to give significant soft-money contributions to the Democrats in order to hedge their bets. In addition, the Democratic Congressional Campaign Committee (DCCC), under the leadership of its new chairman, Patrick J. Kennedy (D-RI), aggressively pursued large donors by exploiting the "celebrity" fund-raising prowess of President Clinton. As the National Republican Congressional Committee (NRCC) chair, Thomas M. Davis III (R-VA), noted derisively about the president, "(a)ll he does is raise soft-money."[12] When comparing the relative costs of the Republican Party having to raise soft-money through direct mail versus the Democrats using Clinton, Davis complained, "it costs us 50 cents per mailing. They raise money by bringing Bill Clinton into a room."[13] DCCC chairman Kennedy was also able to parlay his status as a member of the Kennedy clan to bring in cash for the Democrats. The result was a very competitive money race between the parties, much more so than in past elections.[14]

Nonetheless, the Republicans did well. The NRCC raised more than $90 million by July, compared to $60.2 million for the Democratic Party.[15] However, the Republicans spent far more than the Democrats by the summer and actually had less cash on hand going into the fall. Of the $90 million it had raised, the NRCC had spent $68 million, while the DCCC had spent only $22.8 million of the $60.2 million it had raised.

The differential in spending raised questions about the GOP's campaign strategy, but this early spending did bear fruit. For example, the Republicans spent aggressively against Rep. Michael P. Forbes (D-NY), who had switched to the Democratic Party. Forbes eventually lost his race. They also spent heavily in the state and local races that they hoped would help them control the redistricting process in 2001 and were successful there as well.[16]

In contrast, Democrats waited until the fall to spend heavily. They did provide some support to various House members in tight races, but on a much more limited basis than did the Republicans. Apparently some Democrats were concerned about last-minute ad blitzes against Democratic incumbents from Republican issue-oriented nonprofits, known as 527s. Holding money in reserve was an effective strategy against such an attack. Of course, all of this money raised by the parties was only part of the picture during the 2000 race. Numerous other groups, such as organized labor, business groups, environmental groups, and trial lawyers, spent millions of dollars on issue ads and get-out-the-vote efforts in House and Senate races throughout the nation. All of this money coming from sources outside the two parties made it very difficult to determine if the Democratic Party's success in fund-raising would translate into a real advantage in November.

Dealing with the Political Endgame

The second challenge the House Republicans faced in 2000 was political. At the end of each fiscal year, the government has to pass appropriations bills to fund its operations for the next year. Since the Republicans had regained the House in 1994, President Clinton had consistently managed to win those year-end budget battles decisively. His most notable victory was in 1995, when the stalemate between Clinton and the GOP forced a shutdown of the government. Clinton effectively swayed public opinion against the Republicans by blaming them for the shutdown. Eventually the Republicans relented on virtually all of their demands, giving Clinton a huge political boost going into the 1996 race and the Republican Congress a large black eye going into the 1998 elections.

Republicans were faced with the same endgame in 2000, but there were additional complications. Since the 2000 campaign promised to be close, many incumbent Republicans were anxious to get out of Washington quickly so they could return to their districts and campaign. Furthermore, large federal surpluses seemed to give the political advantage to the Democrats, who favored spending money on popular programs like education. House Republicans, as the summer began, had little stomach for another public relations disaster at the hands of the president. In July 2000, many observers were expecting the GOP to surrender early rather than risk another defeat by Clinton. But the political landscape had changed by the time the Republican convention was held during the summer of 2000. The GOP was unified behind Speaker Hastert in the House. Republicans also knew that Vice President Gore was not going to have coattails to carry Democrats in close districts. But their own polling showed that Governor Bush was not going to have coattails either. As one of our interviewees noted, "We knew we were on our own."[17] Furthermore, in 1998 the Republicans had conceded a lot to President Clinton in the final budget in order to get out of Washington and back to their districts to campaign. They were not going to do it again.

As a result, the Republicans were far more sensitive to their legislative record in 2000 than they were in 1998. The Republicans decided to send the president bills they knew he would not sign in order to give their candidates some issue cover. In this way, the GOP leadership tried to win the issue campaign that Herrnson argues is important in any congressional race. Instead of sending President Clinton a budget with increased spending for his priorities, the Republicans sent him a wave of relatively popular tax cuts that the GOP wanted but knew he would never sign. By forcing President Clinton to veto bills that overturned the estate tax and marriage penalty, the Republicans believed that they had an issue that would appeal to moderate, middle-class voters.[18] They wanted to run against Clinton's policy, not simply his personality.

The GOP's Strategy for 2000

Not only did the Republicans take a different legislative track as they approached the 2000 elections, but they also undertook much more extensive and well-coordinated fund-raising and public relations efforts.

The increase of money in the political arena and the ability of national parties to divert resources to competitive races quickly and efficiently were evident in the 2000 campaign. Even at the most local level, there was an element of national strategy at work. Just as national political leaders such as Hastert and J. C. Watts would travel to the sites of competitive races to provide support to candidates, so did national party fund-raisers. Both the GOP and Democratic Party focused their legislative and monetary resources on a select number of congressional districts in order to produce the desired majorities to control both the House and Senate.

Traditionally, Republican Party fund-raisers have been much more successful than their Democratic counterparts. The GOP often raises three times as much in hard-money donations. However, during the 2000 cycle, the DCCC aggressively pursued traditional and nontraditional donations and outperformed previous fund-raising records. The strength of fund-raising on both sides ensured that each party would have enough resources to communicate with the voters and its core constituencies.

Both political parties were able to use local organizations for fund-raising and political activities when necessary, thereby providing a legal means by which the national parties could increase the amount of money devoted to individual races without violating the statutory limits. For example, according to the Center for Responsive Politics, the Republican Party transferred $43.5 million to parties in the four most competitive states (Florida, Missouri, Michigan, and Pennsylvania) last year.[19]

While the Democratic Party was initially competitive overall with business and other interest groups, its fund-raising efforts foundered as donors realized that the House would likely not flip control. As a result, Republican fund-raisers were able to make a strong case to business and like-minded issue and ideological groups to donate exclusively to the GOP. Furthermore, as attention shifted from competitive races in the House to the Senate, so did the money. Table 9.1 indicates the total amounts the political parties raised and spent in the 1999–2000 election cycle.

Ron Bonjean, former communications director for the House Republican Committee, coordinated the media-oriented themes for the Republican House. Republican polling showed that three issues were far and away the most important to voters in 2000: educational improvement, prescription drugs, and debt reduction. George W. Bush ran on the first two issues; the Republican House ran on the third in conjunction with tax cuts. Throughout the fall, the House leadership decided to emphasize tax relief and debt reduction as a way to use efficiently the growing budget surpluses. Initially, the Democrats pushed debt reduction as their principal issue, but when polls indicated that the GOP had inoculated itself against attacks on the debt, the Democrats switched to prescription drugs. Nonetheless, the Republicans stayed focused on debt reduction.

The Republican House leadership created a media team of about thirty people to press its issue agenda and respond to Democratic attacks. The group met every morning and some afternoons. They studied news coverage, analyzed what issues were working in different regions, and planned responses to Democratic messages. This group also coordinated Republican appearances on talk radio and television, columns in op-ed sections of major newspapers, and Special Orders, one-minute speeches on the floor of the House. In addition to keeping their members focused on campaign themes, the Republicans were also helped by external events such as the attack on the U.S.S. *Cole,* flare-ups in violence in the Middle East, and the crash of the Concorde, which drew attention from Democratic attempts to regain the policy initiative.

Table 9.1

Financing the 2000 Congressional Elections

	Total	Hard money	Soft money
Democratic Party			
Raised:	$513,059,203	$269,934,401	$243,124,802
Spent:	$485,378,245	$253,376,597	$232,001,648
Cash on hand:	$51,872,873	$37,815,764	$14,057,109
Republican Party			
Raised:	$691,804,099	$447,363,945	$244,440,154
Spent:	$644,020,285	$406,566,378	$237,453,907
Cash on hand:	$46,158,676	$36,340,661	$9,818,015

Source: Federal Election Commission, "Party Fundraising Escalates," January 12, 2001.

Although the GOP mounted a national public relations campaign, the party's congressional campaign committee made its funding and strategy decisions on a seat-by-seat basis. Out of necessity, the committee spent a lot of its resources on district-level campaigns. Satellite feeds were used to allow candidates to communicate with their districts while Congress was in session. Regional media training workshops, held in Las Vegas, Pittsburgh, New York City, and Chicago, focused on issues and strategies unique to those areas. The NRCC also had eight regional representatives operating at the grassroots level. Despite the size of its effort, the NRCC tried to maintain a low profile, fearful that voters would resent Washington consultants getting involved in their district elections.

The Results

After the dust settled, little had changed in the partisan composition of the House. The Republicans had cause to celebrate although the GOP held the slimmest margin in the House since 1952, a 221 to 212 majority. The large Voter News Service exit polls revealed that each party held its core supporters.[20]

Three factors allowed the Republicans to hold onto their majority. First, they did a good job winning in districts where they had incumbents stepping down due to retirement. Second, they also picked up a number of seats that incumbent Democrats had left, thereby offsetting other Republican losses. Finally, Republicans successfully defended a number of their most vulnerable incumbents. The Democrats won only four of these marginal Republican seats, three in California. However, they were unable to oust a number of sitting Republican House members elsewhere, especially in the Midwest, who had been singled out by observers as facing tough races.

The election, however, was hardly a ringing endorsement of the GOP. It was one of the closest House elections in recent memory, with at least five races decided by fewer than 2,000 votes. Although the electorate did not provide a mandate to the Republicans, it did enable them to survive.

In the long run, this election may have been the one that helped to seal the Republican majority for the near future. Observers in both parties believe that the Democrats now may face a large number of potential retirements from among their ranks in the wake of their failure to win the majority. Democratic retirements would mean more open seats and therefore more opportunities for the GOP to increase its majority.

What may prove to be another future advantage for the Republicans is that they strengthened their position in many state legislatures, thereby putting their candidates in a better position to survive the redistricting that follows the decennial census. In short, the Republicans not only withstood the Democratic challenge of 2000, but positioned themselves well to withstand future challenges in that legislative body.

Notes

1. Anonymous interview.
2. Keating Holland, "Poll: More Americans Disapprove of Congress," November 16, 1998, <http:www.cnn.com.ALLPOLITICS/stories/1998/11/16/impeach.poll/index.htm>.
3. Ibid.
4. Dan Carney, Karen Foerstel, and Andrew Taylor, "A New Start for the House," *Congressional Quarterly*, December 22, 1998: 3333.
5. Ibid.
6. It is worth noting that Hastert was not the only new member of the House Republican leadership chosen after the 1998 elections. One of the most prominent leadership changes involved Representative J. C. Watts of Oklahoma. Watts is widely

considered a rising star in the GOP. He's a former college football star who is telegenic and hardworking. He's also African American, and after the 1998 elections Republicans were acutely aware of their problems attracting minority votes. Watts ran for the conference chairman's position and won. This gave the House Republicans a new and, hopefully for them, friendlier public face as they looked ahead to the 106th Congress.

7. "GOP Leaders Pledge to Work with Democrats on Key Issues," February 21, 1999, <http:www.cnn.com/ALLPOLITICS/stories/1999/02/21/gop.letter/index.html>.

8. "New Speaker Calls for End to Partisan Stalemate," January 6, 1999, <http:www.cnn.com/ALLPOLITICS/stories/1999/01/06/newcongress/index.html>.

9. John Patterson, "A Leader in Background at GOP Convention," August 1, 2000, <http://www.cnn.com/2000/LOCAL/westcentral/08/01/ahd.hastert/index.html>.

10. Stuart Rothenberg, "A Battle for the House: GOP Has the Lion's Share of Vulnerability," *Roll Call*, May 15, 2000, <http:www.rollcall.com/pages/columns/rothenberg/00roth0515.html>.

11. Paul S. Herrnson, *Congressional Elections: Campaigning at Home and in Washington* (Washington, DC: Congressional Quarterly, 1995), 2.

12. Karen Forestel and Derek Willis, "DCCC Rakes In New Money as Business Hedges Its Bets," *Congressional Quarterly*, July 15, 2000: 1709.

13. Ibid.

14. During the 1997–1998 election cycle, business associations and corporations contributed 63 percent of their donations to the NRCC and only 37percent to the DCCC. By July 2000, those same groups had given slightly more than 50 percent of their contributions to Democrats. In particular, high-tech firms were significant contributors to the DCCC during the 2000 cycle. Microsoft, which gave the DCCC only $20,000 in the 1997–1998 cycle, gave the Democrats $130,000 during the 1999–2000 cycle. Telecommunications companies such as AT&T, Bell Atlantic (now Verizon), and BellSouth also dramatically increased their soft-money contributions to the DCCC. (Ibid., 1708).

15. Ibid., 1712.

16. Ibid., 1710.

17. Interview with anonymous Republican staffer, January 2001.

18. In July, the Republicans had proposed nine different tax cuts including elimination of the so-called marriage penalty, the estate tax, and the limit on income earned by Social Security recipients. They also pushed for increases in the amount that individuals could contribute to tax-free retirement accounts and that parents could set aside in pretax dollars for their children's education. See Lori Nitschke, "Divide-and-Conquer Tax Cuts: GOP Sees Strategy Paying Off," *Congressional Quarterly*, July 22, 2000: 1783. Interestingly, the Republicans decided to use "real people" to illustrate their positions on those tax cuts. They brought married couples to their press conference announcing their marriage penalty bill and ranchers and farmers to their events on the estate tax, which they dubbed "the death tax." Interview with Ron Bonejan, communications director for the house Republican Conference, December 14, 2000.

In 1998 and 1999, the Republicans had been unable to make their appeals for tax reduction work, but after President Clinton vetoed a large tax cut in 1999, the House leadership regrouped and decided to send him the popular reductions one by one. The political landscape in 2000 made this strategy more effective. The continued economic growth made voters more interested in tax reduction, particularly since the government surplus had grown to record levels. But the Republicans themselves had also changed some important parts of the bill.

19. Center for Responsive Politics, "Soft Money," <http://www.opensecrets.org>.

20. Each major party received 49 percent of the congressional vote with the remaining two percent going to minority party candidates. Voter News Survey, Exit Poll, November 7, 2000.

IV

Legacies

IV

Legacies

10

Women in the 107th Congress
The Past Meets the Future

Sue Thomas, Courtenay Daum, and Beth Stark

"Everyone else is here because of their win; I'm here because of my loss."
—*Missouri Senator-elect Jean Carnahan, appointed to fill the seat*
her husband won posthumously

"For too long, the powerful special interests have controlled the agenda in our nation's capital, ignoring the people's interest while serving their own narrow interest. That's why I'm spending more of my time talking to the citizens of Washington state than going to Washington, D.C., to solicit campaign contributions."
—*Washington Senator-elect Maria Cantwell, responding to criticism*
of her self-funded, $10 million campaign

"Sixty-two counties, sixteen months, three debates, two opponents and six black pantsuits later, because of you, we are here."
—*New York Senator-elect Hillary Rodham Clinton in her victory speech*

The congressional elections of 2000 were an illuminating microcosm of the historical and current circumstances of women who seek and win federal legislative office. Jean Carnahan entered the Senate after the tragic preelection death of her husband and son in a plane crash. Mel Carnahan had been running for Senate in Missouri and, after the election, which he won, the Missouri governor appointed Mrs. Carnahan to the seat. This is a familiar scenario since, historically, the bulk of the women who have entered Congress did so as widows of successful politicians.

At the other extreme, Maria Cantwell, a successful businessperson, a self-made multimillionaire, a former member of the Washington state legislature, and a former member of the United States House of Representatives, beat a long-term incumbent to win her Senate seat. In a race that eerily reflected the early stages of the presidential recount, Senator Cantwell won her seat narrowly after a recount by presenting a picture of a woman who created her political career in much the same way that successful male politicians have done. She illustrates the modern trend of women in politics whose careers are of their own making.

And, in the middle, is Senator and former First Lady, Hillary Rodham Clinton. A new chapter in U.S. political history has been written in which a wife of a president runs for office on her own and wins. While women may get their start in politics with a family connection, it is clear that women can fashion their own political careers in ways that are new and creative. And, of course, men in politics have long used connections or a famous name to "go into the family business." Whether it is the dramatic illustration of Robert Kennedy being named attorney general in his brother's administration, or sons of former presidents running for the same office and winning, family connections have long been important in politics. Senator Clinton has given them a new twist—one that is deeply evocative of women's experience as helpmates.

The 2000 Results

Women Winners

A record number of women serve in the United States Senate in the 107th Congress. Thirteen women (ten Democrats and three Republicans) serve in the Senate. Four newcomers—Maria Cantwell (D-WA), Hillary Rodham Clinton (D-NY), Jean Carnahan (D-MO), and Debbie Stabenow (D-MI)— join three reelected incumbents—Dianne Feinstein (D-CA), Kay Bailey Hutchison (R-TX), and Olympia Snowe (R-ME)—and six incumbents who were not running this cycle.

Similarly, the 2000 elections brought more women than ever to the U.S. House of Representatives. Fifty-nine women (41 Democrats and 18 Republicans) and two nonvoting delegates (from the District of Columbia and the Virgin Islands) sit in the 107th Congress. All fifty-two incumbents who ran for reelection won as did seven newcomers—Hilda Solis (D-CA), Betty McCollum (D-MN), Susan Davis (D-CA), Jane Harman (D-CA), Melissa Hart (R-PA), Shelley Moore Capito (R-WV), and JoAnn Davis (R-VA). See Table 10.1 for historical comparisons that show women's incremental gains as well as the fairly significant jump that women achieved this elec-

Table 10.1

Number of Women in Congress Historically

Congress	Years	Senate	House	Total in Congress
101st	1989–91	2	29	31
102nd	1991–93	4	28	32
103rd	1993–95	7	47	54
104th	1995–97	9	48	57
105th	1997–99	9	54	63
106th	1999–01	9	56	65
107th	2001–03	13	59	72

Source: Center for American Women and Politics, Eagleton Institute, Rutgers University, Fact Sheet, December 2000.

toral cycle. In all, 13 percent of Congress is composed of women in 2001—the highest level ever.

More women of color also serve in the 107th Congress than ever before. Of the twenty-one women of color in the House, fifteen are African Americans (including two nonvoting delegates), six are Latinas, and one is an Asian American. No women of color currently serve in the U.S. Senate.

The postelection selection of congressional leaders also shows women's gradual increase in impact. In the 107th Congress, the House contains four women in leadership positions. The Republican Conference vice chairman is Deborah Price (OH) and the conference secretary is Barbara Cubin (WY). The Congressional Black Caucus is headed by Eddie Bernice Johnson (D-TX) and the head of the Democratic Congressional Campaign Committee is Nita Lowey (NY). In the Senate, Kay Bailey Hutchison (TX) is the Republican Conference secretary. For the Democrats, Barbara Milkulski (MD) is the conference secretary and Patty Murray (WA) is the Democratic Senatorial Campaign Committee chair. The fact that the heads of the Democratic fund-raising operations for the House and Senate (the DCCC and the DSCC) are women suggests that women have demonstrated their ability to raise money as effectively as their male colleagues. The sources of this expertise are discussed later in the chapter. There are, however, no women committee chairs in the House of Representatives.

As noted earlier in this book, our national political leaders have interesting and daunting challenges ahead: The House is Republican controlled and the Senate Democrats have only a slim one-seat advantage; further, many congressional races were competitive ones, and no overriding national themes emerged to suggest a widespread mandate. The women who take on these leadership posts both within their parties and their chambers will, therefore, have to prove their skills in a somewhat uncertain political environment.

Women Candidates

Candidates for the U.S. Congress and those who recruit them carefully plan all dimensions of their races—timing, fund raising, media strategy, public appearances, and message. Over the course of the last decade, the women who ran for these high offices became increasingly successful in each of these dimensions.

Table 10.2 illustrates the number of women who ran for the House and Senate in 2000 and how many prevailed at each stage of the process. Interesting additional data show that women's campaigns set some records this electoral season as well. The three Republican women who won open seats in the House—Hart (PA), Capito (WV), and Davis (VA)—are the first Republican women ever elected to serve in Congress from their respective states. In addition, a new record for the number of women winning House primaries—122—was set in 2000. The previous record was set in 1998 when 121 women won primaries.

In the Senate, all six nominees prevailed—a better record than in 1992, the heralded Year of the Woman. Additionally, three states, California, Maine, and Washington, are now each represented entirely by women in the Senate, and ten states now have female senators: Arkansas, Arizona, California, Louisiana, Maine, Maryland, Michigan, Missouri, New York, Texas, and Washington.

As Table 10.2 reflects, in the House, 168 women ran, 122 won primaries, and 59 won in the general election. Of those now on Capitol Hill, 5 women won open seats, 2 challengers were victorious, and the vast bulk of women in the House are returning incumbents. Also, as is typical in legislative races, most of the women who ran were challengers and most of those lost (52 of the 63 who lost were challengers). Comparing this year to previous years reveals that the record for the number of women filing to run in races for the House of Representatives was set in 1996, when 217 ran. Also, this year, there were 11 woman-versus-woman races—although the record for this sort of competition was set in 1998, when 13 woman-versus-woman races were fought.

Tables 10.2 and 10.3 also show that the year 2000 was a banner year for women in the Senate compared to previous years. Fourteen women ran in 2000, 6 won primaries, and all 6 won their general election contest. The previous record of 9 women in the Senate is surpassed by the 13 who took their seats in 2001. The record for the number of women

Table 10.2

Number of Women Candidates 2000

	House	Senate
Total women running	168	14
Open seats	38	1
Challenger	78	10
Incumbent	52	3
Number winning primaries	122	6
Open seats	16	1
Challenger	54	2
Incumbent	52	3
Number winning general	59	6
Open seats	5	1
Challenger	2	2
Incumbent	52	3

Source: Center for American Women and Politics, Eagleton
Institute, Rutgers University, Fact Sheet, December 2000.

filing to run for the Senate is still from the Year of the Woman in 1992,
when 29 women filed to run and 11 won their primaries. As Table 10.3
shows, the 2000 election cycle featured the highest percentage of victorious
women candidates in both houses for the last ten years.

The 87 Percent Club—Why Are Women Still Underrepresented?

Our discussion so far illuminates women's historic successes in achieving
increased federal-level representation. But, as Table 10.3 illustrates, despite
these gains, women are still vastly underrepresented in Congress compared
to their proportion of the population. Why is this the case? In the past, it
was not uncommon for women candidates to face discrimination by party
elites, fund-raising difficulties, and bias by the media and voters. While
these barriers are not obliterated, they have diminished greatly.[1] When
women choose to run, they have an even chance of winning their races.

A case in point from this election cycle is the victory of Hilda Solis,
Democrat of California, who defeated a longtime incumbent in her primary.
In a personal interview on December 4, 2000, Solis said enthusiastically
that it was definitely "advantageous" to be a woman running for office in
her district. She said that women candidates do well in her district, and
many candidates for office are Latinas. "I think it is an indication that the
community has matured, that it senses that women have the needed talent

Table 10.3

Women Candidates and Winners Over the Decade

		Senate candidates	Winners	Percent who won	House candidates	Winners	Percent who won
2000	Total	6	6	100	122	59	48
	Incumbents	3	3		52	52	
	Challengers	2	2		54	2	
	Open seats	1	1		16	5	
1998	Total	10	4	40	121	56	46
	Incumbents	4	3		50	50	
	Challengers	4	0		54	0	
	Open seats	2	1		17	6	
1996	Total	9	2	22	120	51	42.5
	Incumbents	0	0		41	40	
	Challengers	3	0		65	6	
	Open seats	6	2		14	5	
1994	Total	9	3	33	112	47	42
	Incumbents	2	2		44	36	
	Challengers	5	0		52	3	
	Open seats	2	1		16	8	
1992	Total	11	5	45	106	47	44
	Incumbents	1	1		26	23	
	Challengers	7	1		41	2	
	Open seats	3	3		39	22	
1990	Total	8	1	12.5	69	28	41
	Incumbents	1	1		24	24	
	Challengers	6	0		37	1	
	Open seats	1	0		8	3	

Source: Center for American Women and Politics, Eagleton Institute, Rutgers University, Fact Sheet, December 2000.

and ability, and that they are risk takers. My record of experience [in the state legislature] proved that women have what it takes."[2]

In fact, women candidates are enjoying unprecedented party support. June Gold, who ran unsuccessfully in Connecticut, says party officials literally "chased her down" in their search for qualified women candidates.[3] Melissa Hart, running in Pennsylvania, and Shelley Moore Capito, running in West Virginia, were among a group of only eleven nonincumbents to receive over $100,000 worth of support from the Republican Party. The party focused on these candidates and their competitive races. Majority Leader Dick Armey called Hart's race the most important in the country for his party's strategy to maintain control of the House.

But women are still only a small portion of members of Congress for other reasons—most importantly, they are candidates far less often than men. One reason this is the case is the historical success rate of incumbents and the high proportion of officeholders who seek reelection each term. The results of the incumbency advantage mean that any newcomer group to politics has a hard time breaking in.[4] This is certainly more true for national office than state or local, but it is a serious concern at all levels, and the incremental gain by women in Congress is in fair measure a reflection of this reality.

What political scientists call the social eligibility pool (SEP) is another reason why fewer women run for office. The SEP concerns expectations citizens have about the backgrounds of those who are quality candidates. These expectations include certain occupational backgrounds, military service, educational accomplishments, type and number of previous electoral experiences, and the like. Although there has been much progress, women today are still less likely than men to come to office from legal careers, for example, and are more likely to have entered politics from community volunteerism or women's groups. Hence, women may be viewed by others and by themselves as less viable candidates. The ripple effect of such judgments is that women may have fewer political contacts, less access to power structures, and less access to traditional fund-raising opportunities. While the effects of the social eligibility pool have lessened over time and comparable opportunities have opened up elsewhere (such as women's PACs, discussed below), the remaining effects mean that women have greater or different hurdles to overcome.[5]

Maria Cantwell, the first businesswoman candidate to finance her own Senate campaign, expressed her sense that her background was not a common one for political women. "[I] can go to the United States Senate and say, 'I do have business experience. I do understand the Internet economy.' If a woman can stand up and say that, I think it would be unique."[6] In fact, Cantwell is the only high-tech executive, male or female, currently in the Senate.

Because of their differing backgrounds and credentials, women see themselves as viable candidates for public office less often than men do. The very socialization that impels fewer women to seek out careers in corporate business positions or law firms results in their lower levels of confidence about becoming candidates for political office.[7] One reason why potential women candidates exhibit reluctance to run may be related to media treatment of those who do. Studies of media treatment of women and men on the campaign trail show that women, especially those running for high-level offices such as the U.S. Senate, receive less coverage than men, and when they are covered, it is in a negative fashion. Emphasis is placed on low probabilities of success rather than on issues or candidate appeals. Further, the press is more likely to cover the policy priorities of men than women and more likely to highlight the personality and physical traits of women.[8]

Examples of differential attention to women candidates come from Joe Solmonese, chief of staff at EMILY's List, who noted that a number of newspaper articles on Hillary Rodham Clinton remarked on how tired she looked, whether or not she should "get her eyes done," and how often she wore her "brown pantsuit with her pink shirt." Another candidate, Mary-anne Connelly, was consistently portrayed by her opponent as "silly, scatterbrained" and not strong enough to stand up to others on issues. He ran commercials with actresses portraying Connelly as a "ditz."[9] Women also face questions from the press about their families in a way that does not often affect men. Joe Solmonese noted, "Members of the media ask women questions like 'What does your husband do?' 'What are you going to do with your kids when traveling?' They ask questions that they would not ask male candidates."[10]

Shelley Moore Capito, Republican of West Virginia, faced this sort of press inquiry during her 2000 House race. The *Charleston Daily Mail* ran a front-page feature on "Mr. Mom" Charlie Capito. According to the article, he "is preparing to take care of the home front while she commutes to Washington," which included taking his 15-year-old daughter shopping for a homecoming dress. Never fear, the paper assured its readers: "Despite the demands of the campaign, Representative Capito carved out time to attend important events for her son and daughter [during the campaign]. She attended all of Moore's (her son) high school football games, except for a playoff game . . . during that game, her husband gave her a play-by-play over a cellular phone."[11]

Family questions are in part a reflection of women candidates' and office-holders' life experiences as compared to men's. Recent research suggests that despite women's high profile and time-consuming careers as politicians, they are still the ones who have primary responsibility for home life, including child care and house maintenance.[12] This reality may suppress women's ambitions to seek congressional careers, given the all-consuming nature of the commitment.

Electoral structures may also contribute to low proportions of women in office. Political science research indicates that women have more success in multimember districts than single-member districts, and congressional races are, of course, single-member districts.[13] Theories about why women are more successful in multimember districts suggest that when voters can make several ballot choices rather than one, they are likely to want to balance and diversify those choices.

Overall, when women run, they win. When women mount serious campaigns, they find they connect with voters and have something important to bring to national politics. "I have three children and years of dedication to their education, sports, schools," says Capito, "that gave me an ease in discussing children, family, and health issues. I was able to convey a closer, in-touch kind of feeling to voters. It was clear that I understood what families and children are going through on a personal level."[14] But to make a major dent in the remaining 87 percent of Congress that is still a male bastion, more women have to run.

Gender Gap in Voting

One aspect of women's campaigns for elected office that gets much media attention is the gender gap in voting for political candidates. This gap first appeared in the 1980 election of Ronald Reagan as president and was in clear evidence in the year 2000 as well. Women voters have tended, more than men, to respond to the generally more liberal tendencies of women candidates, especially women of the Democratic Party, who focus especially on issues of education, health care, the economy, and social security.

Women voters' preferences for moderate to liberal views of the above-mentioned issues were evident in Senate races. There were sizable gender gaps in three of the six Senate races in which women were candidates. Women voters favored Hillary Clinton over Rick Lazio by 60 percent to 39 percent, whereas men split their votes equally, 49 percent for each. Fifty-four percent of women favored Debbie Stabenow and Maria Cantwell; 54 percent of men supported their opponents. This means that women voters provided the margin of victory for Clinton, Cantwell, and Stabenow. Of the three incumbents who ran and were reelected, one race evidenced a gender gap. A fourteen-point gap appeared for Dianne Feinstein (although a majority of women, 65 percent, and a majority of men, 54 percent, voted for her). The two Republican Senate incumbents who were reelected, Olympia Snowe and Kay Bailey Hutchison, showed a different pattern. Equal proportions of women and men voted for Snowe, but Hutchison garnered 68 percent of men's votes and 63 percent of women's.

As Table 10.4 indicates, in generally similar proportions to earlier years in the decade, a nine-percentage-point gender gap was evident in races for the U.S. House of Representatives. Nationally, 53 percent of women voted for the Democratic congressional candidate in their district whereas 44

Table 10.4

Gender Gap in the U.S. House During the Decade, 1990–2000*

	Voters (in percent)	
	Women	Men
1990	52	48
1992	55	52
1994	54	43
1996	53	44
2000	53	44

* Percent supporting the Democratic candidates.
Source: Center for American Women and Politics, Eagleton Institute, Rutgers University, Fact Sheet, December 2000.

percent of men voted similarly. Thus, a majority of women voted for Democratic House candidates while a majority of men voted for Republicans.

Campaign Finance

Earlier in this chapter, we spoke about women's ability to raise campaign funds successfully. The 2000 electoral cycle illustrates the continuation of women's prowess in fund raising. The Federal Election Commission reports that six women were among the top fifty Senate fund raisers and three were in the top ten. Clinton, Feinstein, and Cantwell were numbers three, five, and nine respectively. Stabenow, Hutchison, and Snowe were numbers twelve, thirty-one, and forty-two. Each of these six was a winner: three incumbents, two challengers, and one candidate running for an open seat.

Fourteen women vying for seats in the House were among the top fifty fund raisers. Of these, eight women won (six incumbents and two challengers) and six lost (two challengers and four candidates for open seats):

Anne Northrup (R-KY-9)	Won
Elaine Bloom (D-FL-18)	Lost
Heather Wilson (R-NM-22)	Won
Shelley Berkley (D-NV-24)	Won
Carolyn McCarthy (D-NY-30)	Won
Loretta Sanchez (D-CA-31)	Won
Dianne Byrum (D-MI-34)	Lost
Maryanne Connelly (D-NJ-41)	Lost

Nita Lowey (D-NY-42)	Won
Susan Davis (D-CA-44)	Won
Nancy Keenan (D-MT-46)	Lost
Susan Bass Levin (D-NJ-48)	Lost
Jane Harman (D-CA-49)	Won
Lauren Beth Gash (D-IL-50)	Lost

Maria Cantwell financed most of her campaign and, as a result, was able to eschew all PAC contributions. She spent more than $10 million of her own money, prompting *USA Today* to write that her campaign "represents a milestone of sorts in the quest of female politicians for true gender equality. She is the first self-funded female candidate who is lavishing her own money, not an inheritance or a husband's riches, on a campaign for major office. The Senate has more than its share of self-made millionaires, but they are all men."[15] Shelley Moore Capito, who raised more than $1.3 million for her House race, advises that women candidates should no longer be viewed as timid in the fund-raising arena. "You have to be aggressive," however, in order to keep up.[16]

Women incumbents outraised their male challengers in all but one race—in Maryland's eighth district, where Terry Lierman raised $1,036,917 more than incumbent Connie Morella. Morella kept her seat nevertheless.

Women only outraised their male opponents in open seat races in four out of thirteen contests (not including Hilda Solis). Only two of those four were able to win (JoAnn Davis, R-VA-1, and Melissa Hart, R-PA-4). One woman who was greatly outraised by her opponent was able to win—Jim Humphrey raised $5,661,263 more than Shelley Moore Capito (R-WV-2). Capito enjoyed considerable party support, including independent expenditures, that helped her to win despite being outspent.

Women challengers raised more money than their incumbent male opponents in only four out of thirty-seven races. Of those four, only Susan Davis (D-CA-49) was able to turn her fund-raising success into victory.

As Table 10.6 suggests, women candidates for Congress now raise and spend as much or more than male candidates. They are competitive in the primaries and general elections as well as in open seat, incumbent, and challenger contests.[17] Part of the reason this is true is that fund raising specifically for women has become an important presence on the political scene.

According to the Center for American Women and Politics, the most recent count in 1999 indicates that there were forty-six Political Action Committees (PACs) and donor networks dedicated to raising money for

Table 10.5

House Campaign Finance in 2000*

All House races
Total receipts for Campaign 2000

	Number	Receipts (in dollars)
House	1,362	539,092,695
Democrats	418	266,633,096
Incumbents	207	167,736,795
Challengers	179	65,298,379
Open seats	32	33,597,922
Republicans	401	267,012,982
Incumbents	196	185,255,051
Challengers	173	419,000,266
Open seats	32	39,857,665

	Average for all House candidates (in dollars)
All:	651,582.51
Incumbents	875,910.29
Democrats	810,322.68
Republicans	945,178.83
Challengers	304,541.61
Democrats	364,795.41
Republicans	242,198.07
Open seats	1,147,743.55
Democrats	1,049,935.06
Republicans	1,245,552.03

Total receipts for women (in dollars)		Average receipts for women (in dollars)	
All:	86,372,197	All:	751,062.58
Incumbents	44,425,247	Incumbents	854,331.67
Democrats	28,026,376	Democrats	737,536.21
Republicans	16,398,871	Republicans	1,171,347.93
Challengers	21,641,231	Challengers	460,451.72
Democrats	18,104,622	Democrats	624,297.31
Republicans	3,536,609	Republicans	196,478.28
Open seats	20,305,719	Open seats	1,269,107.44*
Democrats	14,839,538	Democrats	1,349,048.91*
Republicans	5,466,181	Republicans	1,093,236.20

Races in which a woman ran against a man or had no opponent (races in which a woman ran against another woman are excluded)

Average receipts	Average receipts	Difference in average receipts
Incumbent women	Incumbent men	Incumbent women vs. Incumbent men
$780,122.53	$1,002,753.11	$-222,630.57
Challenger women	Challenger men	Challenger women vs. Challenger men
$468,645.16	$401,188.36	$67,456.80
Open seat women	Open seat men	Open women vs. Open men
$1,304,866.14	$1,939,786.54	$-634,920.40

* Includes Hilda Solis, CA-31, who beat incumbent in primary and ran unopposed in general election.

** All House figures do not include the following candidates for lack of Federal Election Commission data. The Center for American Women and Politics reports these women as candidates, but Federal Election Commission has no record for them: Bailey, KY-5; Rogilio, LA-6; Boyd-Fields, MI-15; Henry, NY-8; Brown, NY-10; Cahill, NV-2; Kerin, VT-AL; Christian-Christensen, VI-AL.

Source: Federal Election Commission Web site, <www.fec.gov.>.

Table 10.6

Senate Campaign Finance in 2000

All Senate races
Total receipts

	Number	Receipts (in dollars)
Senate	156	369,188,885
Democrats	34	203,406,485
Incumbents	11	43,409,572
Challengers	18	54,815,350
Open seats	5	105,181,563
Republicans	34	163,310,579
Incumbents	18	84,878,033
Challengers	11	18,611,981
Open seats	5	59,820,565

Total receipts women (in dollars)	Average receipts women (in dollars)
All 76,637,121	12,772,853
Incumbent	
Democrats (Feinstein only)	10,324,844
Republicans (Snowe, Hutchison)	5,625,568
Challengers	
Democrats (Stabenow, Cantwell)	19,169,037
Republicans (none)	
Open seats	
Democrats (Clinton only)	41,517,672
Republicans (none)	

Source: Federal Election Commission Web site, <www.fec.gov.>

female candidates and consisting of a nearly exclusively female donor base. Of these forty-six organizations, ten are national donor networks or PACs and thirty-six are state or locally based. The national organizations include EMILY's List, WISH List, National Organization for Women (NOW) PAC, National Women's Political Caucus (NWPC) PAC, the Susan B. Anthony List (dedicated to electing pro-life women to Congress), and the Women's Campaign Fund (dedicated to electing pro-choice women to local, state, and federal office).

Donor networks have been key organizations behind the financial support of women's candidacies for Congress. The earliest and most successful PAC for women candidates is EMILY's List, which stands for Early Money Is Like Yeast. EMILY's List was created in 1985 as a donor network to elect pro-choice Democratic women to national office by making women candidates as competitive in fund raising as their male counterparts. Since its inception, EMILY's List has become the largest financial network for women candidates. Its 60,000 members raised $9.2 million for candidates in the 2000 cycle. It was the biggest PAC in the nation in terms of money raised.

EMILY's List endorsed five Democratic women for the Senate in 2000 and solicited funds for four of them; all were victorious. One of them, Debbie Stabenow of Michigan, noted, "When I announced my candidacy, there weren't a lot of people who believed I could defeat the incumbent Republican Senator, Spencer Abraham. . . . After months of solid support from EMILY's List and EMILY's List members across the country, I surged ahead and won a seat in the U.S. Senate for pro-choice Democratic women."[18]

EMILY's List endorsed fifty Democratic women for the House and solicited funds for sixteen of them. Forty of these candidates won. Of the forty who won, thirty-six were incumbents, two were challengers (Davis and Harmon, both of California), and two were running for open seats (Hilda Solis of California and McCollum of Minnesota). Solis also benefited from staff and technical support from EMILY's List and the endorsements of many other women's groups. "They are always players in my campaigns. I know the importance of having them on your team," said Solis.[19]

EMILY'S List has become the model for other networks for women candidates. During the 1992 election cycle, for example, WISH List (Women in the Senate and the House), which funds pro-choice Republican women, was created. Since inception, WISH List has provided more than $2 million in direct contributions to its endorsed candidates. WISH inaugurated a campaign in this election cycle called the 200 for 2000 Campaign to recruit and elect more Republican pro-choice women candidates for state and national office. The campaign was successful and WISH endorsed candidates in forty states. WISH List endorsed two women for the Senate— both incumbents—Kay Bailey Hutchison and Olympia Snowe, and both won their races handily. Twenty women were endorsed for the House and ten of them won—nine incumbents and one open seat contender. Shelley Moore Capito's victory in West Virginia is WISH List's biggest success story for this election cycle.

With women's PACs working to make sure that women candidates raise as much or more than similarly situated men, today's female congressional candidates have the ability to stage well-funded professional efforts to gain seats and increase their influence in the national legislature. The effect of early and consistent money on women's candidacies bodes well for women's future efforts to break the glass ceiling.

Conclusion

Why Do We Want Women in Congress?

The implicit question about the topic of women's gains in Congress is why we write about this at all. The answer is multilayered and starts with the principle of democratic legitimacy. A government that is democratically organized cannot be truly legitimate and stable, enjoying a reasonable degree of trust from its citizenry, if all its citizens do not have the opportunity and potential interest to serve their community and nation.

It is important for women to be members of Congress for symbolic reasons as well. If children grow up seeing women and men as political leaders, each sex will be likely to choose from the full array of options when deciding to shape adult lives. The women elected today are role models for future generations of members of Congress.

Making Congress open to the widest range of potential officeholders insures increased competition for office, thereby increasing the talent pool of candidates and making room for a full array of ideas and perspectives. And political science research of the last quarter century suggests that women's and men's differing life experiences and society's ongoing division of labor can translate into distinctive perspectives in the larger legislative arena, from the construction of legislative solutions to the nation's problems, to bill passage, to policy priorities, to influence at each stage of the bill passage process, to leadership styles.[20] It is important, then, that women inhabit Congress so that the concerns with which they are generally more familiar than men make their way squarely onto policy agendas.

Women's Congressional Future

Women in Congress have made incremental but appreciable gains in the last decade, and the future suggests that this pattern will continue. While women still face obstacles, including the general strength of incumbents, the difficulties of managing the intersection of their personal and political lives and the social eligibility pool, there are reasons to be optimistic about increasing the number of women in Congress.

One very good reason is that in the 2002 electoral cycle, there will be a number of open seats due to redistricting. Every ten years, after the census, when population shifts get reflected in legislative apportionment, opportunities are available for those who wish to vie for congressional seats. Indeed, the much-heralded Year of the Woman, which occurred in 1992 after the last redistricting, created opportunities for women to seek open seats—the best chance of newcomers to be victorious—and they won in historic proportions. Ambitious politicians seek out and prepare for those once-every-ten-year opportunities created by the redrawing of lines, the shuffling of incumbents, and the creation of new seats. It is likely that 2002 will usher in another new era for women in office, especially in the U.S. Congress. The states of California, Nevada, Arizona, Colorado, Texas, Georgia, North Carolina, and Florida will all gain seats in the U.S. House, thereby creating opportunities for women to vie for seats in which no incumbent has the upper hand. And the 2002 elections should continue the pattern of increasing numbers of women who arrive in Congress having pursued political careers of their own.

Notes

1. See Elizabeth Adell Cook, Sue Thomas, and Clyde Wilcox, *The Year of the Woman: Myths and Realities;* R. Darcy, Susan Welch, and Janet Clark, *Women, Elections, and Representation;* Susan J. Carroll, *Women as Candidates in American Politics;* Sue Thomas and Clyde Wilcox, *Women and Elective Office: Past, Present, and Future.*
2. Personal interview with Hilda Solis, December 4, 2000.
3. Personal interview with June Gold, November 19, 2000.
4. See Darcy, Welch, and Clark, *Women, Elections, and Representation;* Carroll, *Women as Candidates in American Politics;* Gary Jacobson, *The Politics of Congressional Elections.*
5. See Darcy, Welch, and Clark, *Women, Elections, and Representation;* Richard Logan Fox, *Gender Dynamics in Congressional Elections.*
6. Walter Shapiro, "She Is Start-up Millionaire, But Cantwell Is No Upstart."
7. National Women's Political Caucus, *Why Don't More Women Run?*
8. Kim Fridkin Kahn, *The Political Consequences of Being a Woman: How Stereotypes Influence the Conduct and Consequences of Political Campaigns.*
9. Personal interview with Joseph Solmonese, December 1, 2000.
10. Ibid.
11. Jim Wallace, "Mr. Capito Becoming Mr. Mom: Wife's New Role Will Often Keep Her in DC."
12. Sue Thomas, "Legislative Careers: The Personal and the Political."
13. See Darcy, Welch, and Clark, *Women, Elections, and Representation;* Richard E. Matland, "District Magnitude's Effect on Female Representation in U.S. State Legislatures"; Wilma Rule and Joseph Zimmerman, *The United States Electoral Systems: Their Impact on Women and Minorities*; Susan Welch and Donley Studlar, "Multimember Districts and the Representation of Women."
14. Personal interview with Shelley Moore Capito, December 6, 2000.
15. Shapiro, "She Is Start-Up Millionaire."
16. Ibid.
17. Barbara Burrell, *A Woman's Place Is in the House.*
18. Letter to donors from Debbie Stabenow, January 2001.
19. Personal interview with Hilda Solis, December 4, 2000.
20. See Barbara Boxer and Nicole Boxer, *Strangers in the Senate: Politics and the New Revolution of Women in America;* Diane D. Blair and Jeanie R. Stanley, "Gender

Differences in Legislative Effectiveness: The Impact of the Legislative Environment";
Debra L. Dodson, *Gender and Policymaking: Studies of Women in Office;* Debra L.
Dodson and Susan J. Carroll, *Reshaping the Agenda: Women in State Legislatures;*
Michelle A. Saint-Germain, "Does Their Difference Make a Difference? The Impact of
Women on Public Policy in the Arizona Legislature"; Sue Thomas, *How Women
Legislate.*

Bibliography

Blair, Diane D., and Jeanie R. Stanley. "Gender Differences in Legislative Effectiveness:
The Impact of the Legislative Environment." In *Gender and Policymaking: Studies
of Women in Office,* ed. Debra L. Dodson. New Brunswick, NJ: Center for American
Women and Politics, 1991.

Boxer, Barbara, with Nicole Boxer. *Strangers in the Senate: Politics and the New
Revolution of Women in America.* Washington, DC: National Press Books, 1994.

Burrell, Barbara. *A Woman's Place Is in the House: Campaigning for Congress in the
Feminist Era.* Ann Arbor: University of Michigan Press, 1994.

Carroll, Susan J. *Women as Candidates in American Politics.* 2nd ed. Bloomington:
University of Indiana Press, 1994.

Center for the American Woman and Politics. *Fact Sheet: Women in the U.S. Congress,*
2000.

Clark, Janet. "Women at the National Level: An Update on Roll Call Voting Behavior."
In *Women and Elective Office: Past, Present, and Future,* ed. Sue Thomas and Clyde
Wilcox. New York: Oxford University Press, 1998.

Cook, Elizabeth Adell, Sue Thomas, and Clyde Wilcox, eds. *The Year of the Woman:
Myths and Realities.* Boulder, CO: Westview, 1994.

Darcy, R., Susan Welch, and Janet Clark. *Women, Elections, and Representation.* New
York: Longman, 1987.

Dodson, Debra L., ed. *Gender and Policymaking: Studies of Women in Office.* New
Brunswick, NJ: Center for American Women and Politics, 1991.

Dodson, Debra L., and Susan J. Carroll. *Reshaping the Agenda: Women in State Legislatures.* New Brunswick, NJ: Center for American Women and Politics, 1991.

Dolan, Kathleen, and Lynne E. Ford. "Are All Women State Legislators Alike?" In
Women and Elective Office: Past, Present, and Future, ed. Sue Thomas and Clyde
Wilcox. New York: Oxford University Press, 1998.

Duerst-Lahti, Georgia. "The Bottleneck: Women Becoming Candidates." In *Women and
Elective Office: Past, Present, and Future,* ed. Sue Thomas and Clyde Wilcox. New
York: Oxford University Press, 1998.

Duke, Lois Lovelace, ed. *Women in Politics: Outsiders or Insiders?* 2nd ed. Upper
Saddle River, NJ: Prentice Hall, 1996.

Fox, Richard Logan. *Gender Dynamics in Congressional Elections.* Thousand Oaks,
CA: Sage, 1997.

Friedman, Sally. "Committee Advancement of Women and Blacks in Congress: A Test
of the Responsible Legislator Thesis." *Women & Politics* 13 (1993): 27–52.

Gehlen, Freida. "Women Members of Congress: A Distinctive Role." In *A Portrait of
Marginality: The Political Behavior of the American Woman,* ed. Marianne Githens
and Jewell Prestage. New York: McKay, 1977.

Gertzog, Irwin, N. *Congressional Women: Their Recruitment, Treatment, and Behavior.*
2nd ed. Westport, CT: Praeger, 1995.

Jacobson, Gary. *The Politics of Congressional Elections,* 3rd ed. Boulder, CO: Westview, 1993.

Kahn, Kim Fridkin. *The Political Consequences of Being a Woman: How Stereotypes Influence the Conduct and Consequences of Political Campaigns.* New York: Columbia University Press, 1996.

Kathlene, Lyn. "Power and Influence in State Legislative Policy Making: The Interaction of Gender and Position in Committee Hearing Debates." *American Political Science Review* 88 (1994): 560–576.

———. "Alternative Views of Crime: Legislative Policymaking in Gendered Terms." *The Journal of Politics* 57 (1995): 696–723.

Margolies-Mezvinsky, Marjorie, with Barbara Feinman. *A Woman's Place: The Freshman Women Who Changed the Face of Congress.* New York: Crown, 1994.

Matland, Richard E. "District Magnitude's Effect on Female Representation in U.S. State Legislatures." *Legislative Studies Quarterly* 17 (1993): 469–492.

Mayhew, David R. *Congress: The Electoral Connection.* New Haven: Yale University Press, 1974.

National Women's Political Caucus. *Why Don't More Women Run?* A Study Prepared by Mellman, Lazurus, and Lake. December 15, 1994.

Norris, Pippa. "Women in Congress: A Policy Difference?" *Politics* 6 (1986): 34–40.

Norton, Noelle. "Women, It's Not Enough to Be Elected: Committee Position Makes a Difference." In *Gender, Power, Leadership, and Governance,* ed. Georgia Duerst-Lahti and Rita Mae Kelly. Ann Arbor: University of Michigan Press, 1995.

Postman, David. "Cantwell to Turn Down PAC Cash in Senate Bid." *Seattle Times,* May 5, 2000.

Rosenthal, Cindy Simon. *When Women Lead: Integrative Leadership in State Legislatures.* New York: Oxford University Press, 1998.

Rule, Wilma, and Joseph Zimmerman, eds. *The United States Electoral Systems: Their Impact on Women and Minorities.* New York: Greenwood Press, 1992.

Saint-Germain, Michelle A. "Does Their Difference Make a Difference? The Impact of Women on Public Policy in the Arizona Legislature." *Social Science Quarterly* 70 (1989): 956–968.

Shapiro, Walter. "She Is Start-Up Millionaire, But Cantwell Is No Upstart." *USA Today,* September 22, 2000: 10A.

Swers, Michelle L. "Are Congresswomen More Likely to Vote for Women's Issues Bills Than Their Male Colleagues?" *Legislative Studies Quarterly* 23 (1998): 435–448.

Tamerius, Karen L. "Sex, Gender, and Leadership in the Representation of Women." In *Gender, Power, Leadership, and Governance,* ed. Georgia Duerst-Lahti and Rita Mae Kelly. Ann Arbor: University of Michigan Press, 1995.

Thomas, Sue. "Voting Patterns in the California Assembly: The Role of Gender." *Women & Politics* 9 (1990): 43–56.

———. *How Women Legislate.* New York: Oxford University Press, 1994.

———. "Why Gender Matters: The Perceptions of Women Officeholders." *Women & Politics* 17 (1997): 27–54.

———. "Legislative Careers: The Personal and the Political." In *Women Transforming Congress,* ed. Cindy Simon Rosenthal. Norman, OK: University of Oklahoma Press, forthcoming.

Thomas, Sue, and Clyde Wilcox, eds. *Women and Elective Office: Past, Present, and Future.* NY: Oxford University Press, 1998.

Vega, Arturo, and Juanita M. Firestone. "The Effects of Gender on Congressional Behavior and the Substantive Representation of Women." *Legislative Studies Quarterly* 20 (1995): 213–222.

Wallace, Jim. "Mr. Capito Becoming Mr. Mom: Wife's New Role Will Often Keep Her in DC." *Charleston Daily Mail,* November 14, 2000: 1A.

Welch, Susan. "Are Women More Liberal than Men in the U. S. Congress?" *Legislative Studies Quarterly* 10 (1985): 125–134.

Welch, Susan, and Donley Studlar. "Multimember Districts and the Representation of Women: Evidence from Britain and the United States." *Journal of Politics* 52 (1990): 391–412.

Werner, Emmy E. "Women in Congress: 1917–1964." *Western Political Quarterly* 19 (1966): 16–30.

Whicker, Marcia, and Malcolm Jewell. "The Feminization of Leadership in State Legislatures." In *Women and Elective Office: Past, Present, and Future*, ed. Sue Thomas and Clyde Wilcox. New York: Oxford University Press, 1998.

11

The Clinton Effect

How a Lame-Duck President Impacted His Vice President's Election Prospects

Margaret Tseng

Was it Clinton fatigue or Clinton nostalgia? No matter—both factors seemed to have worked against Gore. Either Bill Clinton was too scandal-ridden and Al Gore was a mere extension of his presidency or Clinton was a politician in a class of his own and Gore never reached similar expectations. Any way you put it, Gore was in trouble. To make matters worse, he waffled on his strategy dealing with this dilemma.

When he announced his candidacy, Gore put himself at arm's length from the Clinton presidency. During the primaries, Gore embraced the accomplishments of the Clinton-Gore administration. But during the Democratic National Convention, he proclaimed himself as his "own man" and made strides in coming out of Clinton's shadow by nominating Senator Joseph Lieberman as his running mate and presenting a populist, non-Clinton-like agenda.

This chapter will map out the Clinton fatigue/nostalgia phenomenon: where it came from, how it influenced Gore's campaign strategy, and how it ultimately played out in the election.

What Is Clinton Fatigue?

David Kaplan gave birth to the idea of Clinton fatigue in 1990. As a writer for the *Congressional Quarterly Weekly Report*, Kaplan speculated that

Arkansas was tired of Clinton's ten-year gubernatorial rule.[1] The same catch phrase reemerged in the wake of Clinton's lame-duck term.[2]

After maneuvering through a string of scandals and avoiding removal from office, the Clinton administration began to show signs of its own fatigue. The inactivity common to lame duck presidencies seemed to sweep over the Clinton White House. Despite the administration's subdued tone, the electorate could not forget the roller coaster that it rode on for seven years amid Clinton's policy successes and personal failures. From the enactment of deficit reduction legislation to the defeat of health care, from high job approval to surviving impeachment—what a ride!

In March 1999, the Pew Research Center for the People and the Press identified Clinton fatigue as a significant phenomenon within the electorate. Nearly three-fourths of voters were "tired of all the problems associated with the Clinton administration." Only 29 percent said they wished Clinton was eligible for a third term.[3] A *New York Times* poll taken in August 1999 found respondents' attitudes toward Gore closely linked to Clinton's personal ratings rather than to his job approval rating.[4] An incumbent vice president during good economic times normally benefits from the administration's good fortune. However, Clinton's personal attributes seemed to be hurting Gore before the campaign and provided a motivation for him not to embrace the administration's achievements. In a *Washington Post* poll taken around the same time, over 55 percent of respondents conceded, "I'm just plain tired of Bill Clinton."[5]

Respondents were tired not just of Clinton as a person, but also of his policies. In February 1999, 54 percent of respondents wanted to carry on the Clinton administration's policies. Six months later, only 44 percent of respondents wanted to continue them.[6] As primary season grew closer, the electorate's desire for Clinton and his policies waned even more.

In 1999, Clinton fatigue seemed to be a real drag for Gore. As Marjorie Williams of the *Washington Post* put it, "[Gore is] the political spouse who got placed in an impossible spot."[7] Consequently, in June 1999, when Gore officially announced his candidacy, he attempted to keep himself at arm's length from the President. Apparently, the impeachment and the Lewinsky matter, which had been resolved in the Senate four months earlier, still lingered in Gore's mind. Gore referred to the Lewinksy scandal and the impeachment as "that awful year we went through."[8] He also said he had had many disagreements with Clinton regarding campaign strategy and the role that Clinton would play in Gore's election campaign. Specifically, Gore was extremely resentful about the lies Clinton fed him about the Lewinsky affair. According to one Democrat insider, Gore's personal frustration with Clinton physically manifested itself in the vice president's own indecision and inarticulateness. Gore would get knotted up and stammer at the mere mention of Clinton's involvement in his campaign.[9]

Survey data two weeks before the election reinforced this judgment. Only 17 percent of voters indicated that Clinton's presence on Gore's campaign trail would cause them to vote for Gore. However, 40 percent of voters said that Clinton's presence would cause them not to vote for Gore. Forty percent of voters said that Clinton would not affect their vote. Independent voters showed even greater disapproval of Clinton's assistance in Gore's campaign. If Clinton were to campaign for Gore, 45 percent of independents would be less likely to vote for Gore and only 10 percent of independent voters would be more likely to vote for Gore.[10]

Even residents of Clinton's own home state of Arkansas revealed great skepticism about the president's role in Gore's campaign. Bryan Fink, a Methodist pastor from Conway, Arkansas, said, "If Gore weren't so close to Clinton, it would probably help him out." Donald Parks, who owns a telephone company in Prairie Grove, Arkansas, said he was a big fan of Clinton, though he wanted to "wring his neck" at times. Parks said he was "a little apprehensive" about the effect Clinton was having on Gore.[11] The reservations these citizens had reflected their conflicted feelings about Clinton as a good president, but a flawed person.

During the Nomination Process (January 2000–August 2000): Evidence of Nostalgia

With so much at stake, Gore began his quest for the presidency without Clinton's help. However, after a series of campaign blunders and a drop in his standing in the polls, Gore shifted his campaign strategy by embracing the achievements of the Clinton administration. He even began taking wardrobe advice from Clinton![12]

Sensing a sluggish start in the Gore campaign, Clinton took it upon himself to coach Gore to loosen up and dress down, all in the hopes of getting him to connect to the electorate. "You do not have the feeling that the Gore campaign is moving in a positive, forceful, determined way to prepare themselves," said an anonymous source, recounting his conversations with Clinton about Gore.[13] Clinton's concern caused him to take a behind-the-scenes role in the Gore campaign, unlike his predecessors, Ronald Reagan and Dwight Eisenhower, who were criticized for their lack of activity in their vice presidents' campaigns.

In private, the president was critical of the vice president's efforts. A close confidant of Clinton stated, "He thinks Gore needs to stop worrying . . . and shouldn't be terribly concerned about who manages the [campaign]

Table 11.1

Public Opinion of Country's Direction, January 2000–August 2000
(in percent)

Fox News/Opinion Dynamics Poll
"Considering how things are today, would you say that the U.S. is generally headed in the right direction, or is it off on the wrong track?"
N = 900 registered voters (Margin of error +/ −3)

	Right track	Wrong track	Not sure
8/23–24/00	60	28	12
8/9–10/00	53	33	14
7/26–27/00	54	34	12
7/12–13/00	55	33	12
5/24–25/00	53	35	12
4/5–6/00	51	35	14
3/8–9/00	51	34	15
1/26–27/00	58	27	15

Source: The Polling Report, <http://www.pollingreport.com>.

on a day-to-day basis and spend his time instead on what he says to the American people."[14] In public, Clinton praised Gore. At a fund-raising event in Arkansas, Clinton said, "Whatever anybody thinks about whether I was right or wrong about a given issue, when the history of the last six-and-a-half years or next year-and-a-half is written, there is one thing that no one will be able to question, and that is that Al Gore was by far the most influential and effective and productive Vice President in the history of the United States of America." [15]

Heading into New Hampshire, Gore embraced Clinton's accomplishments after months of downplaying his own tie to the administration. Specifically, Gore focused on his partnership with the president and America's unparalleled economic prosperity at the end of the Clinton–Gore era. Perhaps the change in strategy came from Gore's acknowledgment that the economic boom far outweighed Clinton's personal scandals, particularly among Democratic partisans.

Recent research suggests that voters base their votes primarily on retrospective evaluations of the party in power. Voters' judgment of the current administration's past acts in office affects their vote more than the promise of future acts. According to polls taken throughout the primaries, Gore looked poised to benefit from the past acts of the Clinton administration. Throughout the primary season, a majority of respondents noted that the United States was on the right track (Table 11.1). Also, a majority of

Table 11.2

Public Opinion of Economic Conditions, January 2000–August 2000
(in percent)

The Gallup Poll
"How would you rate economic conditions in this country today—as excellent, good, only fair, or poor?"
N = 1,026 Nationwide (Margin of Error +/−3)

Date	Excellent	Good	Only fair	Poor	No opinion
8/18–19/00	25	49	21	4	1
7/25–26/00	26	48	21	4	1
5/18–21/00	17	49	24	9	1
4/3–9/00	14	46	30	9	1

Source: The Polling Report, <http://www.pollingreport.com>.

Table 11.3

Public Opinion of Bill Clinton and Al Gore (in percent)

CBS News Poll and CBS News/New York Times Poll
"Is your opinion of Bill Clinton/Al Gore favorable, not favorable, undecided, or haven't you heard enough about Bill Clinton yet to have an opinion?"

	Bill Clinton[1,2,3]		Al Gore[4,5,6]	
	Favorable	Unfavorable	Favorable	Unfavorable
July 2000[1,4]	43	40	35	34
May 2000[2,5]	44	41	34	36
February 2000[3,6]	43	39	30	36

Source: Compiled by the author from polls from The Polling Report. <http://www.pollingreport.com>.
Registered voters: [1] 953; [2] 947; [3] 947; [4] 596; [5] 716; [6] 1,265.

respondents viewed economic conditions as good or excellent. The most compelling data that may have pushed Gore into using Clinton during the primaries were favorability ratings. Clinton consistently had higher favorability ratings than Gore during the primary season (Table 11.3). These data suggest that Gore made the right decision to embrace the Clinton administration during the primary season because Clinton remained popular among Democratic activists.

Into the General Election: Evidence of Clinton Nostalgia

It took Clinton two minutes to walk to the podium and forty-four more to finish his speech at the convention. Yvonne Vozinski, a delegate from Pennsylvania, summed it up perfectly: "This is an emotional night for him because he doesn't want to give it up. . . . He loves the limelight, I can tell."[16] Clinton's desire for the limelight clearly perturbed the Gore camp. One Gore strategist said that the battle between Clinton's desire for the spotlight and Gore's struggle to get out of his shadow had continued for fourteen months. "Is he having a tough time ceding the limelight? Listen, nothing's more important to this president than ensuring Al Gore gets elected president. But I think it's a tough process for him to move off center stage, as it would be for anybody," said Terry McAuliffe, a close Clinton friend, Democratic fund-raiser, and later chairman of the Democratic National Committee (DNC).[17]

Fellow Democratic candidates also expressed reluctance about Clinton moving from center stage. With a lackluster campaign, Democrats running for office all around the country wondered if there would be any presidential coattails to ride on in November. Rather than depending on a change of fortune, leaders of Democratic state party organizations encouraged Clinton to play an active role in their get-out-the vote efforts. Party organization chairs from Washington State to New Jersey to Wisconsin chimed in unison that Clinton would be an asset in their states. They sensed that Gore was not connecting as well to core Democrats as Bush was to core Republicans, a perception that found some empirical support in the polls. Therefore, many state party leaders did not want to enter the election *without* Clinton. "I think Bill Clinton could carry this state for Al Gore," said Jim Edmunson, the chairman of the Oregon Democratic Party.[18] Clinton's undying desire to play a role in his party's 2000 victory caused him to work the campaign circuit all around this country throughout the election cycle. He stretched himself from New York in his wife's Senate race to House races all over California in his goal to raise $100 million for Democratic candidates. (Appendix 11.A shows hundreds of campaigns Clinton participated in on behalf of politicians other than Gore.) Even protesters outside one fund-raising event mockingly called him "Fund-Raiser in Chief." Clinton's campaigning assisted Democrats on all levels, in House, Senate, and presidential races.

He took away a significant portion of the campaign burden from fellow Democrats. Almost half of the $100 million Clinton raised went to the DNC to help Gore and Lieberman.[19] "Earlier in the year, Clinton's fund raising took a lot of weight off the vice president," Jake Siewert, spokesperson for the White House said. "That's 100 fund-raisers that Al Gore and Joe Lieberman didn't have to do."[20] Clinton helped House Democrats gain a $2 million edge over the Republican Party in soft money and raised over $10 million for Democratic Senate races. He also fund-raised on behalf of gubernatorial candidates all over the United States.

Clinton continuously worked the campaign circuit, initially targeting states considered vulnerable in the November election. Officials running in these key states wanted to jump on the coattails of Clinton's historical job approval ratings. Lame-duck presidents usually suffer a decline in job approval ratings, but Clinton did not.[21] In fact, his approval ratings were higher than when he was reelected in 1996 (51 percent, Zogby International American Poll). Polls during the 2000 campaign showed him in the high 50s to mid-60s. The final Election Day exit poll had him at 57 percent approval. Eisenhower at the end of his tenure had a 49 percent approval rating. Reagan did a little better than Eisenhower at the end of his term with a 54 percent approval rating.

Despite Clinton's fund-raising and campaigning activities, especially in California and New York, Gore did not mention Clinton's name on the campaign trail or even in the debates. Only during the last of the three debates did he venture to trumpet the economic accomplishments of the last eight years. Why would Gore change gears when indicators during the primary season showed the benefits of using Clinton?

After securing the Democratic nomination, Gore asked the public to look to the future and vote for him based on what he could do for them. The polls at the time did not clearly indicate that the public wanted a fresh start and showed some division over Clinton (Table 11.4). At the beginning of the primary season, the public saw Gore too closely tied to Clinton to give the country a fresh start (Table 11.5). However, the public gave Gore more favorable marks after he distanced himself from Clinton at the Democratic National Convention.

Two Weeks Before the Election: Gore's Desperation?

Gore's last-ditch effort to garner support came during the last two weeks of the election. "Gore stubbornly has resisted calling on his running mate . . . partly out of pride and partly because of the uneasy relationship between the Gores and the Clintons since the Monica Lewinsky scandal and the impeachment."[22] However, even the Republicans could see how influential Clinton could be in the close race. "Gore is trying to keep at an arm's length from his friend, his companion, his soulmate for the past eight years," said Pennsylvania governor Tom Ridge. "I personally don't see how

Table 11.4

Public Opinion of Bill Clinton and the Country's Direction, August 2000
(in percent)

"Which of these two statements comes closest to your own views? A) After eight years of Bill Clinton, we need to elect a president who can set the nation in a new direction. B) We need to keep the country moving in the direction Bill Clinton has been taking us." This *Washington Post-ABC News* poll was based on telephone interviews with 1,205 randomly selected adults nationwide, including 975 self-identified registered voters, and conducted between August 4–6, 2000. The margin of error for overall results is plus or minus 3 percentage points.

Date	New direction	Same direction	Somewhere in between	Neither	Don't know
August 2000	48	44	2	4	2

Source: The Washington Post, <http://www.washingtonpost.com>.

Table 11.5

Public Perception of Al Gore's Relationship with Bill Clinton (in percent)

Please tell me whether you agree or disagree with the following statement: Al Gore is too close to Bill Clinton to provide the fresh start the country needs. This *Washington Post/ABC News* poll was based on telephone interviews with 1,065 self-identified registered voters nationwide, including 738 likely voters, and conducted between September 4–6, 2000. The margin of error is plus or minus 3 percentage points.

Date	Strongly agree	Somewhat agree	Strongly disagree	Somewhat disagree	Don't know
September 2000	29	13	34	23	2
August 2000	28	11	37	21	1
March 2000	34	15	26	23	2

Source: The Polling Report, <http://www.pollingreport.com>.

you could believe that an incumbent President could do anything but help you."[23] Ultimately and in desperation, Gore bought into that sentiment. Having sworn off Clinton for a year, Gore recanted his "my own man" stance two weeks before the election.[24] "He's going to have to suck it up and say, 'I need all the help I can get,' " a White House official, speaking on condition of anonymity, said of Gore.

Doug Hattaway, a spokesman for Gore, said the president would "take the fight to George W. Bush on his own in several states as part of the get-out-the-vote effort."[25] However, Gore still avoided joint appearances with the president. Only in an obligatory appearance in Jefferson City, Missouri, did the Gores and Clintons make a show of their friendship at the memorial services for the late governor, Mel Carnahan (D-MO).

Gore not only called on Clinton to pinch-hit for him, he even resurrected the name of Bill Clinton in Philadelphia and Michigan. Perhaps Gore felt safe using Clinton's name in front of African Americans in Philadelphia and union members in Michigan because Clinton remained popular among these constituents. "Thank you for allowing Bill Clinton and me to bring change," Gore said at the Morris Brown A. M. E. Church in North Philadelphia.[26] He specifically credited the Clinton administration for the strong economy. Gore pointed out that his "progressive policies are more easily pursued when we have a sound economy."[27] In addressing a crowd in Michigan, he stated "Now, because you gave Bill Clinton and me a chance to change our economic policy, instead of the biggest deficits, we've got the biggest surplus. Instead of repeat recessions, we've tripled the market."[28]

However, as the media caught on to Gore's new strategy to use Clinton on his behalf, Gore quickly retracted Clinton's political leash and kept him from campaigning in key swing states. Despite the statement of Gore's spokesman Hattaway that Clinton would take the fight to several states, ultimately the Gore camp allowed Clinton to focus his time only on California and New York, very secure Democratic states.

Some political pundits speculated that Gore's unwillingness to use Clinton may have cost him the election.[29] The exit polls suggest this as well. Seventy percent of respondents said that their vote was neither in support of nor in opposition to Clinton. Moreover, 65 percent of respondents said that the country was moving in the right direction, 56 percent of respondents said that the country should stay on course, and 57 percent approved of the job Clinton was doing as president.[30] Therefore Gore should not have been so afraid to show off the accomplishments of the last eight years to his base and to independent voters. Table 11.6 shows how some voters factored Clinton into their vote, but Gore may have never been able to court these votes. Only six percent of the sample were non-Republicans who voted for Bush because of the Clinton scandals. Perhaps Gore should have taken advice from California Democratic chair, Art Torres. "I wouldn't be afraid for [Clinton] to stand with the vice president. The voters who might be offended we never had in the first place," Torres said.[31]

Mixed Reviews on Gore's Strategy

Although Clinton did not object in public to the minimal role he played, he did cause a ruckus in the Gore camp by insisting in an interview with *Esquire* magazine that the Republicans owed the nation an apology for

Table 11.6

Select Findings from Voter News Service Exit Poll (in percent)

1996 presidential vote	All	Gore	Bush	Buchanan	Nader
Clinton	46	82	15	1	2
Dole	31	7	91	0	1
Perot	6	27	64	1	7
Other	2	26	52	1	15
Did not vote	13	44	52	0	3
Party identification	All	Gore	Bush	Buchanan	Nader
Democrat	39	86	11	0	2
Republican	35	8	91	0	1
Independent	27	45	47	1	6
Moral condition of country	All	Gore	Bush	Buchanan	Nader
Right direction	39	70	27	0	2
Wrong track	57	33	62	1	3
Reason for your vote	All	Gore	Bush	Buchanan	Nader
To support Clinton	10	94	4	1	1
To oppose Clinton	18	5	92	1	2
Clinton not a factor	70	53	43	0	3

Source: Compiled from the Voter News Service Exit Poll.

impeaching him in 1998. Also, in an interview with Washington D.C., radio host Tom Joyner, he stated, "You can get the next best thing" by voting for Al Gore.[32]

Those close to Clinton remarked that Gore's advisers treated him poorly, yet that did not stop Clinton's eagerness and earnestness to campaign on behalf of Democrats. "Do you want to build on this prosperity and keep it going and extend it to people who aren't part of it yet, or do you want to abandon the path we're on and go back to different economic policy that let us down before?" he asked African American religious leaders during an appearance at a church in Harlem.[33] "I am pleading with you," Clinton told members of Washington's Shiloh Baptist Church as he urged them to get out the vote for Gore. "I have done everything I know to do to turn this country around, to pull this country together, to move us forward."[34]

Initially, the Gore camp intended for Clinton to visit toss-up states like Missouri and Louisiana. However, Gore and his advisers concluded that swing voters like suburban mothers in these key states did not like Clinton. The *New York Times,* quoting anonymous sources, said Gore aides concluded that while Clinton could energize the Democratic base, he would enrage an equal number of Republicans and possibly alienate swing voters. By using Clinton, Gore could push Republicans to come out in greater numbers on Election Day.

Democrats had mixed feelings about Gore's unwillingness to let Clinton campaign on his behalf. "I'd have him [Clinton] out there every day the last two weeks," said Ed Rendell, former Philadelphia mayor, who became Democratic National Committee cochairman and was a friend of both men. "Get the president into big cities and union halls. He'll turn up the heat."[35] Sen. Joseph Biden (D-DE) said Clinton could be a big help because of his appeal to core Democratic voters among minorities and with organized labor. "That base of the Democratic party loves him [Clinton]," Biden said. "I would use it, use it, use it and use it."[36] California governor Gray Davis made an impassioned call for Clinton to stump in his state for Gore and other Democratic candidates. "He's immensely popular here," Davis told reporters. "He's one of the most compelling speakers in American politics."[37] Other Democrats, however, supported Gore's reluctance to use Clinton. Democrat consultant James Carville, chief strategist in Clinton's 1992 campaign, was one of them. He defended Gore's move. "It makes sense, because if he [Clinton] appears with Gore, it just sucks all the air out of everything; it's all people want to talk about," Carville said. "Gore is in a tight, tight, tight race and he's got to make his case himself."[38] David Worley, chairman of the Georgia Democratic Party, echoed similar sentiments. He said, "I for one, am glad he is running his campaign and not relying on President Clinton. . . . He's got to convince independents that he should be president and he's got to do that in his own right."[39] And Gore certainly tried to do so time and time again, repeating, "This is a campaign that I am running on my own." In another rendition of the "I am my own man" theme, Gore said, "I've said on previous occasions, I am who I am."[40]

Gore's Loss: Whose Fault Was It?

In the aftermath of the election, Gore and Clinton shared a "cathartic" moment together when they blamed each other for the loss of the election. Gore blamed Clinton's scandals for Gore's loss. Clinton retorted that he left Gore a strong economy and a high job approval rating, which should have translated into an election victory. The conversation demonstrated the heightened tension and personal frustration that had built up between the two politicians throughout the election as well as Gore's dilemma in his campaign. One Democrat close to both men said, "It was far worse than anyone knew." Although Gore framed the Clinton factor as a political issue, one Democrat said that Gore really saw Clinton as an "emotional hurdle": "Gore had this sort of psychological analysis in which anything Clinton did was inadequate."[41] Gore's camp remained adamant to the end that Clinton was not the solution but the threat to his election victory.

In excluding Clinton, Gore had listened carefully to focus groups discussing Clinton's involvement in the campaign. The thrust of their findings was that voters wanted to hear directly from Gore. Diane Wright of Jackson, Tennessee, said that as a swing voter she could vote for either Gore or Bush. However, she might ultimately vote for Bush because Gore did not distance himself far enough from Clinton: "Gore should have been stronger. He could have distanced himself. A lot of people in Tennessee feel that way."[42]

Did this decision cost Gore the election? Did Clinton fatigue really cost him the election? Did standing as his own man cost him the election? Findings from the National Election Studies (NES) give greater insight into this question. Based on the idea that voters decide their vote on retrospective evaluations, Clinton's favorability ratings should have translated into high favorability ratings for Gore. However, the NES shows that a number of voters defected from the Clinton–Gore camp to the Bush camp. That is, those who voted for Clinton in 1996 and then voted for Bush in 2000 constituted 16 percent of the total electorate in 2000. Analysis of the Voter News Service exit poll shows that of the voters who supported Clinton in 1996, less than 3 percent voted for Bush specifically to oppose Clinton. Less than 5 percent of the 1996 Clinton voters felt that the country's moral condition was deteriorating and voted for Bush. Ten percent of the 1996 Clinton voters felt that Clinton was very or somewhat responsible for the prosperous economy, but voted for Bush. Considering Bush's slim margin of victory, Gore might have won by retaining the voters that defected from the Clinton–Gore camp by proposing Clinton-like policies.

The data also suggest that Gore would have benefited from running on the Clinton record, but not necessarily joining Clinton on the campaign trail. According to the data, these people approved of Clinton's performance and thought the country was moving in the right direction, which suggests Gore may have lost on his own. Gore might have held onto more of Clinton's supporters who defected to Bush. Whether Gore was ahead or behind Bush, Clinton's favorability ratings remained fairly steady during the campaign. But Gore's favorability ratings suffered a drop after the debates. His hemming and hawing as well as his inflated stories during the debates caused voters to question his trustworthiness and character. Gore's character issue developed outside of the Clinton factor. By dismissing the accomplishments of the Clinton administration, Gore inadvertently affirmed the Republicans' sentiment that Clinton's moral failings were more political than personal. As Ronald Brownstein from the *Los Angeles Times* put it, "[I]f Clinton is the gasoline in the room, Gore is the match."[43]

Notes

1. William Safire, "Clinton Fatigue Nothing to Yawn About," *Houston Chronicle,* October 10, 1999, 6.

2. Lame-duck presidents are two-term presidents serving the last two years of their tenure.

3. John F. Harris, "As Term Wanes, 'Clinton Fatigue' Yields to Nostalgia," *Washington Post*, May 1, 2000, A1.

4. Andrew Kohut, "A Clear Case of Clinton Fatigue," *New York Times,* August 5, 1999, A23.

5. Dan Balz and Richard Morin, "Clinton-Weary Public Has Doubts About Gore," *Washington Post,* September 8, 1999, A1.

6. Ibid.

7. Marjorie Williams, "The Clinton Effect," *Washington Post*, November 28, 1999, B7.

8. John Harris, "Clinton and Gore Clashed Over Blame for Election," *Washington Post,* February 7, 2001, A1

9. Ibid.

10. CNN, "Clinton Campaign Effect Could Hurt Gore More Than Help, Poll Suggest," October 24, 2000, available online at <www.cnn.com>.

11. Katharine Q. Seelye, "Gore Stops By: Clinton Plays the Gracious Host," *New York Times*, August 8, 1999, 26.

12. Richard Berke, "Clinton Admits to Concerns As Gore Campaign Stumbles," *New York Times*, May 14, 1999, A1.

13. Ibid.

14. Ibid

15. Katharine Q. Seelye, "Gore Stops By."

16. Geraldine Baum and Elizabeth Mehren, "One Last Date: Clinton Wins Party's Embrace," *Los Angeles Times,* August 15, 2000, 20.

17. James Gerstenzang and Mark Barabak, "Hands Wring Over Clinton's Weekend Splash," *Los Angeles Times,* August 12, 2000, 12.

18. James Dao, "Democrats Seeking Some Clinton Magic For Gore in the Fall," *New York Times*, July 16, 2000, 1.

19. Kenneth R. Bazinet, "Bill's the $100M Man Sets Out on 3-Day Fund-Raising Push Through State," *Daily News (New York)*, October 22, 2000, 5.

20. Ibid.

21. Researchers acknowledge the drop in approval ratings as presidential terms progress. However, researchers like Richard Brody, Sam Kernell, and John E. Mueller do not agree on the source of the decline.

22. Kenneth Bazinet, Thomas DeFrank, and Richard Sisk "Gore Asks Bill's Help: Wants Him On Stump," *Daily News (New York)*, October 21, 2000, 6.

23. Ibid.

24. Ibid.

25. Katharine Q. Seelye and Kevin Sack, "The 2000 Campaign: The Vice President: Focus Is on Crucial States in Campaign's Final Hours," *New York Times*, November 6, 2000, A1.

26. Ibid.

27. Ibid.
28. "President Agreed with Gore to Limit Stumping," *Milwaukee Journal Sentinel*, November 10, 2000, 16A.
29. Marc Sandalow, "Election Battle Finally Coming to California: Clinton to Campaign for Gore, Bush Will Spend Millions on Ads," *San Francisco Chronicle*, October 26, 2000, A1.
30. Calculated by M. Tseng from Voter News Service exit poll.
31. Mimi Hall, "Clinton Resigns Himself to Limited Campaign Role," *USA Today*, November 3, 2000, 11A.
32. Ibid.
33. Ibid
34. Sandy Grady, "Unchain Bubba: It's Time for Gore to Swallow His Pride and Ask Clinton for Help," *The Gazette (Montreal)*, October 25, 2000, B3.
35. Kenneth Bazinet and Richard Sisk, "Gore Tells Prez No Thanks He'll Take His Election Day Chances Without Help from Clinton," *Daily News (New York)*, October 24, 2000, 18.
36. Andrew Miga, "Campaign 2000: Clinton to Enter Political Fray to Shore Up Gore," *Boston Herald,* October 27, 2000, 6.
37. Ibid
38. "Gore Limits Clinton Campaign Help," *Atlanta Journal and Constitution*, November 2, 2000, A.
39. Richard Berke, "The 2000 Campaign: The Strategies, Democrats Remind Gore of the Economy," *New York Times,* October 30, 2000, A15.
40. "Gore Limits Clinton Campaign"
41. Roger Simon, "It All Comes Down to Gore: Clinton and the Party Are Scrambling, But the Candidate Has to Make the Sale," November 6, 2000, <www.usnews.com>.
42. Ibid.
43. Ronald Brownstein, "Gore, Curiously, Fails to Take Credit for Policy Achievements, *Los Angeles Times,* October 16, 2000, 5. Al Gore is bound to suffer from the negatives associated with the Clinton administration no matter what he does. The real issue is that Gore has proven strangely incapable of benefiting from the positives of both Clinton's achievements and political strategy."

Bibliography

Brody, Richard. *Assessing the President: The Media, Elite Opinion, and Public Support.* Stanford, CA: Stanford University Press, 1991.
Kernell, Samuel. *Going Public: New Strategies of Presidential Leadership.* Washington, DC: CQ Press, c1986.
Mueller, John E. *War, Presidents, and Public Opinion.* New York: Wiley, 1973.

APPENDIX
Clinton's Campaign Activities (December 1999–October 2000)

December 2, 1999—Fund-raiser and Tribute to Mayor Edward Rendell (Philadelphia)
December 7, 1999—Reception for Senator Timothy Johnson (Washington, DC)
December 11, 1999—Florida State Democratic Convention (Orlando)
January 11, 2000—Reception for Sheila Jackson Lee for Congress (Houston)
January 13, 2000—Democratic National Commiittee (DNC) Reception (NewYork)

February 3, 2000—Jane Harman for Congress Reception (Washington, DC)
February 8, 2000—DNC Reception (Washington, DC)
February 8, 2000—Dinner for Major Supporters of DNC (Georgetown, Washington, DC)
February 9, 2000—DNC Lunch (McAllen, TX)
February 9, 2000—Luncheon for Representative Ruben Hinojosa (McAllen, TX)
February 9, 2000—DNC Dinner (Dallas)
February 22, 2000—Lieutenant Governor Ruth Ann Minner of Delaware Reception (Washington, DC)
February 24, 2000—DNC Dinner (New York)
February 24, 2000—DNC Mix and Mingle (New York)
February 29, 2000—DNC Fundraiser (Miami)
February 29, 2000—Reception for State Representative Elaine Bloom (Miami)
February, 29, 2000—DNC Lunch (West Palm Beach)
March 3, 2000—DNC Reception (San Francisco)
March 3, 2000—Dinner for Democratic Senatorial Campaign Committee (DSCC) (San Francisco)
March 4, 2000—DNC Reception (Los Angeles)
March 9, 2000—Democratic Congressional Campaign Committee (DCCC) Native American Fund Lunch (Washington, DC)
March 9, 2000—Mel Carnahan for Senator Dinner (Washington, DC)
March 13, 2000—DNC Dinner (Lincolnwood, IL)
March 13, 2000—Dinner for the Women's Leadership Forum and the Saxophone Club of the DNC (Chicago)
March 29, 2000—Debbie Stabenow for Senate Reception (Washington, DC)
March 30, 2000—DNC Lunch (New York)
March 30, 2000—DNC Dinner (New York)
March 30, 2000—Reception after DNC Dinner (New York)
April 1, 2000—Fund-raiser for Hillary Clinton for Senate (Washington, DC)
April 2, 2000—Brunch for DNC (Las Vegas)
April 2, 2000—Reception for DNC and Nevada State Democratic Party (Las Vegas)
April 4, 2000—Patrick Leahy Reception for Senate (Washington, DC)
April 8, 2000—DNC Lunch (New Orleans)
April 14, 2000—Tribute Dinner for Representative John Lewis (Atlanta)
April 15, 2000—President and vice president at DNC Dinner (Los Angeles)
April 24, 2000—Luncheon for Representative Michael Forbes (New York)
April 24, 2000—President and vice president at DNC Dinner (New York)
May 7, 2000—Reception for Hillary Clinton for Senate (Little Rock, AR)
May 8, 2000—Reception for Representative Baron Hill (Bethesda, MD)
May 9, 2000—Reception for Mary Landrieu for Senate (Washington, DC)
May 9, 2000—Reception for Senator Daniel Akaka (Washington, DC)
May 15, 2000—Dinner for Senator Charles Robb (Washington, DC)
May 15, 2000—Reception for Representative Robert Wexler (Washington, DC)
May 16, 2000—Reception following New York State Democratic Convention (Albany)
May 17, 2000—DNC Dinner (Greenwich, CT)
May 19, 2000—DCCC Lunch (Philadelphia)
May 19, 2000—Reception for Representative Joseph Hoeffel (Philadelphia)
May 23, 2000—Reception for Representative Ellen Tauscher (Washington, DC)
May 23, 2000—DNC Dinner (Washington, DC)
May 24, 2000—President and vice president at DNC Gala "National Tribute to President Clinton" (Washington, DC)

June 10, 2000—DNC Luncheon (Minneapolis)
June 13, 2000—DCCC Hispanic Caucus Reception (Washington, DC)
June 15, 2000—Reception for Mayor Williams (Washington, DC)
June 16, 2000—Reception for Representative Ed Towns (New York)
June 19, 2000—Southwest Voters Reception (Houston)
June 19, 2000—DSCC Lunch (Houston)
June 19, 2000—DSCC Dinner (Austin, TX)
June 21, 2000—Hillary 2000 Dinner (Washington, DC)
June 22, 2000—DNC Luncheon (Phoenix)
June 22, 2000—Reception for Susan Davis for Congress (San Diego)
June 22, 2000—DNC Dinner (San Diego)
June 23, 2000—DNC Dinner (Los Angeles)
June 23, 2000—California State Party Reception (Los Angeles)
June 23, 2000—Saxophone Club Reception (Hollywood)
June 24, 2000—Mix and Mingle with Association of State Democratic Chairs (Los Angeles)
June 24, 2000—Brunch for Senator Dianne Feinstein for Senate (Los Angeles)
June 27, 2000—Reception for California State Senator Adam Schiff (Washington, DC)
June 28, 2000—Reception for Brian Schweitzer for Senate (Washington, DC)
June 28, 2000—New Democrat Network Dinner (Fairfax, VA)
June 29, 2000—Reception for Representative Sanford Bishop (Washington, DC)
June 30, 2000—DSCC Lunch (Newark, NJ)
July 10, 2000—Reception for Representative Ron Klink (Philadelphia)
July 26, 2000—Terry Lierman for Congress Reception (Washington, DC)
July 28, 2000—DCCC Reception (Boston)
July 28, 3000—DCCC Dinner (Cambridge, MA)
July 29, 2000—Hillary 2000—Fundraiser Luncheon (New York)
July 30, 2000—DNC Lunch (Chicago)
July 31, 2000—DSCC Lunch (Tampa)
July 31, 2000—DSCC Reception (Palm Beach)
August 4, 2000—New York Senate 2000—Dinner (Nantucket, MA)
August 5, 2000—Dinner for Kathleen Kennedy Townsend (Hyannis Port, MA)
August 6, 2000—New York Senate 200 Reception (Martha's Vineyard, MA)
August 8, 2000—DNC Dinner (Charlottesville, VA)
August 9, 2000—New York Senate 2000—Dinner (McLean, VA)
August 9, 2000—New York Senate 2000—Dinner (Washington, DC)
August 10, 2000—New York Senate 2000—Dinner (New York)
August 11, 2000—Reception for Representative Xavier Becerra (Los Angeles)
August 12, 2000—New York Senate 2000—Hollywood Gala (Los Angeles)
August 13, 2000—DNC Brunch in honor of Cabinet (Los Angeles)
August 14, 2000—Tribute to president by Gov. Davis (Los Angeles)
August 14, 2000—Lunch with American Federation of Teachers (Beverly Hills)
August 14, 2000—National Democratic Institute Luncheon (Los Angeles)
August 14, 2000—DNC Major Supporters Dinner (Los Angeles)
August 15, 2000—President and vice president address (Monroe, MI)
August 22, 2000—Dinner for Debbie Stabenow for Senate (Bloomfield Hills, MI)
August 23, 2000—Reception for Susan Bass-Levin for Congress (Cherry Hill, NJ)
August 23, 2000—Reception for Representative Rush Holt (Princeton, NJ)
September 1, 2000—Hillary 2000—Reception (Syracuse, NY)
September 2, 2000—Hillary 2000—Reception (Cazenovia, NY)
September 8, 2000—New York Senate 2000—Dinner (New York)

September 11, 2000—Luncheon for Representative Jim Maloney (Danbury, CT)

September 11, 2000—New York Senate 2000—Reception (New York)

September 11, 2000—Reception for Representative Anthony Weiner (New York)

September 12, 2000—Reception Honoring Representative Eddie Bernice Johnson of Texas (Washington, DC)

September 14, 2000—New York Senate 2000—Dinner (Washington, DC)

September 14, 2000—IMPAC 2000/Ken Bentsen for Congress Reception (Washington, DC)

September 15, 2000—Hillary 2000—Reception (Washington, DC)

September 17, 2000—New York Senate 2000—Brunch (Philadelphia)

September 19, 2000—Lunch for North Dakota State Attorney General Heidi Heitkamp (Washington, DC)

September 20, 2000—Jeanne Shaheen for governor of New Hampshire Reception (Washington, DC)

September 21, 2000—Michigan Victory 2000—Reception (Livonia, MI)

September 23, 2000—Mike Honda for Congress BBQ (San Jose, CA)

September 23, 2000—DCCC Dinner (Brentwood, CA)

September 24, 2000—California League of Conservation Voters Event (Bel Air, CA)

September 24, 2000—Brunch Reception for Representative Lois Capps (Los Angeles)

September 24, 2000—DNC Dinner (Hidden Hills, CA)

September 25, 2000—New Mexico Campaign Victory 2000—Reception (Santa Fe)

September 27, 2000—Luncheon for DNC Gay/Lesbian Leadership Council (Dallas)

September 27, 2000—Reception for Representative Max Sandlin (Houston)

September 29, 2000—DNC/Democratic Business Council Lunch (Washington, DC)

September 29, 2000—Reception for Representative Richard Neal (Washington, DC)

October 3, 2000—Phone call to DCCC event

October 3, 2000—New York Senate 2000—Lunch (Miami)

October 4, 2000—Reception for Representative Corrine Brown (Jacksonville)

October 4, 2000—Rally for Representative Corrine Brown (Jacksonville)

October 5, 2000—Governor Tom Carper for Senate Dinner (in New York City)

October 5, 2000—Representative Charles Rangel National Leadership PAC Reception (New York City)

October 6, 2000—Reception for Representative Tom Udall of New Mexico (Washington, DC)

October 7, 2000—Telephone remarks to the New York Senate 2000—reception

October 7, 2000—Telephone remarks to the Julia Carson for Congress Reception (Indianapolis)

October 7, 2000—Telephone remarks to the Julia Carson for Congress Rally (Indianapolis)

October 10, 2000—Reception for Representative Bob Wise for governor of West Virginia (Washington, DC)

October 11, 2000—Pennsylvania Democratic Coordinated Campaign (Philadelphia)

October 11, 2000—Ron Link for Senate Event (Philadelphia)

October 13, 2000—Telephone remarks at the Dinner for State Senator Mike Ross for Congress (Little Rock, AR)

October 14, 2000—Colorado Coordinated and State Senate Democratic Fund (Denver)

October 14, 2000—Reception for Governor Gary Locke (Seattle)

Source: Compiled by M. Tseng from Presidential Public Papers, The National Archives online <http://www.clinton.nara.gov/public_papers/public_papers.html>.

12

Election2000.com

Internet Use and the American Voter

Jeffrey A. Wertkin

Introduction

In the first year of the millennium, Americans went online for information about music, movies, financial opportunity, goods, and services. Although the Internet has fundamentally changed the way citizens interact in the business and entertainment worlds, its effect on politics is less clear. Do citizens use the Internet for political information? Are Internet users more likely to choose a candidate from a particular party? Does the Internet reinforce existing dispositions or foster political conversions? As Internet use proliferates among the electorate, political scientists must examine how the Internet might alter traditional understandings of information acquisition, opinion formation, and voting behavior.

The 2000 presidential election affords us the first real opportunity to observe the relationship between Internet use and presidential elections. When the World Wide Web first went online in 1991, it was used by only a handful of researchers.[1] A report released in October 2000 by UCLA's Center for Communication Policy describes a nation in which 67 percent of Americans use the Internet.[2] Of these users, 84 percent have started using the Internet since the 1996 presidential election.[3] Thus, the 2000

I am grateful to Stephen Wayne and Clyde Wilcox for their helpful comments and encouragement. I also wish to thank my parents for their love and support.

presidential election is a seminal event in the evolution of the Internet because it is the first nationwide election since the Internet became a mainstream tool.

Part one of this paper will ask questions about the Internet user: Who used the Internet for election news? Which sites did they visit? Part two will examine what, if any, effect the Internet had on voting behavior. Did Internet use stimulate different political preferences? Did Internet use serve to convert voters or did it simply reinforce their predispositions? Finally, part three will discuss several ways in which the Internet may affect the American electorate in the future.

Data and Methodology

This study relies primarily on data collected by Wirthlin Worldwide and made available to the author in its raw form.[4] The Wirthlin study was conducted in the hours after the election on November 7–8, 2000, between 2:00 P.M. and 1:00 A.M. EST. Interviews were conducted via telephone using a representative random telephone sample consisting of 1,000 respondents who voted in the election and who reside in the continental United States. The margin of sampling error at a 95 percent confidence level is ±3 percentage points for the final sample of 1,000. This chapter also relies on data collected and analyzed by the Pew Research Center for the People and the Press[5] and exit polls conducted by the Voter News Service (VNS) and reported on the ABC News Internet site.[6]

The chapter utilizes logistic regression in analyzing three models. Logistic regression analysis extends the techniques of multiple regression analysis to research situations in which the outcome variable is categorical.

Which Voters Are Going Online and Where Are They Going?

Who Is Going Online for Election News?

As the Internet continues to grow at an exponential rate, online users have access to an astonishing breadth of information and services. While certain online activities draw a wide and diverse audience, other activities are engaged in by relatively homogeneous groups. Those who use the Internet to gather political information are typically thought to be members of a distinct group. The stereotype casts these Internet users as relatively young, white males, highly educated, and holding political views outside the mainstream. According to the Wirthlin survey, 18 percent of those who voted

Table 12.1

Age of Internet Users*

Age group	Percent of voters in same age group	Percent of all voters
18–29	28	23
30–39	20	24
40–49	19	26
50–59	13	15
60–69	9	6
70+	3	4

* Based on voters who used the Internet for election news.

on Election Day stated that they had used the Internet for news about the presidential contest. The Pew Research Center for the People and the Press conducted a similar study and also found that 18 percent of the general public went online for election news.[7] Drawing on survey data, this section investigates the stereotype and questions whether it is possible to generalize about those who go online for political information.

Is the Internet Just for the Young?

Conventional wisdom suggests that young people are more frequent users of the Internet than are their elders. Young people are perceived to be more technologically savvy compared to their parents and grandparents and more likely to turn to the Internet for political information. Therefore, we would expect to find more voters in the younger age cohorts using the Internet for political information. Drawing on the Wirthlin survey, Table 12.1 breaks down Internet use by age. The first column indicates the percentage of voters who used the Internet within each age cohort. The results confirm the conventional wisdom: A voter in the 18 to 29 age group was more than twice as likely to go online for election news as a voter in the 50 to 59 age group. However, the second column reflects the percent of voters in the respective age cohorts. Thus, in absolute terms, a relatively large number of voters over 40 years old also went online for election news in the months leading up to the 2000 election.

Contrary to the conventional wisdom, the Internet actually reached more voters over the age of 40 than under that age in the months leading up to the 2000 election. Thus, in fashioning an Internet strategy for future presidential elections, it would be a mistake for campaign staff to direct online advertising and information exclusively at younger voters.

Is Internet Use Limited to the Highly Educated and Upwardly Mobile?

In addition to being younger, the typical Internet user is commonly thought to be highly educated and professional. Based on these characteristics, we might hypothesize that most users who went online for political information held college degrees and had an income commensurate with professional salaries.

Data from the Wirthlin survey, as displayed in Table 12.2, provide only modest support for the "highly educated" hypothesis. In support of the hypothesis, the data reveal that voters with a college degree were three times as likely to get election news online as voters with only a high school diploma. The Pew Research Center report posted similar results, finding that 33 percent of college graduates got campaign news online in 2000.[8] An earlier Pew study conducted in the months leading up to the 1996 election found that only 9 percent of college graduates went online for news.[9]

In absolute terms, these results can be explained by the overall disparity in Internet use based on education. In comparative terms (as indicated in Table 12.2), higher levels of education may be correlated with higher levels of interest, causing a higher percentage of college-educated voters to use the Internet for election news. However, the hypothesis is undermined by data showing that a higher percentage of those with some college, technical, or vocational training used the Internet than those voters with postgraduate degrees. Further, it is not clear that all those who have a college degree fit the "highly educated" mold.

Descriptive analysis provides more compelling results for the "upwardly mobile" hypothesis. Internet use for political information ranged across income levels: Of those voters earning $30,000 or less per year, only 10 percent used the Internet for election news. Contrasting this number with the 23 percent of voters earning over $60,000 per year reveals a statistically significant divide across voters of varying income levels.

Is It a Male-Dominated Cyberworld?

The UCLA report mentioned earlier found that men have more access and spend more time online than do women.[10] This gender gap is

Table 12.2

Education Level of Internet Users*

Level of education	Percent using Internet
Less than high school	1
High school graduate	12
Some college/technical/vocational	27
College graduate	36
Post-graduate	22

* Based on voters who used the Internet for election news.

reflected in the Wirthlin data, which reveal that while 23 percent of men got at least some news about the election online, only 13 percent of women did.

Do Married Couples or Families Use the Internet?

As the cost of computer hardware and online service decreases, the Internet is becoming more common outside of work and in the home. We might hypothesize that economies of scale make Internet access more affordable and concomitantly increase the use of the Internet for political news gathering among married couples. This hypothesis is not borne out by the Wirthlin data. Of those voters who were married, only 19 percent went online for election information.

The Internet is also becoming more common in households with children. According to the National Center for Educational Statistics, 95 percent of all public schools had Internet access in 1999.[11] As schools around the country increasingly rely on the Internet as a teaching tool, the use of the Internet by children provides greater incentives for their parents to understand and use it as well. However, the Wirthlin data indicate that the presence of children at home has not translated into increased use of the Internet for political information by their parents. Of those respondents who indicated they had children at home, 18 percent used the Internet for political information.

Is There a Racial Divide Among Internet Users?

Despite the fact that Internet access is more financially viable than it was four years ago, conventional wisdom suggests there is still a racial "digital divide" in this country. In 1999, the National Telecommunications and Information Administration (NTIA) released a study entitled "Falling

Through the Net: Defining the Digital Divide." The study tracked computer and modem ownership and online access across income level, education level, race, and location (urban v. rural). The NTIA study found trends suggesting that, despite the general growth in online access, the digital divide was widening.[12] In particular, the study found that white households are 40 percent more likely to have home Internet access than African American and Hispanic households.[13]

Data obtained in the Wirthlin study provide only modest support for the proposition that there exists a racial digital divide among minorities in the *voting electorate*. Of African American voters surveyed in the study, 15 percent indicated that they went online for political information. Of Hispanic American voters, only 7 percent indicated they used the Internet for such information. Only the Hispanic American response represents a statistically significant difference from the national average of 18 percent.

Are Internet Users Concentrated on the Political Left or Right?

Conventional wisdom suggests that the typical online user is at the fringes of the political spectrum or, at least, holds viewpoints outside the mainstream. In contrast, data from the 2000 Wirthlin study indicate little difference between the political affiliations of Internet users and nonusers. Of those going online for political information, 34.6 percent identified themselves as Republicans while 35.1 percent identified themselves as Democrats. Self-identified Independents made up 21 percent of all those who went online for political information, and those voters who indicated they were registered with an alternative party made up 9 percent. This breakdown among Internet users is mirrored by the political affiliations of the electorate as a whole. As mentioned in previous chapters, the VNS exit poll found that Democrats make up 39 percent of the electorate, Republicans make up 35 percent, and Independents comprise 27 percent.[14] Thus, there seems to be little difference between the political affiliations of Internet users and nonusers.[15]

Measuring the Independent Effects of Specific Characteristics

Thus far we have used descriptive analysis to investigate the characteristics of online users. Here a logistic regression analysis is used to measure the independent effects of certain factors on the likelihood of using the Internet for political news about the election. The dichotomous dependent variable is whether an individual went online for election news. The independent

Table 12.3

Factors Affecting Internet Use by Voters

Independent variables	Regression coefficients	Significance
Age	−.19	.00
Income	.05	.25
Education	.21	.00
Gender	−.54	.00
Marriage	.28	.22
Children	−.35	.07
Political affiliation	.06	.49
Ethnicity	−.33	.31
Constant =	−1.713	
Chi-Square =	66.34	.00
N = 929		

variables are age, income, education, gender, marriage, children, political affiliation, and ethnicity. Table 12.3 presents the results of the analysis which confirm our descriptive data.

The regression results reveal that three variables have a statistically significant impact on whether a voter goes online for political information: age, education, and gender.[16] As the age of voters decreases, the probability that they go online for political news increases. In contrast, voters who have completed a higher level of formal education have a higher probability of going online. Finally, women are significantly less likely to go online for election news than men.

Using this model, we can estimate the probability that individuals with certain characteristics used the Internet for political information. Consider four examples:

- A 26-year-old white male with a college degree, a wife and no children, registered as a Democrat, earning $50,000 per year → 45 percent probability
- A 26-year-old black male with a high school diploma, not married, registered as a Democrat, earning $30,000 per year → 17 percent probability
- A 46-year-old white female with a college degree, a husband and two children, registered as a Democrat, earning $50,000 per year → 14 percent probability
- A 46-year-old white female with a high school diploma, a husband and two children, registered as a Democrat, earning $25,000 per year → 7 percent probability

Although the stereotype of the typical Internet user is breaking down, it is still possible to generalize about Internet users as a group. Contrary to conventional wisdom, income, political affiliation, and ethnicity are not significant predictors for whether a person uses the Internet to gather political information. However, individuals with certain characteristics, as defined by age, education, and gender, are still more likely to be overrepresented. Interestingly, the groups that are over-represented are the same groups that have traditionally been more knowledgeable and more partisan. The implications of this result will be discussed again in part two of this chapter.

Where Do Online News Consumers Go?

Internet advocates conceive of the Internet as a populist tool where information and understanding is not shaped by elite "gatekeepers" but by the Internet users themselves. The defining characteristic of the Internet, in contrast to radio or television, is the absence of gatekeepers regulating the form or amount of political information. Specifically, the Internet has the potential to alter political communications in two ways. First, the Internet could expand the content of information available to a mass audience. While the mainstream media tend to focus on polls and the horse race, the Internet could offer alternatives that focus on particular issues. Second, the Internet could potentially elevate political discourse of citizens by providing forums, or chat rooms, for discussions. The chat room allows citizens to overcome geographic and monetary obstacles to engage in intelligent political discourse and organization.

Several factors conspire to undermine the potential of the Internet as an instrument of change. One consequence of the absence of gatekeepers is that reliability and credibility on the Internet are left up to the individual user to determine. As the number of persons using the Internet has increased, the number of information sources available has also increased. Individual users may overcome this problem by restricting themselves to sites operated by mainstream media outlets that they trust. Similarly, voters may be using the Internet for convenience rather than to participate in meaningful political discourse. If voters visit only those sites on the Internet that are maintained by mainstream media sources, avoiding alternative political sites and chat rooms, the potential for the Internet as a tool to alter political dialogue is severely restricted and the potential for reinforcing a voter's existing preferences is enhanced.

Data collected in the months leading up to the 2000 election suggest that, despite its potential, the Internet has not fundamentally changed political communication. The Pew Research Center for the People and the Press asked those who went online for political news where they went most for news about the 2000 election. Fifty-five percent went to major news outlets such as CNN or the *New York Times* or local news organizations in their area, 27 percent responded that commercial online services such as America Online were their primary source, and 19 percent relied mostly on specialized sources such as political Web sites, candidate home pages, issue-oriented sites, and local government sites. In addition to identifying their primary online sources for election news, the Pew survey also asked respondents whether they had ever visited a number of specific Web sites for news or information about the 2000 election. Table 12.4 indicates that mainstream sites dominated, with CNN.com topping the list.

Evidence from the Pew Center study further suggests that those who get election news online are motivated to use the Internet because it is convenient. The Pew survey asked citizens why they chose to go online for election news. Table 12.5 provides a breakdown of the answers by age group. In each age category, convenience is the number one reason why citizens go online for election news. This result across all age groups undermines the notion of the Internet as a populist tool for expanding the scope of political communications. If convenience is the main reason for going online, we can predict that voters are more likely to avoid sites that present challenging views or exigent content.

The Pew study also revealed that only a small minority of Internet users participated in online dialogue. Of those who get campaign news online, only 8 percent joined chat rooms this election year. This result paints a picture of most online users as passive, rather than active, participants in the Internet medium.

Did Internet Communications Affect Voters?

Most Americans believe that the Internet has affected their lives in some way. According to the UCLA report, more than two-thirds of Americans who use the Internet consider the technology to be an "important" or "extremely important" source of information.[17] More specifically, the Pew Research Center study found that 43 percent of those using the Internet believed that online election news affected their vote choice. The question remains whether these subjective self-evaluations reflect an actual disparity that exists between the voting patterns of users and nonusers.

In their seminal work *The People's Choice*, Lazarsfeld, Berelson, and Gaudet describe three ways political communications impact a voter's decision: the activation effect, the reinforcement effect, and the conversion

Table 12.4

Did You Ever Go to . . .

Site	Percent yes	Percent no
CNN.com	59	41
News feature on Yahoo or MSN	57	42
MSNBC.com	52	48
Web sites of broadcast TV networks	45	54
Web sites of national newspapers	33	67
Local community Web sites	29	70
AOL news channel	27	72
Web sites of weekly news magazines	18	82
Special interest groups Web sites	16	83
House, Senate, White House Web sites	16	83
C-Span Web site	15	84
Wall Street Journal Web site	13	86
PBS Online	10	90
Salon or Slate	7	92

Source: Pew Research Center For The People & The Press. "Online Election News Poll." <www.people_press.org/online00mor.html>.

Table 12.5

Content vs. Convenience (in percent)

Why do you go online for election news?	Ages 18–29	Ages 30–49	Ages 50+
Information is more convenient	61	58	45
Other media do not provide enough news	25	30	34
Get information not available elsewhere	11	11	14
Internet sources reflect personal interests	7	6	5

Source: Pew Research Center For The People & The Press, "Online News Poll" <www.people_press.org/online00mor.htm>.

effect.[18] The activating forces of a political campaign bring the voter's predispositions to the level of visibility and expression, transforming the latent political tendency into a manifest vote. The reinforcing effect of political communications secures and stabilizes a voter's intention and translates it into an actual vote. The conversion effect measures the extent to which campaign information convinces voters to vote against their pre-dispositions. Using this interpretative frame, this section will attempt to measure the independent impact of Internet use on American voters.

Activation Effect

Issue Preference

Demographic data presented in part one of this chapter suggest that Internet users no longer represent a distinct demographic subgroup. However, there is some evidence that Internet users are divided by education level and ethnicity. Further, Internet users are often willing to embrace the distinction that they are part of an elite, "connected" class of citizens.[19] This begs the question: Did political communications received through the Internet activate voters on a different range of issues? In other words, did Internet users enter the voting booth with a different set of political preferences compared to nonusers with the same demographic characteristics?

Given the digital divide and the popular conception of the "connected" class, we may expect Internet users to have different sets of priorities for the nation and divergent criteria for their president. Respondents in the Wirthlin study were asked to give their main reason for voting for their candidate. As indicated in Table 12.6, there is not a significant difference between users and nonusers. Almost 19 percent of all users stated that political party was the main reason they voted for their candidate compared to 17 percent for nonusers. Similarly, voters who used the Internet were as likely as nonusers to mention a specific issue in their response. Internet users were slightly more concerned with the abortion issue, protecting the environment, and the economy. Nonusers, on the other hand, were relatively more concerned about social security and education. However, these differences were not statistically significant.

If there was not a significant difference in political preferences between Internet users and nonusers. Then the Internet did not activate a different set of preferences among Gore voters or Bush voters.

Vote Choice

While the Internet did not appear to activate citizens on any particular issue or aspect of character, it is possible that the Internet catalyzed voters to choose one of the candidates and thus affected vote choice.

Table 12.6

Main Reasons for Vote Choice Among Internet Users and Nonusers

Q: What was the main reason you voted for your candidate?	Percent nonusers	Percent Internet users
Party	17.0	18.8
Issue-based	32.3	32.2
• Tax relief	3.4	2.5
• Abortion	8.6	10.0
• Strengthen military	1.6	.6
• Social Security	4.0	2.5
• Long-term health care/Medicare	1.0	1.3
• Education	3.3	1.9
• Economy	3.0	5.0
• Protect environment	1.1	2.5
• Family values	1.3	1.3
• Supreme Court	1.1	1.3
• Gun control	1.7	1.9
• Other issue-based reasons*	2.2	1.4
Candidate-based	41.8	37.1
• Dislike other candidate	11.6	8.1
• Honest person	5.1	8.3
• Time for a change	2.3	.6
• Restore integrity to White House	3.0	0
• Thinks like me	2.1	3.1
• High ethical standards	2.7	1.9
• Clear vision for future	1.7	3.8
• For the working people	2.4	1.3
• Positive past performance	4.7	5.0
• Other candidate-based reasons**	7.2	5.0
Other	8.5	10.2

* Includes: Tough on crime, prescription drugs, plan for surplus.
** Includes: Personally strong; has new ideas; gets things done; cares about people like me; makes me feel secure; debate performance; like candidate—unspecified.

Here a logit model is used to investigate whether the Internet had an independent effect on whether an individual voted for Bush or Gore. The dependent variable is whether a voter chose Bush or Gore. This model thus excludes voters who chose Ralph Nader or Pat Buchanan. However, given these candidates' minimal impact on the popular vote tally, this is not viewed as problematic. Regression results for model are listed in Table 12.7.

Three clusters of independent variables clearly affected vote choice. First, registration as a Democrat and where voters place themselves on the ideological spectrum ("Ideology") were both strong predictors of a vote for Gore. This result is consistent with the conventional wisdom that voters

Table 12.7

Factors Affecting Vote Choice

Independent variables	Regression coefficients	Significance
Used Internet	.36	.22
Registered Democrat	1.8	.00
Clinton evaluation	−1.4	.00
Black	2.6	.02
Income	.02	.78
Age	.07	.12
Education	.06	.53
Married	−.53	.08
Gender	.30	.25
Ideology	.41	.00
Right track/wrong track	1.0	.00
Constant = −.577		
Chi-Square = 625.13		.00
N = 819		

take cues from their chosen party. Second, whether a voter was African American was a significant predictor. This is consistent with VNS Exit Poll data that found 90 percent of all African American voters chose Gore over Bush. Finally, whether a voter approved of the way Bill Clinton handled his job as president and whether a voter believed that the country was on the "right track" or "wrong track" were statistically significant predictors. If an individual voter disapproved of Clinton's performance, the odds that the voter would cast a vote for Gore decreased dramatically. As noted in the previous chapter, the Gore campaign worried that many disapproved of Clinton's performance in office and attempted to downplay this effect by limiting the role Clinton played in Gore's campaign while in office.

It is worth mentioning that age and income were not significant predictors of vote choice in the model. That age was not determinative is supported by exit poll data that indicated that voting was consistent across age cohorts. That income was not determinative may be suggestive of a flaw in the survey. The uppermost income cohort in the Wirthlin survey was $60,000+ per year, effectively lumping together what may be disparate groups.

Notably, whether voters went online for political information was not a statistically significant predictor of their vote. We may infer from this result that Internet use did not affect vote choice in a systematic way. In other words, political information obtained online did not activate voter dispositions toward Bush or away from Gore, or vice versa. This conclusion is consistent with existing literature on vote choice. In discussing the acti-vation effect, Lazarsfeld et al. stressed that attention is selective: Voters self-regulate their exposure to certain types of information. While traditional media forms such as television and newspapers allow some mea-sure of self-regulation, the individual's ability to control the type and con-tent of information received is far greater on the Internet. Thus two explanations emerge for why Internet use is not a significant predictor for vote choice. First, since neither conservative nor liberal Web sites dominate, Internet users have ample access to viewpoints from both sides of the political spectrum. Second, since reasonable people can disagree on who was the better candidate, it is not clear that increasing access to information will necessarily push a voter in the direction of one candidate.

Reinforcement or Conversion?

Although Internet use did not activate voters on a particular issue or emerge as a reliable predictor for vote choice, the Internet may have had a rein-forcing or converting effect on vote choice. These effects will be measured by dividing voters into two camps: crossover voters and static voters. A static voter is someone who voted with their party (e.g., a registered Re-publican who voted for Bush), while a crossover voter crossed party lines.

Two contrasting understandings of the media and voters can be used to formulate hypotheses. On the one hand, traditional political science theory suggests that the political communications received during a campaign most often serve to reinforce rather than convert the voter. Lazarsfeld et al. found that people who followed the election most closely were reading their own party's propaganda and were most resistant to conversion, and those most open to conversion read and listened least. This theory is echoed by Flanigan and Zingale, who argue that those with the most exposure to the media are among the least affected by it.[20] According to this view, we would hypothesize that those who are more likely to read and pay attention to political news on the Internet are also most likely to have strong predispositions.

On the other hand, technology advocates aver that the Internet represents a unique and potentially revolutionary medium that does not conform to traditional tenets about information effects. One of the great advantages offered by the Internet is that individuals no longer need to rely on a few centralized sources for information about politics. The Internet enables peo-ple to form their own groups, attract followers, and participate in the po-litical process without raising large sums of money. One implication of this argument is that as the Internet grows and networks of political commu-

Table 12.8

Factors Affecting "Crossover" Voting

Independent variables	Regression coefficients	Significance
Used Internet	−.48	.05
Crossed over in 1996	2.65	.00
Age	−.03	.31
Country on the right track	−.32	.17
Clinton fatigue	−.16	.07
Chi-Square = 245.5		.00
N = 859		

nication become available online, individuals will break their traditional ties to political parties. Thus, if the number of voters who turn to the Internet for voting cues increases, then there might be a concomitant decrease in the number of voters who use political parties as a heuristic shortcut for choosing a political candidate. The notion that the Internet undermines the influence of political parties is consistent with the more general argument that the Internet will cause a fragmentation of the public discourse.

These conflicting postulates will be tested through logistic regression analysis by creating a dependent variable called crossover voting. If a registered Democrat voted for a candidate other than Gore, or a registered Republican voted for a candidate other than Bush, that voter is considered a crossover voter. For the purposes of the dependent variable, a voter who crossed party lines was coded 1, and a voter who did not cross party lines was coded 0. Controlling for whether the voter crossed party lines in 1996, age, approval of Clinton, and more general views on the direction of the country, this model measures the effect of Internet use on crossover voters.

As indicated in Table 12.8 whether a voter goes online for political information does provide a statistically significant predictor for whether that voter crosses party lines. However, the coefficient is *negative*. This indicates that going online for election news actually reduces the probability that a voter will cross party lines. It can be inferred from this result that the Internet is a reinforcing mechanism rather than a conversion mechanism.

The nature of the new medium provides some explanation for this conclusion. Individual Internet users choose the content of the political information they receive online. Internet users looking for political information on the Web are more likely to visit and revisit those sites that confirm preconceived notions rather than seek sites that challenge or denigrate those beliefs. Given that Internet users can bookmark one specific site for all their political news, and given that that site most likely confirms many preexisting beliefs, it is not surprising that Internet use reinforces the previously held views and that the odds that Internet users cross party lines actually decrease. Although Internet technology makes available a seemingly limitless number of viewpoints, it also allows individuals to sharply narrow their exposure to alternative viewpoints.

The Internet and the Future

What Can Individual Voters Expect From the Internet in Future Elections?

Based on Internet activities during the 2000 election, users can expect to feel a greater web presence by both Republicans and Democrats in future elections. Six months prior to the election, the Bush team called in Internet consultants who transformed Bush's Web site from a bland online brochure to a slick, interactive site. In reviewing the Web site, the *Los Angeles Times* stated that the Bush site's "bold colors, snazzy graphics and crisp design project an image of George W. Bush as the latest cool product from Silicon Valley."[21] Also, just forty-eight hours before Election Day, Bush's Internet strategy team decided to invest in banner advertisements on Web sites in key states, including Florida. This investment in cyberspace by the Bush team, and the success that followed, suggest that no future presidential campaign will be complete without a fully developed and interactive candidate Web site.

In future elections, voters can also expect to find their e-mail inboxes full of political mailings. Both Republicans and Democrats are increasingly turning to e-mail because it is cheaper, faster, and more likely to be passed on than old-fashioned bulk-rate direct mail. In the months leading up to the 2000 election, the Democratic and Republican national committees launched almost identical initiatives designed to take advantage of the viral potential of e-mail communication. The Democrats called their effort the e-Precinct Leader program. E-leaders agreed to receive weekly messages from the DNC and forward them to at least ten undecided voters they knew. The Republicans called their program e-Champions and asked members to pass e-mails along to as many friends as possible. These e-mail lists are arguably more valuable than traditional direct-mail lists because candidates can communicate with all of the people on their e-mail list almost instantaneously.

Voters in the next election may also find increasing amounts of online solicitation of campaign donations. John McCain, in his race for the Republican Party nomination, enjoyed incredible success through Internet fund-raising. McCain hired the online campaign firm Aristotle International for $30,000 and received access to Aristotle's list of more than 150 million registered voters, online fund-raising technology, and the ability to aim online banner ads at specific voter groups.[22] McCain then went on to raise $6 million online. The unique nature of online fund-raising proved invaluable to his campaign for a number of reasons. First, donors were able to make credit card donations through the Web site, giving the campaign immediate access to donations without having to wait until donors sent checks. Second, the absence of printing and postage costs made online fund-raising much more efficient than traditional fund-raising techniques. Unlike direct-mail solicitations where a candidate must spend as much as 30 percent of a fifty-dollar contribution in overhead costs, the nominal costs of maintaining a Web site allow candidates to receive online donations of as little as ten dollars and still put that money to use. The efficient nature of online fund-raising could make it a dominant form of campaign solicitation, especially if the soft money loophole is closed and candidates must rely on smaller contributions from more voters. Finally, 70 percent of McCain's online donors were giving either their first or second political donation ever. This indicates that fund-raising online may offer access to a new set of donors.

In conclusion, increases in Web campaigning, e-mail communications, and online campaign fund-raising provide ample points of departure for future research. As the Internet becomes the medium for more political communication, its impact on voters' behavior is likely to become more apparent.

Will the Internet Fundamentally Change the Way Americans Vote?

The Florida recount and the legal problems it engendered revealed that our system of running elections is out of date. The Florida counties at the center of the recount dispute used punch cards, the most commonly used device to record votes in the country.[23] The Florida recount brought national attention to the intricacies of vote counting, and the nature of these problems suggests that the time may be ripe for utilizing Internet technology in election counting. An important advantage to voting on the Internet is that it does not require citizens to learn completely new communication methods. Web sites contain pictures, text, and audio for their users, all of which are traditional modes of political communication. Online voting allows citizens to avoid problems caused by traveling to polling places and allows election officials to overcome problems attendant on counting votes and dealing with voting irregularities.

Even before the Florida recount debacle, the idea of Internet voting had arisen in a number of different contexts. In January 2000, the Brookings Institution and Cisco Systems cosponsored a symposium in which senior public officials and experts examined the potential impact of Internet voting.[24] In addition, approximately 350 volunteer military service members scattered around the world actually voted via the Internet using their home computers as part of a Department of Defense pilot project that allowed military personnel to register and cast absentee ballots online. Though the number of participants was small, the entire process went smoothly. Glenn Flood, spokesman for the Department of Defense, said of the experiment, "It's something we wanted to try out in a limited way. Given what has been going on [with the Florida recount] I expect we'll see a lot more interest in it."[25]

Although the technology for online voting exists, a number of problems must be overcome before Internet voting becomes a reality. First, many people are still concerned with privacy and security on the Internet. When asked if "people who go online put their privacy at risk," 64 percent of Internet users and 76 percent of nonusers either agreed or strongly agreed.[26] Closely related to the question of privacy is security. Ninety-one percent of all Internet users indicated they were concerned or very concerned about credit card security on the Web. In trying to implement an effective online voting system, local and state governments may have a difficult time allaying the skepticism about privacy and security of online activity.

Second, under the Voting Rights Act, states must allow federal observers to enter and attend any polling place "for the purpose of observing whether persons who are entitled to vote are being permitted to vote."[27] It would be impossible for federal election officials to visit the many sites where individuals may be voting online. While the law may need to be amended to include the new realities of online voting, the principle behind the law— that the federal government has a strong interest in monitoring fairness— would still need to be addressed.

Ultimately, the greatest barrier to online voting is the massive amount of money that would be needed to fund such a program and ensure its smooth operation. Since presidential elections are run at the state level, state legislatures would be responsible for absorbing the costs. Given that state legislatures will resist prioritizing election procedures over other concerns, the federal government would have to make a substantial financial investment in any such plan.

Is the Internet Erasing Political Boundaries?

Former speaker of the House, Tip O'Neill, once wrote that "all politics is local."[28] At the time, he meant that if you want to make a real difference, you have to find people in the same political jurisdiction who share your goals and beliefs. The Internet age has changed the meaning of local politics by erasing traditional geographic obstacles to collective action. However, the blurring of geographic lines in cyberspace is at odds with the firmly entrenched boundaries of the electoral college system. One example of this disconnect was the vote-swapping scheme developed on the Internet in the last weeks of the 2000 campaign. A review of this scheme and its implications suggests that the Internet may bring about a fundamental change in electoral process.

In the weeks leading up to the election, Internet users on opposite coasts began using Internet technology to "swap" their votes. The idea worked like this: in swing states such as Florida, where Gore and Bush were running even, a vote for Nader by those who would ordinarily vote as Democrats would hurt Gore. In states such as Texas, polls indicated an overwhelming victory for Bush, meaning that a vote for Gore would not make much difference. So voters in Florida and Texas would strike a bargain: Gore supporters in Texas would vote for Nader, while Nader supporters in Florida would vote for Gore. Both parties to this agreement would benefit, since Gore needed Florida's electoral votes while Nader's Green Party needed 5 percent of the popular vote to qualify for matching federal campaign funds in 2004.

Vote-exchange Web sites began to emerge following an online article in *Slate* magazine, "Nader's Traders: How to Save Al Gore's Bacon by Swapping Votes on the Internet."[29] The author, American University law professor Jamin Raskin, introduced the idea as a variation on the "pairing" technique used by United States senators. Raskin proposed that sites could use sorting software to match individual Gore and Nader voters: "If just 100,000 Gore supporters and 100,000 Nader supporters in the key states registered and kept their words, both a Gore victory and federal funding for the Greens could be accomplished."[30]

The following week a number of Web sites were registered to accomplish this goal. Voters could visit votexchange2000.com, voteswap2000.com, voteauction.com, or nadertrader.com to engage in vote swapping. On votexchange2000.com, voters could navigate to a Web page where they were asked three questions: their state of residence, their preferred candidate, and their preferred major-party candidate. The program would inform voters about whether their states were considered "safe" or "swing." The Web site would then invite visitors who wished to contact compatible voters to enter their e-mail addresses. Voters' preferences and e-mail addresses were then stored in a database. A software program matched up citizens with complementary preferences and sent out e-mail addresses to each party. At that point, further discussion or action by any two voters matched by the votexchange2000 software was conducted directly between those parties on an entirely voluntary basis. If the two voters believed each other trustworthy, on Election Day they would each vote the other person's preferences. If the two voters could not reach an understanding, they were invited to return to the Web site to try again.

One week before the election, the operators of this Web site voluntarily shut down following the threat of prosecution by California's secretary of state.[31] The American Civil Liberties Union filed a complaint for injunctive relief on behalf of the site operators and citizens in Massachusetts and California, claiming that the threat of prosecution violated basic First Amendment protections. The district court judge denied the request.

Whether or not the courts extend strict First Amendment protection to the vote swapping, this case raises interesting questions about the relevance of the electoral college in an Internet age. If these types of arrangements proliferate in the 2004 election and if these Web sites are constitutionally protected, political leaders may be forced to reevaluate the viability of the electoral college in an age in which technology bridges the gap between states in ways not contemplated by the Framers of the Constitution.

Conclusion

This chapter has dispelled a number of commonly held views regarding Internet use and the American electorate. Part one demonstrated that voters who used the Internet for political news during the 2000 election campaign were not a discrete group, but represented all ranges of demographic and partisan categories. Given the wide audience, it is not surprising that most of the information voters received over the Internet came from sites operated by mainstream media sources. Part two found that the Internet did not have a significant activation effect for voter preferences or vote choice. Further, not only did the Internet not convert many voters, it served as a reinforcing mechanism. Despite these modest results, part three gave a number of examples suggesting that the Internet is likely to become an even greater force in American politics in future elections.

These conclusions suggest that while the seeds of the Internet revolution have been sown, America is at least a few years from seeing the full bloom. At this stage, the Internet is a useful source of information for a significant portion of the population, but is more of a reinforcing tool of traditional media than a catalyst for political realignments.

Notes

1. The World Wide Web is not identical to the Internet. It is one of many Internet-based communication systems. However, since the Web is the dominant system in the United States, I will use the terms "Web" and "Internet" interchangeably.
2. ULCA Center for Communication Policy, "Surveying the Digital Future," p. 10 (hereinafter ULCA Report). The study found that 47 percent of Americans use the Internet at home and 42 percent use the Internet at their place of employment.
3. Ibid., p. 10. In 1997, 19 million Americans were using the Internet. That number tripled in 1998 and then exceeded 100 million in 1999.
4. Wirthlin Worldwide is an opinion research firm headquartered in McLean, Virginia.
5. Pew Research Center for the People and the Press, "Online Election News Poll" (hereinafter Pew Research Center Report).
6. "ABC News National Exit Poll," available online at <www.abcnews.go.com/sections/politics/2000vote/general/exitpoll_hub.html>.
7. This finding was supported by a national exit poll conducted by Voter News Service that found that 30 percent of voters went online for political information about the campaign.
8. Pew Research Center Report, 1–2.
9. Ibid.
10. UCLA Report, 12–13.
11. Catrina Williams, "Internet Access in U.S. Public Schools and Classrooms: 1994–1999."
12. National Telecommunications and Information Administration, "Falling Through the Net: Defining the Digital Divide" (hereinafter NTIA Report).
13. Ibid.
14. The poll asked: "No matter how you voted today, do you usually think of yourself as a: (1) Democrat; (2) Republican; (3) Independent."
15. This conclusion is consistent with the UCLA Report that found no difference between the political affiliation of users and nonusers. UCLA Report, 30.
16. It is not clear that age correlates with education for voters. Because all voters are older than 18, and most citizens complete their formal education at age 22, colinearity does not present a major obstacle here.
17. UCLA Report, 33.
18. Paul Lazarsfeld, Bernard Berelson, and Hazel Gaudet, *The People's Choice: How the Voter Makes Up His Mind in a Presidential Campaign,* ch. 3–9.
19. This is an ethic that many Internet Service Providers (ISPs) have sought to nurture in their marketing campaigns. ISPs promise access to unlimited information that in theory translates into a more substantive and complex understanding of the world.
20. William H. Flanigan and Nancy H. Zingale, *Political Behavior of the American Electorate,* 146.
21. Karen Kaplan, "E-Review: A Look at the Net Results of Presidential Hopefuls," C1.

22. Shawn Zeller, "Clicking on e-Dollars."

23. Richard Morin, "The Voting Technology Gap," B5.

24. Brookings Institution Symposium, "The Future of Internet Voting."

25. Stephen Hegarty, "Military Ballots Brook Varying Rules," B1.

26. UCLA Report, 32.

27. 42 U.S.C. 1973(f).

28. Tip O'Neil, *All Politics Is Local, and Other Rules of the Game.*

29. Jamin Raskin, "Nader's Traders: How to Save Al Gore's Bacon by Swapping Votes on the Internet."

30. Ibid.

31. On October 30, 2000, the secretary of state of California sent e-mail correspondence to the founders of a Web site known as "voteswap2000.com" threatening criminal prosecution under the California Elections and Penal Codes and demanding that the operators "end [the Web site's] activity immediately."

Bibliography

"ABC News National Exit Poll," available online at <www.abcnews.go.com/sections/politics/2000vote/general/exitpoll_hub.html>.

Brookings Institution. "Symposium: The Future of Internet Voting." Transcript available: <www.brook.edu/comm/transcripts/20000120.htm> (last visited 09/10/2001).

Flanigan, William H., and Nancy H. Zingale. *Political Behavior of the American Electorate.* 7th ed. Washington, DC: Congressional Quarterly Press, 1991.

Hegarty, Stephen. "Military Ballots Brook Varying Rules," *St. Petersburg Times,* November 22, 2000, B1.

Kaplan, Karen. "E-Review: A Look at the Net Results of Presidential Hopefuls," *Los Angeles Times,* August 17, 2000, C1.

Lazarsfeld, Paul, Bernard Berelson, and Hazel Gaudet. *The People's Choice: How the Voter Makes Up His Mind in a Presidential Campaign.* 3rd ed. New York: Columbia University Press, 1968.

Morin, Richard. "The Voting Technology Gap." *Washington Post,* January 28, 2000, B5.

National Telecommunications and Information Administration. "Falling Through the Net: Defining the Digital Divide," Department of Commerce, July 1999 <www.ntia.doc.gov/ntiahome/fttn99/contents.html>.

O'Neil, Tip. *All Politics Is Local, and Other Rules of the Game.* New York: Times Books, 1994.

Pew Research Center for the People and the Press. "Online Election News Poll." <www.people-press.org/online00mor.htm>.

Raskin, Jamin. "Nader's Traders: How to Save Al Gore's Bacon by Swapping Votes on the Internet." *The Slate.* <http://slate.msn.com/Concept/00–10–24/Concept.asp>.

UCLA Internet Report: UCLA Center for Communication Policy. "Surveying the Digital Future," <www.ccp.ucla.edu/pages/internet-report.asp>.

Williams, Catrina. "Internet Access in U.S. Public Schools and Classrooms: 1994–1999." Department of Education, National Center for Education Statistics, spring 2000, <http://nces.ed.gov/pubs2000/qrtlyspring/4elem/q4–8.html>.

Zeller, Shawn. "Clicking on e-Dollars." *National Journal* 32, no. 42 (October 14, 2000): 3248–3249.

13

Platforms, Promises, and the Agenda for the New Government

Lynn C. Ross

Charles O. Jones argues that the Framers of the Constitution intentionally set elections and presidential terms of office to coincide with the calendar, not the emergence of issues. No part of the Constitution provides even hints at holding elections "as a result of a crisis or some issue configuration."[1] Yet presidential elections are often viewed as representations of which candidate's policy proposals the public endorses. This has led some presidents to conclude that they have a mandate to enact the policy proposals they set forth during the campaign. Indeed, even presidential hopefuls like George W. Bush have invoked the language of mandates: "If you give me your trust, I will honor it. . . . Grant me a mandate, and I will use it."[2] It is for this reason that the party platforms and the promises set out during presidential campaigns take on special meaning. They are the precursors to the agenda of every new administration. And the success or failure of presidents in enacting that agenda is often evaluated in terms of whether they had the mandate of the people. Further, the salience of the issues and the clarity of candidates' issue positions during the presidential campaign affect the extent to which issues matter when voters go to the polls. This, in turn, determines the agenda for the new government, which often contributes in a significant way to public policy outcomes.

I am especially grateful to Stephen J. Wayne, whose guidance and encouragement made this chapter possible. I am also thankful to Jeff and Sam Yarnell for their seemingly limitless patience.

The 2000 Election: Apathy, Indecision, and a Very Close Race

By all accounts, the 2000 election was unusual. Obviously, the events sur-rounding the final result were like none witnessed in American history. Much of the election's uniqueness stemmed from what was predicted from the beginning to be a very close race. And close elections are unusual in the United States. In the twenty-five elections in the twentieth century, only three resulted in the president-elect winning with less than 300 electoral votes. Similarly, only three presidents in American history have been elected without winning the popular vote—none in the twentieth century.

The 2000 election was also one in which a president was not running for office. Of the twenty-five elections in the twentieth century, this was the case in only six. When a sitting president runs for reelection, "it's a vote of confidence or no confidence . . . should we keep the person we've known, or should we throw the rascal out."[3] But when no incumbent is on the slate, voters must make a more complicated assessment, projecting who they think will do a better job based in part on past experience.

Interestingly, the closeness of the race and the relatively complex de-cision (given no incumbent) did not seem to pique voter interest. Poll data from the early summer showed that Americans were not particularly en-gaged in the election. The Pew Research Center for the People and the Press found that only a small minority, 15 percent, looked for campaign news, and the vast majority, 83 percent, came across such information only serendipitously.[4] In its report, Pew attributed this relative apathy to two main factors. First, measured against comparable questions from polls at around the same time for the 1992 and 1996 elections, many citizens said that who is elected president is not as important as it once was. Twenty percent of the respondents agreed with the statement that who is elected president is not as important as it was in the 1970s and 1980s. Almost one-third said it did not make much difference to them who is elected president, up from 18 percent in Pew surveys conducted in 1992 and 1996. Second, younger Americans seemed more cynical and disconnected from politics than even in the recent past. Cynicism over what the next president could achieve was comparable to that expressed in polls from August 1976, when the country was still recovering from Watergate and the oil shortages of the mid-1970s. In the 1976 survey, as in 2000, Pew found that nearly half of the respondents agreed that "things will pretty much be the same" no matter who is elected.[5]

While apathy and cynicism may explain the lack of electoral engage-ment in the earlier part of the race, there also seemed to be an element of genuine indecision and an inability to draw distinctions between the choices. A month before the conventions, Pew found that 37 percent of respondents were having trouble choosing between Al Gore and Bush because they believed *neither* was qualified, but almost as many said they were having trouble because *either* would be qualified. And only a bare majority of respondents thought Gore and Bush had different positions on issues.[6]

The peace and prosperity of the time may have lulled voters into complacency, whereas party elites saw a stark contrast between "the public disinterest, disengagement, and the extraordinary high stakes in this election . . . [and] the stakes in Social Security, and in taxes, and what to do with the surplus, and the future of the Supreme Court, and so on."[7] In short, prior to the national nominating conventions, much of the electorate did not perceive the presidency as critical to the future, was not particularly excited about either candidate, did not perceive high stakes in terms of the issues of the campaign, and was unclear about what the issue differences between the candidates were. Taken together, these factors help to explain why many Americans did not perceive the choice between Bush and Gore as a clear or important one.

In the end, the horse race that was predicted from the beginning of the 2000 election campaign materialized. The Voter News Service (VNS) exit poll showed that a sizable number of voters (17 percent) were still making up their minds about how they would vote one week before the election.[8] While electoral apathy and cynicism were not new phenomena in the 2000 election, and while there were myriad factors contributing to the closeness of the race, greater electoral engagement might have changed the outcome. An estimated 51.4 percent of people who were old enough to vote cast ballots in the 2000 election. This turnout rate was not as dismal as 1996, when about 49 percent of those old enough to vote cast ballots—the lowest turnout since 1924. But it was not as high as 1992, when about 55 percent voted.

Party Platforms: A Critical Link Between Parties, Candidates, and the Electorate

Platforms are a linchpin between the parties, the candidates, and the electorate. First, they are a means through which candidates can influence their parties' policies. There is evidence in both the Democratic and the Republican platforms of 2000 that the candidates had significant influence. Al Gore and George W. Bush are mentioned more than any other person in their respective platforms, 98 times for Gore and 44 times for Bush.

The platforms are also a means by which citizens decide for which party to vote. Clearly the focus of the 2000 platforms on promised benefits like Social Security, health care, and public education was aimed at garnering as many votes as possible.[9] The platforms also link the candidates to the electorate in another way. They provide the blueprint for the more specific promises that will be made to voters in the months following the conventions. And while "platforms are to run on," they may also be to "stand on." Research by Jeff Fishel has found a surprisingly large number of the testable pledges in platforms are fulfilled by the party controlling the presidency (ranging from 91 percent on agriculture and defense to 51 percent on labor).[10] This rate of redemption makes the platform's link to the policy preferences of the electorate even more meaningful. It places the platform drafting process at the beginning of an important, if circuitous, route to public policy outcomes.

Platforms also offer an interesting window into the election itself because they provide voters with important information about the nominees. They are the first test of the nominee's ability to lead his party by putting his mark on its message to the public. Platforms are also explicit statements of political philosophies and issue positions, which distinguish the parties from each other and provide voters with electoral choices. To the extent that platforms provide specific action, the electorate's choice of party also becomes a choice of policy preferences.[11]

Platforms are examined seriously by only a very small number of voters,[12] but the process of deriving party platforms has an important, if indirect, influence on voters. While the average citizen might not read the parties' platforms, policy statements reach voters indirectly through interest groups, the media, political speeches, and the like.[13] Further, the construction of the party platform is a trade-off between what policies the various factions within the party will tolerate and the leadership's desire to garner broader support in the electorate.[14] Consequently, party platforms have grown in size (length) and diversity (of issue positions) as parties cast wider nets, attempting to appeal to as many voters as possible.[15] In 1948, for example, the Democratic platform contained about 2,800 words and the Republican platform about 2,000 words. By 1984, the Democratic platform was almost twenty times as long, and the Republican platform almost fifteen times as long, as it had been four decades before.[16] In 2000, the Democratic platform contained more than 24,000 words and the Republican plan almost 35,000 words,[17] and both covered a huge array of policy issues, from agriculture and defense, to energy, and technology.

Since the party's goal is to win elections, it makes sense that in developing platforms, parties try to anticipate voters' policy interests. Gerald Pomper argues that in order to contribute to winning the election, platforms

Table 13.1

Importance of Issues and Voter Preferences on Issues (in percent)

Gallup poll July 25–26, 2000 issue	Extremely important	Very important	Extremely/very important	Better performing candidate (percent point difference)
Education	43	46	89	Gore (+2)
Economy	35	51	86	Bush (+7)
Health care	37	47	84	Gore (+6)
Social Security	37	45	82	Gore (+2)
Handling the budget surplus	32	47	79	Bush (+11)
Medicare	34	44	78	Gore (+10)
Taxes	33	44	77	Bush (+15)
Creating jobs	28	44	72	Gore (+4)
Environment	29	42	71	Gore (+28)
National defense	30	40	70	Bush (+27)
Gun issue	30	32	62	Bush (+9)
Foreign affairs	18	40	58	Bush (+14)
Abortion	25	27	52	Gore (+6)
Foreign trade	15	36	51	Bush (+13)

Source: Gallup Polling, <www.gallup.com/Election2000/>, July 25–26, 2000. Question asked: "Now I am going to read a list of some of the issues that will probably be discussed in this year's presidential election campaigns. As I read each one, please tell me how important the candidates' positions on that issue will be in influencing your vote for president—extremely important, very important, somewhat important, or not important."

need to deal only with policy questions that contribute to victory, present comparisons of the parties' past records to win voters concerned with the "nature of the times," and make promises that are consistent with the voters' positions on the issues.[18] A brief examination of the issues that Americans were most concerned about before the election reveals that the parties were paying keen attention to what Americans were saying. Just prior to the conventions, a Gallup poll asked people about the most important issues influencing their vote in the upcoming election and which candidate they preferred on each of these issues. Table 13.1 summarizes those results.

Pomper tells us that topics like foreign policy, defense, and economic policy do not tend to have a direct or personal effect on individuals. Because they are less salient, vague platform pledges are sufficient. Other issues like labor, natural resources, and social welfare require more specific platform pledges because they have a more direct and personal effect on voters, who tend to be more knowledgeable about them.[19] As Table 13.1 shows, Gallup's data are fairly consistent with Pomper's finding. Three of the top four most important issues people mentioned were education, health care, and Social Security. Defense and foreign policy issues (foreign affairs and trade) fell below the top ten. The economy, which was deemed the second most important issue in determining vote choice, is the exception to Pomper's theory of voters' focus. A plausible argument could be made, however, that respondents were focused more on their personal economic situation ("pocketbook") when asked about the economy, rather than on the more general economic policy ("sociotropic") to which Pomper refers.[20]

Gallup also reported that major concerns about war or other foreign policy issues on the national scene were "conspicuously absent" from the list of concerns that American voters mentioned before the 2000 election. In contrast, during the Cold War era, polls had shown that foreign affairs were a primary focus in the 1952, 1968, 1972, and 1980 presidential campaigns.[21] This finding may be emblematic of the very nature of these issues, as discussed above, but in the context of the 2000 election, it may also provide evidence that during times of peace and prosperity, Americans perceive these issues as less relevant to them in their personal lives.

Interestingly, respondents uniformly thought Bush would better handle those issues on which voters tend to be least informed, the most ephemeral ones, and Gore engendered more confidence on issues on which voters tend to be most informed, that is, those that were more directly personal and focused on group benefits. One interpretation of this finding could be that voters, unclear about the differences between the candidates, reverted to the traditional partisan stereotypes: the Republicans' strength being a vibrant free-enterprise system and a defense that ensures the nation's security, and Democrats' strength being generous group benefits and protection for the poor and needy.[22]

Having a platform that emphasized issues on which the party was weak worked to counter the stereotype. In particular, the Republican platform gave considerable attention to traditional Democratic issues. "Education and Opportunity: Leave No American Behind" was the second section of the seven in the platform; its fourth section was "Retirement Security and Health Care: Our Pledge to America." With "American Partners in Conservation and Preservation: Stewardship of Our Natural Resources" (the fifth section) added, the Republican platform focused almost half of its contents on issues that have traditionally been considered Democratic strengths.[23] This emphasis served two purposes for the Republicans: to appeal to voters on issues on which the party has not traditionally fared well and to provide specificity on issues on which (given their salience) voters tend to be knowledgeable.

It is also interesting that the Republican platform was longer than the

Democratic platform by more than 10,000 words. Although the length of a platform does not provide conclusive evidence that it offers more specific policy proposals, the 2000 platforms were notably different from historical patterns. Specifically, in the four decades that Jeff Fishel examined, the Republicans had a shorter platform than the Democrats in nine out of ten elections.[24]

In sum, getting specific allowed the Republicans to co-opt Democratic issues, which were important issues to the public. At the same time, giving prominence to these issues downplayed the Republicans' differences from the Democrats, who had led the nation through record prosperity. This strategy persisted as the campaign hit full stride. E. J. Dionne Jr. a senior fellow at the Brookings Institution, remarked:

> [After the primaries] I think by reducing perceived issue differences between himself and Gore on questions such as education, healthcare, housing, and other areas of federal action, [George W. Bush made] himself look like a different kind of Republican, a Republican who is not against government action in these areas, [and] he has succeeded in convincing a very substantial number of Americans that the difference on issues between electing Bush and electing Gore are much smaller than they might have thought.[25]

While there were differences between the parties on such issues as abortion, guns, and the role of government, those issues were ones on which the parties' electoral coalitions disagreed. On other issues, there seemed to be more limited disagreement. Table 13.2 provides a comparison on several selected issues to illustrate both the differences and the similarities between the party platforms.

Issues, Promises, and Voting Behavior: A Review of the Literature

Most literature on issue voting has focused on whether partisanship, candidate traits, or issues most influence decisions about how to vote. An underlying assumption in most of the research (even in the early social-psychological models) is that voters must be able to understand their policy options if they are to vote for candidates who hold policy positions similar to their own. Page and Brody confirmed this dynamic by examining "candidate ambiguity" in the 1968 presidential campaign. They found that both Richard Nixon and Hubert Humphrey provided vague information to the public vis-à-vis their positions on the Vietnam War.[26] Because there was little objective information about the issue positions, voters relied on more subjective processes and then retrospectively rationalized their vote choice

Table 13.2

Comparison of Major Party Platforms on Selected Campaign Issues

Issue	Democratic platform	Republican platform
Abortion	"Stands behind the right of every woman to choose, consistent with Roe v. Wade, and regardless of ability to pay." However, explicitly welcomes others into the party who may hold differing positions on these and other issues.	Supports a human life amendment to the Constitution and legislation to make clear that the Fourteenth Amendment's protections apply to unborn children. Opposes using public revenues for abortion and funding organizations that advocate it.
Education	Calls for "major national investment [in public schools]; a demand of accountability from all; a genuine expansion of public school choice; and a renewed focus on discipline, character, and safety." Calls for 1 million new teachers, starting with reduced class sizes by hiring 100,000 new teachers. Promises expenditures for teacher development and salaries. Says "Al Gore will make education his top domestic priority."	Advocates reduced federal influence in education, and school choice as the best way to improve standards. Also calls for return of voluntary school prayer, equal access to student religious groups, and increased funding for abstinence education. Opposes school clinics that provide referrals, counseling, and related services for contraception and abortion.
Economy/ taxes	Calls for surplus to be kept by government to offset future publicly held debt over the next 12 years. Advocates "tax cuts that are specifically targeted" to help poorer citizens save for college, invest in job skills, pay for health insurance and child care, care for elderly or disabled loved ones, invest in clean cars and homes, and build additional retirement savings. Advocates eliminating the marriage penalty for working families.	Argues that budget surpluses are the result of overtaxation of the American people and calls for "return[ing] half a trillion dollars to the taxpayers who really own it." Argues that federal tax code "penalizes hard work, marriage, thrift, and success." Calls for doubling the child tax credit, eliminating the marriage penalty, and promoting charitable giving. Endorses the principles of Governor Bush's "Tax Cut with a Purpose" and supports legislation requiring a supermajority in Congress to raise taxes.
Social Security	Calls for new ways to invest retirement funds in tax-free vehicles, while keeping Social Security plan intact. Cites Gore's Retirement Savings Plus, a private savings account with government match. Calls for "using budget surplus to strengthen the Social Security Trust Fund."	Calls for giving citizens still contributing to Social Security the option of putting part of their payroll deductions into privately held, privately controlled investment vehicles. Makes Social Security surplus "off-limits and off budget." Calls for restructuring without tax increases with personal savings accounts as the cornerstone.

Table 13.2 *(continued)*

Issue	Democratic platform	Republican platform
Health care/ Medicare	Promises a Patient's Bill of Rights with the right to see a specialist, to appeal decisions to an outside board, guaranteed coverage of emergency room care, and the right to sue when denied coverage. Calls for guaranteed, universal prescription drug benefit in Medicare; guaranteed access to affordable health care for every child; expanded coverage for working families, dislocated workers, and small businesses. Calls for "a Medicare Lock Box" on trust fund surpluses.	Calls for expanded coverage by providing tax breaks to individual citizens to buy private insurance. States commitment to "change federal law to give small employers the liberty to band together to purchase group insurance for their employees at reduced rates." Urges the federal government to "respect the states' traditional authority to regulate health insurance, health professionals, and practice guidelines." Argues Medicare should be "modernize[d] to match current medical science," improved in terms of financial stability, and federal regulations should be significantly streamlined.
Role of government	Says "we must ensure that government has the tools to provide high-quality services." Also argues that "partnerships with faith-based organizations should augment—not replace—government programs."	Government's role is as a "partner . . . to the armies of compassion," to "community and faith-based providers."
Crime/guns	Advocates increasing community police, DNA testing in death penalty cases, and effective counsel for defendants. Calls for mandatory child safety locks, photo license identification, full background check, and gun safety test to buy a handgun. Supports hiring more federal gun prosecutors, and 10,000 state and local prosecutors. Calls for an end to racial profiling.	Advocates reducing crime through no-frills prisons, with productive work requirements; deters crime by increasing penalties and resources to combat escalating drug abuse. Supports community-based diversion programs for first-time, nonviolent offenders. Proposes a constitutional amendment to protect victims' rights. Supports enforcing current gun laws and conducting background checks, but opposes federal licensing of gun owners and national gun registration.
Defense/ national security	Calls for policy of "Forward Engagement" and leadership and engagement in global affairs. Advocates continuing to increase military pay, further reforming military retirement system, and im-	Denounces previous administration's reduction of forces and extensive use of peace-keeping missions. Promise to renegotiate 1972 ABM treaty or give Russia a 6-month notice, as the treaty al-

(continued)

Table 13.2 *(continued)*

Issue	Democratic platform	Republican platform
	proving other benefits. Calls for "continued cutting stockpiles of weapons of mass destruction and halt to testing." Rejects Republican plans to construct a missile defense system.	lows, that it will be voided, in order to clear the way for development of an antimissile program. Calls for "deploy[ment of] effective missile defenses . . . at the earliest possible date." Argues that "multilateral agreements and international institutions are not ends in themselves."

Source: Summary of positions derived from the respective party platforms. Full text of the Democratic and Republican platforms can be found at <www.democrats.org/hq/resources/platform/> and <www.rnc.org/2000/2000platformcontents/>.

(i.e., voters tended to think that the candidate for whom they voted held the same position they did on the war). Thus, ambiguous candidate positions led to unclear differences on issues, which, in turn, muted the impact of issues in the 1968 election outcome. Interestingly, in the 1972 election, in which the candidates' issue differences were perceived to be less ambiguous, Abramson, Aldrich, and Rohde found that the war played a more important role in voting.[27]

Converse, Miller, Rusk, and Wolfe argued that the 1968 candidacy of George Wallace was an "issue candidacy." Specifically, voters who opted for Wallace showed higher correlations between their approval ratings of him and their personal stances on the issues that marked his campaign (civil rights, law and order) than did voters who opted for either Nixon or Humphrey. Thus, the clarity with which issues were presented and the differences between the candidates appeared to be factors in whether voters used issues to make their decisions.[28]

Edward Carmines and James Stimson distinguish between "easy" and "hard" issues in national elections. Hard issues are those that require a high level of information and sophistication on the part of voters (e.g., withdrawal from the Vietnam conflict).[29] According to this research, such issues provide material influence vis-à-vis vote choice only for those few who have a lot of political information. Easy issues, on the other hand, are important to *all* voters (i.e., those who have lots of information and those who have only a little). Because of the accessibility of easy issues, Carmines and Stimson assert that political realignments are more likely to occur around them and, in fact, in later work suggest that such a realignment did occur in the late 1960s around race, which was the easy issue they had previously identified.[30]

Thus, several facets of the candidates' presentation of issues as well as the nature of the issues themselves seem to contribute to whether voters use issues in the vote calculus. Clearly, voters must understand the candidates' positions and be able to discern the difference between them. Voters are also more likely to pay attention to and, therefore, understand issue positions when they consider the issue important. Further, when an issue is, by its nature, complicated and requires a lot of sophistication and study, the average voter tends *not* to base his or her vote on it. While the literature still focuses on the effects of partisanship versus voting based on issues versus voting based on candidate traits, including perceived issue competence, the more recent literature has concluded that each of those variables can be a factor affecting vote choice. It is more a matter of *when* each is important and *which* particular issues are paramount at a given time.[31] Some have argued that it is impossible to disentangle the effects of partisanship, issues, and candidate qualities with the data currently available.[32] Though there may not be conclusive evidence, the literature does, at least, provide a strong basis for believing that substantive understanding, ability to discern differences in candidate positions, salience, and the complexity of issues themselves all contribute to the likelihood of voters casting their ballots based in part on issues and the candidates' positions on them.

Issues and Promises in the 2000 Election

In the 2000 election, most of the factors that contribute to issue-based voting seemed to be conspicuously absent. In particular, throughout the campaign, Gallup found that voters were not clear about the differences between the candidates on the issues of the election. In June, for example, most Americans knew about one or the other candidate's policy proposals, but few knew both positions.[33] After the debates, the polls showed that neither candidate's positions were favored over the other's, leading pollsters to believe that the public was still unclear about what the differences were. Gallup reported that "by almost identical margins, voters say that Gore's policies—and separately, Bush's policies—would move the country in the right rather than the wrong direction."[34] Like the party platforms, the candidates offered markedly different positions on some issues, but their perceptions of the most salient issues converged in the areas of education, Social Security, taxes, and health care. Table 13.3 below summarizes the

Table 13.3

Comparison of Candidates' Promises/Positions on Selected Campaign Issues

Issue	Gore's position	Bush's position
Abortion	"Strong" supporter of the *Roe v. Wade* decision. Opposed to the "gag rule." Supports public funding for abortions.	Opposes abortion except in cases of rape, incest, or to save a woman's life. Supports parental notification, no use of taxpayer funds for abortion, and ban on partial birth abortion.
Education	Supports spending $170 billion over 10 years to help children in public schools to achieve high standards. Supports a 10-year, $115 billion plan paid for by an education trust fund. Opposes vouchers for private and home schools. Supports national education standards. Proposes creation of 401(j) Life-Long Learning Accounts. Proposes mandatory teacher testing for all new teachers and rigorous evaluations after granting teacher licenses. Supports teacher merit pay. Supports raising teacher pay and will hire 100,000 new teachers to reduce class sizes in lower grades. Supports funding to help recruit, hire, and train 1 million new teachers over ten years, with incentives for those who commit to work in a high-need school. Supports modernizing schools, including rebuilding outdated buildings, wiring every classroom to the Internet, and training students and teachers to use that technology.	Supports federal requirements for states to set education standards and a three-year testing period for each school. Supports further development of charter schools by investing $300 million in a homestead fund to provide $3 billion in loan guarantees to 200 new charter schools. Would triple federal funding for "character education." Supports establishment of Education Savings Accounts. Would allocate $5 billion to establish "Reading First" initiative so every child can read by the third grade. Supports providing $1 billion over five years to increase Pell Grants by $1,000 to students who take college-level math and science courses in high school. Would recruit math and science teachers by providing $345 million to increase from $5,000 to $17,500 the amount of student loans that may be forgiven for science, math, technology, and engineering majors who teach for at least five years. Would provide $2 billion in new funding for after-school programs.
Economy/ taxes	Proposes using the $2.17 trillion non–Social Security surplus for the following: $480 billion in targeted tax cuts; $360 billion to shore up Medicare; $870 billion on domestic programs; $300 billion left in reserve.	Proposes using the $2.17 trillion non–Social Security surplus for the following: $1.3 trillion tax cut; $475 billion in spending on domestic programs; and $265 billion in reserve.

Table 13.3 *(continued)*

Issue	Gore's position	Bush's position
Economy/ taxes	Proposes $480 billion in targeted tax cuts over 10 years, with no change in the overall rate structure.	Proposes a 10-year, $1.3 trillion tax cut that includes an overhaul of the current rate structure.
	Would eliminate the national debt by 2012.	Supports cutting the maximum tax rate for the middle class to 25 percent from 28 percent and capping the top tax rate at 33 percent.
	Supports the current child tax credit of $500.	
	Supports increasing the Earned Income Credit earnings threshold.	Would cut the current 15 percent tax bracket to 10 percent for the first $6,000 of taxable income for singles, the first $10,000 for single parents, and the first $12,000 for married couples.
	Supports providing marriage penalty relief by doubling the standard deduction for joint filers.	
	Supports the creation of Universal Savings Accounts for low- and middle-income families.	Would eliminate the national debt by 2016.
	Supports expanding the low-income housing tax credit to expand and improve the quality of available low-income housing.	Supports doubling the child tax credit to $1,000.
	Would simplify estate tax exemptions and raise the tax exemption for small businesses and farms.	Supports reducing the marriage penalty by restoring the 10 percent deduction for two-earner families, allowing them to deduct up to an additional $3,000.
		Supports eliminating the estate tax by 2009.
		Pledges to veto any income tax increase.
Social Security	Supports setting aside the entire projected Social Security surplus of $2.39 trillion.	Supports setting aside the entire projected Social Security surplus of $2.39 trillion to shore up the program.
	Supports using $2.2 trillion of the Social Security surplus to shore up the program and pay down the debt, ensuring the solvency of the Trust Fund until 2050.	Supports partial privatization of Social Security by allowing participants to invest a portion (2 percent) of their payroll taxes in the stock market.
	Supports placing a "lock box" on payroll taxes to prohibit borrowing against the Social Security trust fund.	Supports placing a "lock box" on payroll taxes to prohibit borrowing against the Social Security trust fund.
	Supports the elimination of the earnings limit.	Does not rule out raising the eligibility age for baby boom–era recipients as trade-off for private investment accounts.
	Supports an increase in benefits for widows and eliminating the "motherhood penalty."	

(continued)

Table 13.3 *(continued)*

Issue	Gore's position	Bush's position
Social Security	Supports the creation of "Retirement Savings Plus Accounts," which would allow tax-deductible annual contributions of up to $2,000.	Supports elimination of the earnings limit. Supports the system's current provision to pay benefits to widows, widowers, and the disabled. Opposes an increase in the current 12.4 percent payroll tax.
Health care/ medicare	Supports providing 25 percent tax credit for individuals lacking employer-based health coverage to purchase private insurance. Supports providing low-income seniors with "catastrophic" prescription drug coverage for chronic illnesses. Supports Patient's Bill of Rights legislation that includes direct access to specialists; the right to use the nearest emergency room; choice of providers; and right to appeal a health plan's decision. Proposes a Medicare Trust Fund "lock box" plan that would extend the life of the program until at least 2030. Supports using $432 billion to shore up the Medicare program and include prescription drug benefit. Supports using part of the surplus for a voluntary prescription drug benefit for Medicare beneficiaries. Supports allowing seniors 55–65 to buy into the Medicare program. Supports a $3,000 tax credit for long-term care.	Supports offering medical savings accounts to all Americans. Supports a limited patients' right to sue HMOs over care denials. Would provide a $2,000 health credit to families ($1,000 for individuals) who do not qualify for Medicaid and are not covered by an employer-sponsored plan. Supports allowing small businesses to purchase "Association Health Plans" to lower the cost of insurance. Supports private prescription drug benefit for Medicare beneficiaries. Supports prescription drug subsidies for low-income seniors. Supports providing taxpayers with a 100 percent above-the-line deduction for long-term care insurance premiums.
Role of government	Supports giving the government tools to do its job. Supports continued efforts to "reinvent government" to make it more customer-focused and streamlined.	Would establish an "Office of Faith-Based Action" in the Executive Office of the President that would remove federal regulations that bar faith-based organizations from participating in federal programs. Calls for streamlining the federal bureaucracy.

Table 13.3 *(continued)*

Issue	Gore's position	Bush's position
Crime	Wants to hire and redeploy up to 50,000 more community police. Supports an expansion of the death penalty for those who murder federal law enforcement officers. Supports expanding cutting-edge, crime-fighting technology with law enforcement around the country. Advocates banning convicted violent juveniles from owning guns for life, and using the resources of the FBI to break up violent teen gangs. Supports mandatory child safety locks, photo license I.D., full background check, and gun safety test to buy a handgun; opposes laws that allow people to carry concealed weapons. Supports hiring more federal gun prosecutors, and 10,000 state and local prosecutors. Calls for an end to racial profiling.	Supports federal and state partnerships to develop advanced technology to help police. Supports background checks at gun shows and pawn shops, and expanding "instant check" system. Supports increasing the minimum age from 18 to 21 to possess a handgun without parental supervision. Supports semiautomatic assault weapons ban for juveniles. Supports voluntary child safety locks for all handguns, but would sign legislation requiring mandatory trigger locks for all new handguns. Would enforce federal gun laws and provide more funding for aggressive gun law enforcement. Supports criminal justice initiatives, such as the abolition of parole and truth in sentencing.
Defense/ national security	Supports a policy of "forward engagement" that includes a limited national missile defense that would not threaten the antiballistic missile (ABM) treaty with Russia. Supports the administration's proposed 3.7 percent across-the-board pay budget increase, as well as providing adequate housing and medical care for military personnel. Supports providing military retirees over 65 years of age with prescription drug coverage. Supports ratification of the Comprehensive Test Ban Treaty. Supports lifting the ban on gays in the military.	Supports deployment of a large scale national missile defense system and would cancel the ABM treaty with Russia to do so. Supports reducing the U.S. nuclear stockpiles to "lowest possible number" without sacrificing readiness; would order a review of overseas deployments, but maintain U.S. commitments. Supports an increase in defense spending, including a $1 billion increase in military pay. Supports spending an additional $20 billion on defense R&D for post–Cold War weapons systems. Opposes lifting ban on gays in military; supports current "Don't Ask, Don't Tell" policy.

Source: Summary derived from promises listed on candidates' Web sites. Complete issue positions can be found at <www.algore.com and www.georgewbush.com>.

candidates' stands on some of the most debated policy issues in the 2000 election.

As discussed, polling data showed that voters lacked a clear understanding of the candidates' policy differences, but they also did not perceive the issues as overwhelmingly salient. In November 2000, Gallup reported that the election was different from other presidential elections because no "majority or near majority of Americans could point to one or two issues as being the most important problems facing the country." The most cited issues, education and ethics/moral decline, were mentioned only by 17 and 12 percent of the public in open-ended questions.[35]

Historically, larger percentages of Americans had focused on particular problems during election years. For example, in 1992, the general economy was identified by 37 percent of the public as the most important problem. In 1976 and 1980, 44 and 52 percent respectively identified inflation/cost-of-living. In 1968, 44 percent of the public said Vietnam was the most pressing problem.[36] After the 2000 election, one of the only pressing issues cited by more than 10 percent of respondents was "unite the country" (13 percent). Further, when Gallup asked voters what the Bush administration should focus on most immediately, issues that had received attention during the campaign were only mentioned by small percentages of the population: education—8 percent, health care—7 percent, taxes/tax reduction—6 percent, the economy—6 percent, and Social Security—5 percent. In fact, the second most popular response following the vote was to have no opinion about the most pressing problem (12 percent).[37]

Consistent with Carmines and Stimson's notion of easy and hard issues, there also appeared to be no major cleavage issue in the 2000 election. Perhaps the complicated nature of the issues, combined with other factors already discussed, contributed to public ambivalence. For example, Gallup found that parents of school-age children were very satisfied with the quality of education their children received, but much less satisfied with the country's educational system in general: "Americans gave higher grades to the schools in their local community than they did to schools nationally."[38] Similarly, Americans perceived greater health care problems at the national level than at the local level. Although people expressed their general concern about the adequacy of health care in the United States, most were satisfied with various aspects of their own health care situation.[39]

On tax relief, a position trumpeted by both major party candidates, data indicate that people virtually always support tax cuts, but when presented with trade-offs they were more likely in 2000 to favor increased expenditures for some government programs (such as education, health care, and Social Security) and paying down the national debt over large tax cuts.[40]

Thus, while interesting and important issues dominated the public discourse during the 2000 campaign, none stood out as *the* issue. Given the peace and prosperity of the previous eight years and the general cynicism toward government, it is not surprising that Americans were relatively hard-pressed to come up with urgent problems for the government to fix. The public was also unclear about the differences between the candidates, and the issues themselves were quite complicated. This left the candidates in a somewhat precarious position, having to debate issues that were confusing and not overly salient to them.

Important Issues and Vote Choice in the 2000 Election: Did They Carry the Day?

Did issues matter in the 2000 election? Survey data indicate that the electorate consistently favored Gore's positions over Bush's. On such issues as education, Medicare prescription drugs, Social Security, and handling the budget surplus, Gore beat Bush. The VNS exit poll showed that almost five times as many voters favored funding as the answer to bad schools, not vouchers (78 versus 16 percent); 57 percent thought Medicare should be responsible for helping seniors with drugs rather than private insurance companies; and 35 percent favored using the budget surplus to shore up Social Security, while 24 percent thought it should be used to pay down the debt (compared with only 28 percent who favored a tax cut).[41] On personal traits, however, such as honesty, leadership, and likability, Bush won hands down. As Table 13.4 shows, Gore and Bush present almost mirror images of each other on the issue/attribute continuum. Gore won three out of the four issues about which the electorate cared the most, but Bush won on the top three personal qualities that voters considered most important.

Despite the importance that voters say they attach to policy issues, personal traits seemed to have more influence on their vote. When asked what they liked most about their choice for president and what factors influenced their vote decision, Gore voters stressed their candidate's "experience and intellect" and Bush voters their candidates "strong leadership qualities" rather than issue congruence, that is, "he thinks like me on the issues." For Bush voters "moral/ethical values" were more important to their decision than any of the substantive policy issues. For Gore voters, it was "jobs/the economy." Table 13.5 illustrates these responses.

So what do these results tell us about voters in the 2000 election? At this point, it is trite to say "it was too close to call," but in effect, that's what the voters seemed to be telling us. While they favored Gore on the substance of the traditional Democratic issues, as well as in terms of his

Table 13.4

Exit Polls on Issues and Candidate's Qualities (in percent)

Which issue mattered most?	All	Voted for Gore	Voted for Bush	Winning candidate (points difference)
Economy/jobs	18	59	37	Gore (+12)
Education	15	52	44	Gore (+8)
Taxes	14	17	80	Bush (+63)
Social Security	14	58	40	Gore (+18)
World affairs	12	40	54	Bush (+14)
Health care	8	64	33	Gore (+31)
Medicare/prescription drugs	7	60	39	Gore (+21)
Which quality mattered most?	All	Gore	Bush	
Honest/trustworthy	24	15	80	Bush (+65)
Has experience	15	82	17	Gore (+65)
Strong leader	14	34	64	Bush (+30)
Good judgment	13	48	50	Bush (+2)
Understands issues	13	75	19	Gore (+56)
Cares about people	12	63	31	Gore (+32)
Likable	2	38	59	Bush (+21)
Which is more important?	All	Gore	Bush	
Issues	62	55	40	Gore (+15)
Qualities	35	35	62	Bush (+27)

Source: Voter News Service Exit Poll as reported on CNN: <www.cnn.com/ELECTION/2000/results/index.epolls.html>.

ability to understand the issues (having the "intellect" to be president), they favored Bush on character issues, leadership, and morals—arguably areas in which the Republicans have tried to claim the advantage over the last several years.

Putting Promises into Action: Deciphering Presidential Mandates

Scholars like Charles O. Jones, Raymond Wolfinger, and Robert Dahl have argued that the conception of a presidential mandate is not only unrealistic in the American political system, but it is a notion that runs counter to the ideals set forth by the Framers.[42] Specifically, the institutions of government were set up to protect against the whims and demagoguery often associated with salient issues of the day and the candidates' promises on how they will deal with the issues. In a separated system of government, presidents must pursue their policy goals with the cooperation of the other branches

Table 13.5

Exit Poll on Factors Deciding Vote Choice (in percent)

Choice in 1996	Clinton		Dole		Other	
	Bush	Gore	Bush	Gore	Bush	Gore
Most liked about choice	voters	voters	voters	voters	voters	voters
He has the experience and intellect to be president	12	53	17	30	16	45
He thinks like me on the issues	17	14	25	17	19	13
He has strong leadership qualities	23	15	24	19	19	14
He shares my values	17	10	28	18	19	8
He cares about people like me	13	21	10	17	14	20
He has honesty and integrity	17	6	28	15	16	4
He understands average Americans' problems	13	15	7	13	10	15
An overall good opinion of my candidate	14	10	14	6	19	11
He has a clear vision of the future	7	11	9	5	11	8
He is personally likable	11	4	6	10	7	3
None of the above	10	5	3	12	5	12
Number of respondents	459	3,053	2,192	141	459	738
Most important issues deciding vote						
Moral/ethical values	41	16	64	28	44	19
Jobs/economy	22	36	13	31	20	35
Education	23	31	18	24	24	31
Social Security	24	27	15	25	17	19
Taxes	17	9	28	12	21	9
Abortion	12	11	19	11	14	14
Environment	2	14	2	10	3	15
Health care	7	12	5	9	5	9
Medicare/prescription drugs	11	11	5	11	6	7
Budget surplus	6	6	6	13	5	7
Foreign affairs	4	5	6	5	4	4
None of the above	4	3	2	2	7	5

Source: Author analysis of data from *Los Angeles Times* Poll, <www.Pollingreport.com>, Tuesday, Nov. 7, 2000. Based on interviews with 8,132 voters as they exited 140 polling places. Question's asked: "What did you like most about your choice for president?" (up to two responses accepted), and "Which issues, if any, were most important to you in deciding how you would vote for president today?" (up to two responses accepted).

of government. But Jones also acknowledges that the notion of a public mandate has become a convenient way to explain election outcomes, and the perception of a mandate may drive its reality.[43]

In deciphering what message elections send, Jones examines four possibilities for mandates: the perceived mandate for change, the status quo mandate, the mixed or nonmandate, and the unmandate, which is Jones's way of reiterating his belief that presidential mandates do not, in fact, exist.

The mandate for change is characterized by publicly visible issues, clear differences between the candidates, a substantial victory for the winner and the winner's party in Congress, and a postelection declaration of party unity. Elections that come the closest to meeting these criteria according to Jones are Lyndon Johnson's victory in 1964, Ronald Reagan's 1980 election, and, arguably, Clinton's 1992 election.

Of all the types of mandates, the one for change provides the strongest ammunition for those wanting to claim policy endorsement on the part of the public. Although, as Jones would argue, the policy preferences of the voters are not necessarily clear based on the outcomes of elections, the candidate who meets the relatively stiff criteria for claiming such a mandate is in the strongest position to leverage presidential power and to convince others in government that his policy program would be good for them. Thus, even if a real mandate does not exist, the claim of one can serve as an indirect source of influence in articulating and achieving a legislative agenda. In this sense, the claim of a mandate for change becomes a self-fulfilling prophecy.

The mandate for the status quo occurs when presidents win reelection by a strong margin but their party does not win both houses of Congress. Thus, there is a personal endorsement of a candidate and an implied endorsement of the continuance of his policy agenda. This mandate, Jones argues, demonstrates public confidence in an individual leader and that leader's policy objectives. Jones says that Eisenhower's reelection in 1956, Nixon's reelection in 1972, and Reagan's reelection in 1984 represent postwar cases of this kind of mandate. Clinton's election in 1996 should also be added to this list.

The mixed or nonmandate is marked by an extremely close election, and it is interpreted as falling between a status quo mandate and no mandate at all. Jones includes Harry Truman, John Kennedy, Jimmy Carter, George H. W. Bush, and Clinton's first election in this category. While Truman, Kennedy, Carter, and Clinton enjoyed Democratic majorities in Congress, the Republicans were in the minority in both houses during the Nixon and Bush terms.

Responsible party scholars interpret control of both the White House and Congress as a strong signal that the party in power has been given the authority to govern and, perhaps more germane to the conception of a mandate, that it has been given the nod to enact the policy priorities it and its standard bearers set out during the campaign. Given the president's narrow victory, there may be reticence to claim such a mandate. In cases where the other party wins the majority in Congress, claims of a mandate are even fewer and more muted.

Was a Mandate Conferred by the 2000 Election?

Even if presidential mandates do exist, the 2000 election does not meet the criteria for a mandate for change, nor would it have if Gore had won a narrow electoral college victory. Clearly the issues dealt with in the campaign did not rise to the level of public interest that the social, economic, and international crises of racial segregation, widespread poverty, oil embargoes, and hostage taking did during the 1964 and 1980 elections. Nor was there a clear victory for the president's party. Although the Republicans will control the White House and have a majority in the House, their lead in that body is slim and fragile.

On the other hand, the 2000 election was not a mandate for the status quo either. Republican George W. Bush replaced Democrat Bill Clinton. Moreover, Bush did not win a plurality of the popular vote. Had Al Gore won an electoral college majority, a mandate for the status quo might be more debatable. However, since Gore ran away from the Clinton administration, not with it, it would have been difficult to argue for a status quo result. In distancing himself from Clinton's policies and behavior, Gore also obfuscated his stand on the issues. Thomas E. Mann of the Brookings Institution says, "Gore never felt comfortable running on the Clinton–Gore record. His obsession with separating himself from Clinton and running on the future, not the past, kept him from sharply framing the election as a referendum on good times."[44]

For those who believe in presidential mandates, Bush's victory will undoubtedly be interpreted as a mixed or nonmandate because of the disparity between the popular and electoral votes. Such a mandate puts George W. Bush at a disadvantage in exercising power on other elected officials. Nonetheless, Bush determined that the best way to establish his legitimacy was to lead as if he had a mandate. His decision to pursue his campaign goals and redeem his promises was designed to satisfy his electoral constituency, reinforce his credibility, and leave some room for compromise.

Platforms, Agendas, and Governance

Regardless of the common perception that politicians do not follow through on their promises, the empirical evidence suggests that they do. They use their party platforms and campaign promises as the framework by which they develop a legislative agenda and manage the government, and they frequently enjoy impressive success in implementing those pledges.[45] Thomas Mann says,

> Political scientists have discovered from research on party platforms and policy-making over the past half-century, [that] the vast majority of platform promises eventually are adopted. Departures in public policy initiated by Ronald Reagan after the 1980 election and Clinton after his 1992 victory, for example, were explicitly previewed in their respective party platforms. Adjustments were made, of course, in response to changing economic and political conditions. But the direction of Reagan's and Clinton's administrations was crystal clear well before the election. . . . Party platforms do indeed make a difference.[46]

While the party platform informs the agenda, there are also unique powers that presidents bring to agenda implementation by virtue of their office. First, they have the formal authority to veto legislation and appoint their own advisers. They also have organizational clout, the "support" of the large bureaucracy of policy and program experts within the federal government. Finally, presidents are in a unique position to command public attention, which can be used to build and maintain a majority coalition. For all these reasons, presidents tend to be in the driver's seat regardless of their margin of victory.

However, as John Kingdon points out, "Presidents can dominate the congressional agenda, but they have much less control over the alternatives members of Congress consider."[47] Thus, Congress will always create critical legislative hurdles as new administrations design, sell, and modify their agendas. In the current milieu, in which the government and the electorate are virtually divided, the devil will be in the details of George W. Bush's agenda. If we are to believe the data, the public sides with Gore on many of the important issues of the election. While it is unlikely that Bush will adopt the Democratic positions on these issues, he will undoubtedly be cognizant of them as he works with a Congress that begins with a large minority from that party and after Jefford's defection a Senate majority. Thus, leaders of both parties in Congress have incentive to provide many policy alternatives, as they, too, will look to garner support from a majority of Americans. In the end, this translates to an incentive to generate lots of ideas and foster open debate about important public policy matters. In our system of government, these are among the best circumstances for stimulating the policy-making process and connecting electoral judgments to governing decisions.

Notes

1. Charles O Jones. *The Presidency in a Separated System* (Washington, DC: Brookings Institution, 1994), 148.
2. From George W. Bush's acceptance speech at the 2000 Republican National Convention, Philadelphia, Pennsylvania.
3. Quoted from Stephen Hess in "A Brookings Press Briefing—The American

Voter 2000: Dissatisfied? Distracted? Or Just Don't Care? A New Survey from the Pew Research Center," www.brookings.org, July 14, 2000.

4. The Pew Research Center for the People and the Press, "Fewer See Choice of President as Important: Voter Turnout May Slip Again: Introduction and Summary," www.people-press.org/june00rpt.htm, July 13, 2000.

5. Ibid.

6. Ibid.

7. Quoted from Thomas Mann in "A Brookings Press Briefing."

8. Question asked during survey: "When did you decide your vote?" <www.cnn.com/ELECTION/2000/results/index.epolls.html>.

9. Gerald M. Pomper, *Elections in America: Control and Influence in Democratic Politics*, 2d ed. (New York: Longman, 1980), 140.

10. Jeff Fishel, *Presidents and Promises* (Washington, DC: Congressional Quarterly Press, 1985), 27.

11. Pomper, *Elections in America*, p. 129.

12. Fishel, *Presidents and Promises*, p. 27.

13. Pomper, *Elections in America*, p. 152.

14. Fishel, *Presidents and Promises*, p. 27.

15. Ibid.

16. Ibid., p. 28. Fishel provides a table of party platform word length covering the 1948–1984 period.

17. Word counts taken from the 2000 Democratic and Republican platforms and rounded to the nearest 100 words.

18. Pomper, *Elections in America*, p. 131.

19. Ibid., pp. 140–41.

20. Some scholars argue that voters pay most attention to their own personal economic situations ("pocketbook voters"), while others have argued that voters use judgments about the general economic health of the nation ("sociotropic voters"). Both camps argue that voters assess the economic situation and punish or reward the incumbent accordingly. Gregory B. Markus provides a summary of the basic arguments of the two schools of thought and the controversies in this literature in "The Impact of Personal and National Economic Conditions," *American Journal of Political Science* 32 (1988): 137–54.

21. Gallup Polling, www.gallup.com/Election2000/, July 25–26, 2000.

22. Pomper, *Elections in America*, p. 146.

23. This is not meant to imply that more policies are offered in these categories; it is simply notable that the major headings of the platform, which offer a crude measure of prominence, are significantly focused on traditionally Democratic issues.

24. Fishel, *Presidents and Promises*, p. 28. It is important to note that in 1964, the Democrats presented a shortened platform outline (5,500 words) with a separate appendix (13,000 words). I have counted both pieces of this platform in the comparison to the 1964 Republican platform.

25. Quoted from E. J. Dionne Jr., in "A Brookings Press Briefing."

26. Benjamin I. Page and Richard A. Brody, "Policy Voting and the Electoral Process: The Vietnam War Issue," *American Political Science Review* 66 (1972): 979–995.

27. Paul R. Abramson, John H. Aldrich, and David W. Rohde, *Change and Continuity in the 1980 Elections*, rev. ed. (Washington, DC: Congressional Quarterly Press, 1983), Chapter 6.

28. Philip E. Converse, Warren E. Miller, Jerrold G. Rusk, and Arthur C. Wolfe, "Continuity and Change in American Politics: Parties and Issues in the 1968 Election," *American Political Science Review* 63 (1969): 1083–1105.

29. Edward G. Carmines and James Stimson, "The Two Faces of Issue Voting," *American Political Science Review* 74 (1980): 78–91.

30. Edward G. Carmines and James Stimson, *Issue Evolution: Race and Transformation of American Politics* (Princeton, NJ: Princeton University Press, 1989).

31. Richard G. Niemi, and Herbert F. Weisberg, *Classics in Voting Behavior* (Washington, DC: Congressional Quarterly Press, 1993), 10.

32. William H. Flanigan and Nancy H. Zingale, *Political Behavior and the American Electorate,* 9th ed. (Washington, DC: Congressional Quarterly Press, 1998), 179–180.

33. Gallup Polling, "Voters Generally Unaware of Bush-Gore Differences on Issues, But Know Position of Either Bush or Gore on Several Issues," <www.gallup.com/Election2000/>, June 5, 2000.

34. Gallup Polling, "As Race Narrows, Voters See Little Difference Between Bush and Gore on Leadership Qualities and Effectiveness of Their Policies: Once Again, Bush's Lead Within Poll's Margin of Error," <www.gallup.com/Election2000/>, October 24, 2000.

35. Gallup Polling, "In Election Year 2000, Americans Generally Happy With State of the Nation: Most Americans Satisfied with Economy and Political Institutions," <www.gallup.com/Election2000/>, November 7, 2000.

36. Ibid.

37. Gallup Polling, <www.gallup.com/poll/releases>, December 15–17, 2000. Question asked: "In your opinion, what should be the top priority for the Bush administration in its first 100 days? [Open-ended]"

38. Gallup Polling, "Education: A Vital Issue in Election 2000: Public Much More Positive about Education in Their Local Community than about Education Nationally," <www.gallup.com/Election2000/>, October 2, 2000.

39. Specifically, during the 2000 election, 82 percent said that they were satisfied with the quality of health care they and their family receive, 70 percent said that they were satisfied with their health insurance coverage, 69 percent said they were satisfied with their health insurance plans, and 59 percent said they were satisfied with the cost of their health care. Complete results of this poll can be found at <www.cnn.com/ELECTION/2000/results/index.epolls.html>.

40. Gallup Polling, "Voters Continue to Say Economy Is Important Issue in Presidential Race, Prefer Targeted Tax Cuts for Low- and Middle-Income People over Across-the-Board Tax Cut," <www.gallup.com/Election2000/>, September 26, 2000. This poll showed that 74 percent of Americans favored a federal income tax cut, about the same number who expressed that view in March 1999, but down slightly from the 80 percent in 1994. However, while Americans seemed to support a tax cut in principle, they had reservations about "broad, across-the-board cuts." And when given specific alternatives, Americans generally preferred that the budget surplus be used for education, Social Security, paying off the national debt, and health care over tax relief. In its September 15–17 poll, Gallup found that a relatively small minority of voters (11 percent) would choose a tax cut over these other priorities. Of the alternatives mentioned, 24 percent said that they preferred either reforming health care and prescription drugs or improving education to a tax cut. Slightly fewer said that they would use the surplus to strengthen Social Security or pay off the debt.

41. Complete results of this poll can be found at <www.cnn.com/ELECTION/2000/results/index.epolls.html>.

42. Jones, Presidency in Separated System, p. 153. Jones also cites the works of Wolfinger and Dahl as follows:
Raymond E. Wolfinger, "Dealignment, Realignment, and Mandates in the 1984 Elec-

tion," in Austin Ranney, ed., *The American Elections of 1984* (Washington, DC: American Enterprise Institute, 1985), 293; Robert A. Dahl, "Myth of the Presidential Mandate," *Political Science Quarterly* 105: 358–359.

43. Jones, *The Presidency in a Separated System,* p. 153.

44. Thomas E. Mann, "Reflections on the 2000 U.S. Presidential Election," *Politique Etranger,* January 2001.

45. See especially Pomper, *Elections in America,* pp. 161–167, and Fishel, *Presidents and Promises,* p. 27.

46. Thomas E. Mann, "Party Platforms Provide Glimpse into Future," *USA Today,* August 15, 2000.

47. John W. Kingdon, *Agendas, Alternatives, and Public Policies* (Glenview, IL: Scott Foresman, 1984), 4.

14

Conclusion

Stephen J. Wayne and Clyde Wilcox

Lessons of the 2000 Election

Campaigns matter—this is the simplest and most obvious lesson of the 2000 presidential election. Those who focused solely on the environment in which the election occurred—which was an extended period of economic prosperity, relative social tranquility with no major threat to the country's national security, a period during which the sitting president received high public approval despite the personal and political scandals that marred his presidency and culminated in his impeachment—all predicted that the incumbent vice president would win. That he did not suggests that policy, personality, and performance can and do make a difference; that scripting, staging, and strategizing are important and do affect election outcomes.

George W. Bush ran a better campaign, and he won, although barely. He overcame his opponent's incumbency advantages: good times, experience in national office, demonstrated political skills and policy knowledge. How did he achieve his victory? Why did Bush win and Gore lose? The chapters in this book suggest some of the reasons.

As Anne Marie Camissa points out, "It wasn't just the economy, stupid." That Gore did not get a sufficient boost from the strong economy to put him over the top may be attributed to his failure to indicate that he deserved credit for the economic gains of the past eight years or that those gains in and of themselves should be a principal reason to vote for the candidate of the party and the administration on whose watch they occurred. As for the future, voters placed almost as much confidence in Bush as they did in Gore to maintain the economic prosperity. It may also be the case that a strong economy has less political benefit than a poor economy has adverse political consequences. Contrast the 55 percent turnout in 1992 with the 51.4 percent in 2000.

Experience and knowledge in government should also have worked to Gore's advantage. Not only was he a former representative, senator, and sitting vice president, but his principal opponent, George W. Bush had no national governing experience. Nor was Bush considered well versed in foreign policy, having failed a well-publicized pop quiz in which he could not name the leaders of four countries which were involved in controversy and as a consequence, featured in news reports.

Although foreign policy issues, per se, were not salient to most voters in 2000, Bennett and White point out that foreign policy competence remains a principal criteria for judging qualifications for the presidency. After all, the foreign policy making and implementation as well as the commander-in-chief roles are considered to be primarily presidential responsibilities. Two performance-related events, Gore's perceived temporizing of the Cuban-American community in the Elian Gonzales affair and Bush's competent presentation of his foreign policy views in the second presidential debate, together leveled the foreign policy competence issue, nullifying another potential incumbency-related advantage.

Trends

Whereas the campaign enabled Bush to overcome Gore's environmental and experiential advantages, issues of race, gender, and religion were played out pretty much as expected in the 2000 election. Group activity and voting behavior, based on similar demographic and attitudinal characteristics, were evident throughout the campaign. Despite attempts by both major parties to extend their appeals to a broad cross-section of the electorate, demographic and attitudinal divisions continued to be evident in the issue positions, group support, and coalitional bases of the two major parties.

Within these groups, certain trends also stand out: the increasing turnout and heightened cohesion of African-American voters and their support for Democratic candidates; the steady progress women have made as viable candidates, their success in raising money and winning elections, and the distinctive views, partisan appeals, and voting behavior of which they and their male counterparts demonstrate in American politics; the activism of the Christian Coalition and the role of Christian fundamentalist policies in

Republican party nomination politics, but the increasing pragmatism of this group in general elections; the persistence of a sectarian-secular divide with its cultural implications for the American polity (discussed in the following section of this conclusion); and the growing size and impact of Latino voters and the partisan battle for their allegiances.

Another trend that has persisted into the twenty-first century has been the tepid participation levels of the youngest group of eligible voters, Generation X. Despite attempts by the parties and candidates to reach out to this population group, "apathy, ignorance, and inaction" continues to characterize Xers in the electoral process. Those in the eighteen to twenty-nine age bracket had the lowest participation rates by far. When they do vote, however, the Xers have mirrored the population as a whole.

Demographic, religious, and age groups reinforce partisan voting patterns. Despite the weakening of party loyalty among the general population over the last three decades, the continued growth of candidate-centered campaigns, the persistence of split-ticket voting, and the decline of strong party organizations at the grass-roots level, partisanship remains highly correlated with voting behavior at the national level. In 2000, partisan identifiers voted overwhelmingly for their party's nominees.

Ideological orientations also correlate with partisanship, conservatives voting Republican and liberals voting Democratic. Ideological differences are apparent in party platforms, candidate positions, and in the partisan support which elected officials provide for their party's policy stands in government. Here, too, the campaign works to reinforce rather than challenge the partisanship-ideological linkage.

With the major parties nearly evenly divided and partisan voting patterns apparent, close presidential elections are not surprising, particularly those in which an incumbent president is not running. Nor is the persistence of divided government in a system in which presidential and congressional elections are relatively autonomous, election cycles and constituencies differ, incumbency continues to be a major advantage, and the number of open, competitive seats remains small. These factors serve to limit the impact of campaigns on election outcomes, particularly in House races in which most legislative districts are drawn in such a way as to favor a particular party.

To the extent that congressional elections are resistant to presidential influence, presidential coattails will be short or nonexistent. Under the circumstances, a president's claim of mandates becomes less persuasive to members of Congress who can point to their own elections and usually also to the size of their own votes as reasons for representing their perceived constituency interests rather than some national will which, though claimed, can rarely be expressed in the current election system.

Divided government and congressional autonomy contribute to the newly elected president's leadership dilemma in which a campaign agenda, which normally hypes public expectations by the promises the candidate has made and the image which that candidate has tried to present, combined with the pledges of the party platform to which most nominees indicate their willingness to adhere, becomes difficult to realize. Appeals to partisan unity in government, though necessary, are usually not sufficient, in and of themselves, to achieve policy success. As a consequence, behind the scenes negotiation and external coalition building are required as well.

Uniqueness

In some ways, the 2000 election was also unique. President Clinton's role was highly controversial. The Republicans ran against him, Gore ran away from him, and Democrats ran toward him. The president stayed in the news, remained active, and received high public approval for his job performance. Politically, he raised lots of money for the Democrats, his wife won election to the U.S. Senate from New York, and he helped mobilize core voters.

Gore's decision to sever his ties to Clinton and run "as my own man" did insulate him from some of the personal and political scandals that had marred the Clinton presidency, but it also prevented the vice president from cashing in on the administration's performance-based popularity. Not only did Gore alienate the president and some of his supporters, but by keeping Clinton on the sidelines, the vice president deprived his campaign of the advice of the party's most astute politician as well as the president's verbal and party building skills. In retrospect, Gore's decision to distance himself from Clinton was self-serving and politically incorrect.

A new factor that could have affected the 2000 campaign was the use of the Internet as a new communications vehicle. It did have some influence in helping potential nominees raise money and gain volunteers, but as noted previously, it did not engage many more new voters, particularly those of the younger generation for whom the parties and candidates designed their interactive Web sites to appeal. The Internet-based campaign appealed to those who were already interested, informed, and in many cases, committed, reinforcing their political orientations rather than introducing them to new campaign-relevant information and activity. Here, as elsewhere, the lessons of 2000 are rooted in twentieth-century trends rather than in twenty-first century changes.

Back to the Future: Where Do We Go From Here?

In the aftermath of the 2000 elections, many election observers and political pundits threw away their crystal balls that failed to predict the outcome and turned back to history. During the protracted legal struggle over the Florida recount, journalists and political scientists told their readers and students of the last time that a candidate had lost the popular vote but won the presidency, and of the last time that the Senate had been evenly divided between the two major parties. As the struggle reached its conclusion and Republicans in the Florida legislature and in the U.S. House made their contingency plans, students of elections peered into the even more distant past, to the debates of the founders over the way to elect a president, and the role of the House in early presidential races.

Even after Bush assumed office and proceeded to govern as though he and his party had won the 2000 elections by a comfortable margin, a consortium of newspapers arranged a study of the Florida ballots, to see who really had won the previous November. (Their findings were inconclusive.)[1] Throughout the early months of 2001, Republican partisans talked of how Gore had tried to "steal" the election by forcing a recount, and Democrats complained of the Supreme Court's illogical equal protection argument that ended the recount.

Certainly the 2000 election will be long remembered as one of the closest in history, and as an election where lawyers and justices decided the winner. Historians will debate the tactical decisions and strategic plans: Bush's contingency plan to appeal to electors to support him had he won the popular vote but been behind in the electoral college, or the internal debates in the Bush camp about whether to request recounts in New Mexico and Wisconsin, or to pin their hopes on stopping the recount in Florida.

But despite the anger among Democrats and many Republicans over the post-election struggle, despite Bush's failure to win a plurality of the popular vote, most Americans accepted him as the legitimate president. Within a few weeks, public interest in the election ebbed, and even seasoned observers of American politics were surprised at the absence of a popular drive to eliminate the electoral college or reform voting practices in the states. Soon the political system had moved on to new topics: the defection of Vermont Senator Jim Jeffords from the Republican party, the Bush administration's plans to abandon the Kyoto accords on global warming and the ABM treaties, the coming 2002 elections, and then the terrorist attack. The country's attention came back to the future.

Students of politics often look to past elections for clues about future politics. The 2000 elections provide us with some lessons that may help us understand the early politics of the new millennium. In this section, we will focus on four issues: the financing of the 2000 campaigns, voting patterns in the 2000 elections, post-election debates over voting procedures, and the early actions of the Bush administration.

Financing the 2000 Campaigns: FECA is Dead

In the aftermath of the Watergate scandals, Congress passed in 1974 a set of comprehensive amendments to the Federal Election Campaign Act (FECA) that have provided the framework for financing presidential elections for the past seven election cycles. Over time, candidates have explored and expanded a number of loopholes in the legislation, and the courts have struck down significant portions of them. The 2000 campaigns provided the final nails in the coffin of the FECA regime. The 2004 campaigns are likely to be financed in ways that those who wrote the FECA could not have anticipated.

The FECA had four main components, all of which were significantly undermined by the 2000 campaigns. First, contributions by individuals, groups, and even political parties were limited in size. Second, spending by individuals, candidates, interest groups, and parties was limited. Third, public funding was provided for primary election candidates, for the party conventions, and for the general election campaigns. Finally, the system mandated that financial activity be disclosed to the Federal Election Commission, which would make the information available to the general public.

In the 2000 campaign, contribution limits were made ineffective by contributions of "soft money" of unlimited size given to the political parties to help build the parties and to aid state and local candidates. In theory, this money could not be used directly to help candidates for national office, but by 2000 neither party even maintained the fiction that they were abiding by that principle. Presidential candidates are their party's best fund-raisers, and both Bush and Gore spent much of the fall raising large amounts of soft money, and directing its spending by party committees in ways that would help their campaign.

Limits on spending by candidates were voided by the Supreme Court in 1976, but they remained in place for presidential candidates who accepted public funding. Essentially, candidates who take matching funds sign away their right to unlimited spending in exchange for campaign funds from the public treasury. In 2000, George W. Bush (and Steve Forbes) declined matching funds, and Al Gore could have done so as well had he not feared that such a move would cost him votes. By not accepting matching funds, Bush was free to raise and spend unlimited amounts: his campaign raised about $100 million during the competitive phase of the nomination process, a record amount. It is likely that if one mainstream party candidate foregoes matching funds and thereby avoids the spending limits, his or her competitors will do so as well.

Candidates from the ideological wings of their parties will continue to accept matching funds, which essentially double the value of the small contributions that such candidates raise through the mails. And both parties will continue to accept public funding for their conventions and their general election campaigns. But the original intent of this funding was to free the parties and candidates from the need to raise private contributions—to fully pay for the conventions and campaigns. In 2000, the national conventions were awash in private money, with corporate sponsorship at an all-time high. Moreover, the substantial amounts of soft money raised by the presidential candidates meant that the public grant did not even constitute half of the spending by the presidential campaigns.

Finally, disclosure of contributions and spending remained in effect for candidates, parties, and the political action committees sponsored by interest groups, but interest groups were also free to spend unlimited amounts to advocate issues, not candidates. The distinction between issue ads and candidate ads was a subtle one, understood by parties, interest groups, and the courts but not the voters. As a consequence advertising exploded with ads designed and paid for by the presidential candidates representing only a portion of the political commercials that may have influenced the electorate.

In spring and summer 2001, Congress debated new changes to the campaign finance system, including a ban on soft money and some kinds of issue advocacy. The proposed bans on issue advocacy, however, may violate the First Amendments free speech protections. Any law, if enacted, will face a strict challenge in the courts with its resolution most likely awaiting the judgment of the Supreme Court. Thus, the issue of campaign finance is likely to be salient in future elections.

Cultural Voting?

The much-quoted Clinton campaign mantra in 1992 was, "It's the economy, stupid." In 2000, the Bush campaign might well have replied, "It's the culture, stupid." Bush centered his campaign around a large tax cut that Gore charged would benefit mainly the rich, and downplayed cultural issues such as abortion, gay rights, and gun control. As the Gore campaign came to realize that the battleground states were ones in which the cultural issues would not help them, they too downplayed those issues. Indeed, in the presidential debates, the two candidates took only subtly different positions on gun control, gay rights, and the death penalty.

Yet Bush allied himself firmly with Christian conservatives in his primary election campaign, and sent out carefully targeted appeals to culturally conservative GOP groups. The NRA campaigned aggressively for Bush, at one point rather immodestly claiming that a Bush victory would put the NRA in the White House. Liberal groups like Planned Parenthood and Handgun Control ran ads favoring Gore in battleground states.

Exit polls showed that cultural characteristics divided the voters as much as traditional class cleavages. Gore won by 20 percent among voters with incomes of less than $15,000, but he won by a similar margin among women who identified as "working women." Bush won by 11 percent among those who identified as "upper middle class," but he won by the same margin among men. Bush's margin among voters with incomes of more than $100,000 was 11 percent, but he piled up a 27 percent advantage among those who attended church more often than once a week, and by 25 percent among voters from households with at least one gun owner. Gore won 62 percent of the votes of union members, but 70 percent of the votes of gays and lesbians.

Some cultural identities came close to the power of partisanship and ideology in their ability to sway voters. As we noted in chapter 7, Bush won 91 percent of the votes of Republican voters, but he received 80 percent of those who identified with the Religious Right. Gore won 80 percent of the votes of self-identified liberals, and 79 percent of the votes of Jewish Americans, who, of course, may have augmented their pro-Democratic voting patterns because there was a Jewish vice presidential candidate on the ticket.

The cultural divide was also evident in the issues that drove votes. Again, according to the large Voter News Service exit poll, Gore won by 50 percent among those who thought government should do more, and Bush won by 45 percent among those who thought that government should do less. But cultural issues at least rivaled this traditional partisan issue. Pro-life voters gave Bush a 52 percent margin, and pro-choice voters provided Gore with a 45 percent edge. Bush won by 50 percent among those who opposed stricter gun laws, and by 56 percent among those who favored school vouchers. Bush's margin on these issues was even greater than among that minority of voters who reported that their family's financial situation had gotten worse: among that group, Bush's edge was only 33 percent.

The cultural divide was widely symbolized by geography. Bush carried the vast rural landmass of America, whereas Gore piled up his majorities in the large urban areas. The exit polls showed that Bush won 20 percent among those who lived in rural areas and small towns, and Gore piled up a 45 percent margin among those who lived in large cities.

Clearly Americans are becoming more polarized along cultural lines, but this does not mean that the 2000 election presages a coming culture war. It is worth noting that the exit polls showed 60 percent of voters "between two absolutes" on abortion, neither opposing it under all circumstances nor favoring it without limits. The 2000 national election poll continued to show a sizable moderate middle on issues such as school prayer, gun control, death penalty, and gay rights.

Moreover, the positioning of the candidates on their issue stands demonstrates the importance of taking moderate positions that appeal to moderate voters. Bill Clinton frustrated Republicans because he stole or co-opted their issues. His positions in favor of the death penalty, school uniforms, more police on the beat, and an end to welfare prompted many Republicans and Democrats alike to note that he often sounded more like a Republican than a Democrat.

George Bush was attractive to party elites early in the process because he shared many of Clinton's strategic positioning. Like Clinton, Bush was ideologically agile, able to shift to the right in South Carolina to get around John McCain, then back to the center in the general election. Although Bush emphasized traditional GOP issues like tax cuts, a strong defense, and decreased government interference on business, he was the first Republican candidate in history to run on a platform of increased spending for national education programs, a new national entitlement program for prescription drugs for the elderly, and a slogan that focused on greater educational opportunities for disadvantaged children, "Leave no child behind."

Finally, it is worth noting that the 2000 elections were perhaps optimal for producing cultural voting patterns. Bill Clinton's affair with intern Monica Lewinsky elevated personal morality in the public's mind, and the strong economy and lack of a visible foreign enemy meant that economic issues and foreign policy issues were not as salient to voters as in previous elections. Gore's ill-chosen strategy to focus more on the next four years than the past eight also led to a decreased discussion of the economy. It is likely that the next major economic slowdown will return the economy to the forefront of voter's minds.

Is That Chad Pregnant or Just Plain Fat?

The post-election controversy in Florida focused America's attention, at least for a time, on the mechanics of voting. One of the most memorable images of the long battle over the recount was one county official, squinting bleary eyed at a ballot that he held against the light, searching for any evidence of light shining through. The 2000 Florida election was clearly too close for the voting mechanism in place in that state to decide. Almost certainly the butterfly ballot in Palm Beach County denied Gore votes, but the large numbers of ballots disqualified by machines, and the significant portion of overseas ballots discarded showed the public the high rate of error in our voting system.

Florida received the bulk of the attention because it was extremely close and had a large number of electoral votes. Indeed, Robert Erikson has reported that the expected vote difference in Florida if all voters had simply flipped a coin to decide which candidate to support would have been 600 votes, larger than Bush's actual margin of victory.[2] Other states were also quite close and also had their share of ballot and registration problems.

Five states, Illinois, South Carolina, Idaho, Wyoming, and Georgia had a greater percentage of voided and undercounted ballots than did Florida. In fact, there were more invalidated votes in New York City and Chicago than there were in the entire state of Florida. According to a study by researchers at the Massachusetts Institute of Technology and California Institute of Technology, 4 to 6 million ballots were invalidated because of faulty voting equipment, errors in filling them out and in casting them, and lateness in submitting absentee ballots. In addition, registration problems prevented another three million people from voting.[3]

The federal nature of American elections was clearly on display in 2000. As Florida debated about the absentee ballots, their restrictive rules for counting ballots contrasted sharply with some other states. On election eve, voters were turned away from polls in some areas after waiting in line, because of state or county rules that mandated a strict closing time for polls. In other states or counties, polls remained open until everyone who wanted to vote had cast a ballot. In still others, voters cast ballots over a longer period of time, or mailed them in from their homes.

In the post-election fallout, African American leaders pointed to the high levels of disqualified ballots in black precincts across the country. Antiquated voting machines do a poorer job reading ballots than new ones, and some wealthier states and counties have electronic voting machines that do not permit double voting.

Clearly the magnifying glass put on the 2000 election did not reveal a pretty picture. The Cuban offer to dispatch poll observers to Florida put a humorous edge to what was otherwise an embarrassing election. After years of telling developing democracies to take their time and count every vote, and to do so by hand if the election is close, the U.S. conducted an election where many votes simply did not count or were not properly counted. And those votes might have changed the outcome.

The Constitution gives states the right to administer elections, but allows the national government an additional role. Thus, the national government mandated that states allow citizens to register to vote when they applied for driver's licenses (the so called Motor Voter bill), and earlier in the 1960s sent federal marshals into southern states to ensure voting rights for African Americans. The 107th Congress is considering subsidies for states to modernize their voting apparatus. At the state level, Florida adopted a statewide voting standard in the spring of 2001. Quietly, many counties are dropping punch-card ballots in favor of other voting mechanisms, in part to avoid the embarrassment of Florida counties, but more importantly to avoid the costs of civil lawsuits filed by disgruntled, disqualified voters. Meanwhile, foundations are pouring millions of dollars into research projects designed to develop better voting mechanism.

Yet the 2000 vote may well prime the pump of public opinion on electoral reform. The media will certainly focus on disqualified ballots in the 2002 congressional races, and unions, civil rights groups, and other liberal organizations are primed to try to push the issue to the fore. With control of the Senate shifting to the Democrats, it is possible that hearings on voter disqualification might lead to consideration of various legislative remedies.

To the surprise of many observers, the 2000 election did not result in a concerted push to abolish the electoral college. The Bush camp, anticipating the possibility that Bush would win the popular vote but lose the electoral college, developed contingency plans to encourage electors to defect from their states vote to ratify the national referendum result. On election night, Newt Gingrich told television views that whoever won the popular vote would find a way to win the electoral college—a theme the Republicans promptly dropped when Gore received more popular votes than Bush.

Just Plain Conservative, Thank You

The early actions of the Bush administration may well influence the politics of the next decade. After campaigning as a compassionate conservative, Bush appointed a conservative, business-oriented administration, and sought to govern as though he had won a mandate. By late spring, the

Democrats' stereotype of Bush as a strong or even extreme conservative began to stick. Partisanship was alive and well in Washington as Congress debated budget, tax, and appropriation issues and as political leaders began to position themselves for the 2002 congresstional elections and the 2004 presidential contest. Although the Bush team dismantled the Clinton "War Room" they built their own reelection machinery quickly and regularly consulted the polls, some of which they commissioned.

Congressional elections have been close for several years, as Democrats have repeatedly narrowed the already narrow GOP majority in the House. Contemporary politics are far too mercurial to predict far in advance, as Bush's father's freefalling popularity in 1992 demonstrated. But it is possible to consider many of the factors that might influence electoral politics in the near term.

First, much depends on the outcome of the 2002 congressional elections. In all but two congressional elections in the last century without a presidential candidate running, the party of the president has lost seats. The latest off-year election—1998—was one of the exceptions, so perhaps the trend has eased. Yet the safest prediction, at least before the terrorists' attacks, was that the Democrats would gain seats in the House in 2002, perhaps enough to regain control.

Offsetting that trend is the redrawing of district lines, which will create new seats in GOP strongholds like Florida and Texas. Republican operatives believe that redistricting will net them six or more seats in 2002, a number that they hope will offset any losses. Should the GOP retain control of the House, then it is likely that a number of senior Democratic members may retire before 2004. It is not much fun to be in the minority in the House, particularly after being in the majority and Democrats have held on to the hope that the next election will give them victory. But like Achilles racing the hare in Zeno's first paradox, the Democrats keep cutting into the GOP margin without erasing it. If they do not capture the House in 2002, many will simply give up and go home.

Should the Democrats recapture the House, that may well energize the GOP base and help Bush in his reelection bid. Although the GOP victories in 1994 were bad news for liberal groups and those who favored Democratic policy, they did wonders for Clinton's popularity, and probably were a key factor in the ease of his 1996 reelection. With enemies, like the conservative ideologues in Congress, who needs friends?

If Bush continues to govern from the right, he may engender a public reaction.[4] Political scientist James A. Stimson has described public policy moods, with liberal and conservative preferences rising and falling in response to policies. Reagan's victory in 1980 ended a long trend toward more conservative opinion, and resulted in a sharp increase in liberal sentiments, as the public came to believe that government was too conservative. Similarly, Kennedy's election in 1960 ended the sharp trend toward more liberal opinion, and began a twenty-year trend toward greater conservatism. Conversely, if Bush dances back to the center, like Clinton before him, then it is possible that the Republicans will control government throughout the first decade of the twenty-first century, and more permanently stamp their image on the judiciary in the process.

As the two parties prepare for elections in the new millennium, they do so in a country that is changing rapidly in its ethnic makeup. The 2000 census revealed that previous projections had understated the growth in the Latino population in the United States, and projections are for that population to grow rapidly over the next ten years. Current census projections would have the white, non-Hispanic population declining from 71 to 67 percent of the population, while Hispanics go from 12 to 15 percent. This amounts to 10 million new Hispanic voters, compared with 4 million new white non-Hispanic voters, 4 million new black non-Hispanic voters, and 4 million new Asian voters.

Just how the new changing ethnic composition will change American politics is difficult to predict.[5] What is clear is that it will become increasingly difficult for Republicans to compete without attracting significant numbers of Hispanic votes.

Photo Finishes and Landslides

After three successive elections in which party control of Congress has been closely divided, and in which the winning presidential candidate received fewer than 50 percent of the popular vote, many wonder if the country is entering a time of closely contested elections between evenly matched parties. In 2000, the Democrats significantly narrowed the party fund-raising advantage, and both parties now do extensive polling, conduct countless focus groups, and test their messages to appeal to the largest numbers of voters. Between 1880 and 1888, the country experienced three consecutive close elections, and Grover Cleveland won in 1892 by only 4 percent of the vote. Eventually, a realignment occurred in 1896 which led to three consecutive, relatively easy GOP victories.

In modern times, close elections have often been followed by blowouts. The razor-thin Democratic margin expanded to a landslide in 1964, and Nixon's photo-finish victory in 1968 was followed by a sweeping victory in 1972. The American electorate, like that in many other countries, is increasingly volatile, and public sentiments can move rapidly. It is unlikely that the next election will be as close as the election of 2000, or as contested. But politics is capable of surprising us all.

Notes

1. Dan Keating and Dan Balz, "Florida Recounts Would Have Favored Bush But Study Finds Gore Might Have Won Statewide Tally of All Uncounted Ballots," *Washington Post*, November 12, 2001, <http://www.washingtonpost.com/up-dyn/articles/A12623-2001Nov11.html>.
2. Robert S. Erikson, "The 2000 Presidential Election in Historical Perspective," *Political Science Quarterly* 116 (Spring 2001): 29–52.
3. Massachusetts Institute of Technology and California Institute of Technology, "Voting: What Is and What Could Be," released July 17, 2001.
4. James A. Stimson, *Public Opinion in America: Moods, Cycles, & Swings.* 2nd ed. (Boulder, CO: Westview, 1998).
5. For a more detailed analysis, see Jennifer Hochschild, "The Possibilities for Democracy in America." In *Defining the Conditions for Democracy,* eds. Theodore Rabb and Ezra Suleiman (Princeton: Princeton University Press, 2001).

Index

About the Editors and Contributors

The contributors to this volume are currently or formerly affiliated with the graduate PhD program in the government department at Georgetown University.

Molly W. Andolina (PhD, Georgetown), formerly survey director of the Pew Research Center For the People and the Press, is currently a visiting assistant professor at Loyola University in Chicago. Her principal area of research is generational politics with a particular focus on Generation X. She has published articles in the *Journal of Politics* and contributed numerous book chapters.

Michael A. Bailey (PhD, Stanford) is an assistant professor of government. His teaching and research focus are on Congress and political economy. His articles have appeared in such journals as *World Politics* and the *American Journal of Political Science*. He has also been a Monbusho Scholar at the Graduate School of Policy Research at Saitama University in Japan.

Andrew Bennett (PhD, Harvard) is an associate professor and coordinator of the graduate program in government at Georgetown. Specializing in foreign policy and qualitative methodology, Bennett has written on Soviet, Russian, and U.S. foreign policy. His most recent book is *Condemned To Repetition? The Rise, Fall, and Reprise of Soviet-Russian Military Interventionism, 1973–1996*. Bennett has also served as special assistant to the Assistant Secretary of Defense for International Security Affairs.

Anne Marie Cammisa (PhD, Georgetown) is an associate professor at Suffolk University. She is the author of three books: *From Rhetoric to*

Reform?: Welfare Policy in American Politics; Governments as Interest Groups: Intergovernmental Lobbying and the Federal System; and *Checks and Balances: How a Parliamentary System Could Change American Politics* (with Paul Christopher Manuel).

Courtenay Daum is a PhD candidate at Georgetown and received her BA and MA from the University of Delaware. Her interests lie in the area of judicial politics with secondary fields in political behavior, gender issues, and media.

Melissa Levitt is an adjunct professor at San Francisco State University and founder and director of ELM Research Associates. She has published and presented papers on a variety of topics including political behavior of newly naturalized citizens, sexual minorities in foreign militaries, and new immigrants in the labor force.

G. Patrick Lynch (PhD, North Carolina) was an assistant professor of government at Georgetown. He is now a fellow at the Liberty Fund. His specialties include political economy, urban politics, and quantitative methodology.

Jeremy D. Mayer (PhD, Georgetown) is currently visiting assistant professor in the Department of Government at Georgetown where he teaches courses on American politics. He is author of the forthcoming book, *Running on Race.*

Hayden Milberg is a PhD candidate at Georgetown with a research interest in public opinion and legislative politics. He was legislative director to Representative Tom Latham (IA-R) and presently serves as Director of Public Policy of the National Corn Growers Association. Milberg received a BA from Tufts and an MPP from Georgetown's Public Policy Institute.

Kathy Naff (PhD, Georgetown) is an assistant professor of public administration at San Francisco State University and a senior faculty researcher with the university's Public Research Institute. She has authored numerous articles and book chapters on the impact of gender and ethnicity within the federal bureaucracy and has recently published a book, *To Look Like America.*

Keiko Ono, a PhD candidate in the government department, is a former reporter who covered U.S. institutions and politics for the Nikkei newspapers of Japan. Her research interests included democratic theory, political economy, and legislative politics. She has taught several undergraduate courses at Georgetown.

Lynn C. Ross is a PhD candidate in government at Georgetown. She holds a BA from State University of New York at Binghamton and an MPA from the Maxwell School at Syracuse. She was a presidential management intern in the Office of Personnel Management and worked in the Office of Management and Budget as a budget examiner until recently. Her research interests are bureaucratic politics, the budget, and the presidency.

Beth Stark, a PhD candidate at Georgetown, received her undergraduate degree from Whitman College in Washington state. Her dissertation focuses on civil society and women's political participation.

Sue Thomas (PhD, Nebraska) was an associate professor of government at Georgetown. She is the author of *How Women Legislate* and *Women and Elective Office: Past, Present, and Future.* She is currently working as an educational administrator and independent scholar in Santa Cruz, California.

Margaret Tseng, a PhD candidate at Georgetown, received her undergraduate degree from the University of California at Los Angeles. Her dissertation examines the powers and limitations of lame duck presidents in their final years in office. She is also doing research on acculturation and Mexican Americans.

Stephen J. Wayne (PhD, Columbia) is a professor of government and author of a number of books on the presidency and elections. They include *The Road To The White House 2000; Is This Any Way to Run A Democratic Election?;* and *Presidential Leadership* (with George C. Edwards III). Wayne has also testified before Congress and advisory committees of both major political parties and is a frequent commentator on contemporary national politics.

Jeffrey A. Wertkin is in the joint PhD and JD program at Georgetown. His undergraduate degree is from Haverford College. He is interested in the impact of new communication technology on politics and law.

Troy White is a PhD candidate in the Department of Government. A graduate of the United States Naval Academy, he has an MA in national security studies from Georgetown. His current research focuses on the investigation of trans-state phenomena through the application of both qualitative and quantitative methods.

Clyde Wilcox (PhD, Ohio State) is a professor of government at Georgetown. He has published several books, including *Onward Christian Soldiers* (2nd ed.), and *Religion and Politics in Comparative Perspective: The One,* *the Few, and the Many,* as well as articles on religion and politics, gender and politics, interest groups, and campaign finance, both in the United States and abroad. He has also written on the politics of science fiction. Before joining the department, Wilcox was an analyst for the Federal Election Commission—hence his continuing interest in campaign finance issues.